ENDORSEMENTS

FOREWORD BY TOM ANTION

"I have mentored hundreds of authors and speakers. *The 3 Secret Skills of Top Performers – Powerful Lessons in Transformational Leadership* is high on my list of the best I have read.

The lessons are applied to improving performance in less time for any job, task, skill, or relationship. This is your opportunity to shorten your learning curve modeling what top performers consistently do. This benefit provides an advantage over your competition vying for the same results.

Most people think of motivation as something someone does to them or someone else. Top performers are self-motivated, and you can learn the same skills. Do you know any top performer who ever waited for the approval of another person? Top performers understand how to apply intrinsic motivation principles to satisfy their personal needs and values and goals. For leaders this is imperative to know about those you lead and improve your team.

If you ever thought of becoming a top performer to improve your finances or your team, then this is a must read. The educational 7-module course will teach you The Triad Performance Improvement System and master the 3 secret skills so you can become the top performer that is within you."

> **Tom Antion**, Box 9558, Virginia Beach, VA, 23450 USA.
> Podcast https://www.ScrewTheCommute.com, Mentor Program
> https://www.GreatInternetMarketingTraining.com, School https://www.IMTCVA.org,
> Documentary "The American Entrepreneur" https://www.Facebook.com/
> americanentrepreneurfilm.

FOREWORD BY DANIEL HALL

"If you ever wanted to be a top performer, then model the 3 secret skills they do. You may already do two of the three but perhaps not all three. Each skill is learned independently but applied interdependently. Like riding a bicycle, once you learn The Triad Performance Improvement System you never forget it. Then you apply it to any job, task, skill, or relationship to shorten your learning curve.

You may be a top performer and this book will confirm that or be your golden ticket to greater success and a rewarding income. As the leader you'll learn how to intrinsically motivate your performers learning their needs and values. This is especially important during these pandemic times with more people working from home.

You'll take unconscious motives to a conscious level of awareness to feel rewarded for your effort and meet your goals. You'll learn better methods to self-evaluate performances and connect reward to reinforce what you are doing well. In these demands to work from home trust is a major factor to get quality performance results. It is the perfect time to retrain and transform your directors, managers, supervisors, teachers, coaches, and CEO's including parents.

I've read books on leadership, but none compare to this content and learning system to transform from extrinsic to intrinsic methods to motivate yourself and those you lead. When you evaluate the personal needs and values of your performers, they feel you care about their life. This motivates each with the desire to improve on the job and be loyal to you, your team, and the company."

Daniel Hall, USA Today and Wall Street Journal Bestselling Author
and host of the www.RealFastResults.com podcast.

FOREWORD BY STEVE HARRISON

"Dr. Pete Andersen is a winner who knows how to achieve extraordinary results. Listen to him. Learn from him. His Triad Performance Improvement System works."

Steve Harrison, Co-Founder www.AuthorSuccess.com

"For years I have been the publicist for notable authors. The Chicken Soup series with Jack Canfield and Mark Victor Hansen was launched by my company. I know what qualities are common to top performers. *The 3 Secret Skills of Top Performers* and The Triad Performance Improvement System aptly describe common skills leaders would do well to model. Order your copy today on Amazon and bookstores and consider enrolling in one of the 7-module courses to benefit you and your performers."

Rick Frishman, www.RickFrishman.com, Bestselling Author,
Publisher & Speaker, publicity & publishing for entrepreneurs & business,
CEO and Founder, https://Author101University.com, the premiere event
for marketing & publishing success.

"*The 3 Secret Skills of Top Performers* can transform how leaders lead more with intrinsic motives and improve performance for their team in less time."

Jay Boyer, CEO, Publisher, https://jjfast.com, training authors
how to market what they publish.

"I have helped hundreds of authors correctly market their courses. *The 3 Secret Skills of Top Performers* will hold your attention and the 7-module course will help anyone who wants to be a top performer master the necessary skills. Get your copy today and start learning The Triad Performance Improvement System to enjoy a higher quality of life."

Chris Kyle, CEO and Founder, Launch Academy,
on-line course building program, https://ChrisKyle.com.

"You may be a top performer and do two of the three secret skills naturally but probably not all three. This is your chance to learn what you are good at and keep improving your performances in all areas of your life. Leadership begins with you, and how you lead others. The Triad Performance Improvement System is your path to success."

Brian Goodell, Double Gold Medalist 1976 Montreal Olympic Games, Mayor of Mission Viejo, CA, Business Owner – Real Estate.

"For over 50 years leading development organizations at Indiana University Foundation, at the University of California at California at Berkeley, at the University of Oregon and the University of Tennessee I have been associated with top performing leaders, both staff and volunteers who have been able to focus on the tasks at hand. Dr. Pete Andersen has authored a masterpiece in teaching leadership skills. His book *The 3 Secret Skills of Top Performers* provides powerful lessons to create new permanent skills to improve performance. Every person whether at the beginning of a career to lead others or mid-career professionals will benefit from his succinct lessons."

Curt R. Simic, President Emeritus, Indiana University Foundation

"The best way to reach a global audience is to have a website to showcase your work and your mission. And great content comes out of you when you are in a top performer state. Dr. Pete and "*The 3 Secret Skills of Top Performers*" is a model to follow on your journey to become a top performer. Get his book today and shorten your learning curve to give you that edge over your competition!"

Christina Hills, www.WebsiteCreationWorkshop.com, CEO and Founder of the International programs: The Website Creation Workshop and the Create Your Online Course Workshop.

"As a top performing speaker and trainer, Dr. Pete Andersen has captured exactly what top performers consistently do in the three secret skills. The key is to model what top performers do. This shortens your learning curve to become the top performer in your field of expertise. Order your copy from Amazon today and get started."

James Malinchak, Featured on ABCs Hit TV Show, Secret Millionaire, 3,000+ Talks · 2,000+ Consultations · 20+ Books, Founder, www.BigMoneySpeaker.com

"I am a retired Navy Rear Admiral who observed and evaluated the performance of all the men and women in my ship and shore commands, having to rank them in priority based on their accomplishments and for future promotions. Dr. Pete Andersen has correctly identified 3 secret skills common of top performers worth modeling. The benefit in using these skills will improve your performance in less time for any job, task, skill, or relationship. So, shorten your learning curve and order his book on Amazon or your bookstore today. Then be aware of your improvement and successes."

John J. Bepko, III, Rear Admiral United States Navy, Retired

"All my life I've coached divers to be top performing champions, and I like Dr. Pete Andersen's transformational lessons in his book *The 3 Secret Skills of Top Performers*. They are spot on. To intrinsically motivate my performers, I followed The Triad Performance Improvement System. I understood the personal needs and values and goals of my divers so I could use that knowledge to motivate their desire to be a champion. Now is the time to model the 3 secret skills of top performers to improve your performance in less time and become a top performer in your field."

> **Hobie Billingsley**, Professor Emeritus Indiana University, retired Diving Coach, author Challenge – How To Succeed Beyond Your Dreams, Five-time Head Olympic team diving coach, 1996 Atlanta Olympic Games Diving Judge and honored to give the oath address to all Olympic judges in opening ceremony. www.HobieBillingsley.com.

"As a healthcare executive, I have been a long-time learner of Dr. Pete Andersen's teachings. He has once again delivered high quality content that will be valuable for me to implement and share with my team. If you need to improve the performance of your team, then Dr. Pete Andersen's 3 secret skills will help you become a transformational leader who maximizes the potential of your team."

> **Cory Geffre**, Vice-President and Chief Nursing Officer,
> Mary Greeley Medical Center, Ames, IA.

"If you ever wanted to be a top performer on the job, doing tasks, getting skills, or in a relationship the 3 Secret Skills will shorten your learning curve to make that happen. The quality of your life will be better once you start practicing The Triad. I recommend you get your copy today."

> **Gary Hall**, Sr., MD, 1972 & 1976 Olympic Swimming Medalist and World Record Holder, honored by fellow Olympians to carry the flag in opening ceremony 1976 Montreal Games, Owner, CEO of the www.TheRaceClub.org improving quality competitive swimming performance.

"As an Emmy Award winning producer director, I know the importance of having a clear, concise, powerful, and quick plan to maximize my time for planning and execution of a motion picture project. *The 3 Secret Skills of Top Performers* is a refreshing wake up call for anyone who wants to shorten their learning curve, increase their financial bottom line, and have the confidence to perform at their maximum efficiency. Do yourself a favor and get this book."

> **Richard Crawford**, www.OneProductionsWeb.com, CEO, Producer, Writer, Director.

"Would you like to accelerate the progress on your dreams and goals? Or, have your efforts to accomplish great things in your life stalled and you are having a hard time restarting your efforts? Dr Andersen has a great secret (actually 3 secrets) to help you restart or accelerate your progress. It is amazing how simple these tactics are and yet, many do not use these to climb the mountain faster with less effort. Do yourself a favor and pick up a copy of Dr. Andersen's book on *The 3 Secret Skills of Top Performers*. You will be glad you did. I have benefited greatly from is insights and performance improvement recommendations."

> **Dr. Serena Reep**, www.Serenasez.com, Founder and CEO: Transformational Communications; Author of the forthcoming book "*Work Life Balance is Dead*" and, Co-Author of "*Success Secrets*" with Jack Canfield, and Co-Author of "*Change Agents*" with Brian Tracy.

"If you own a business or lead others in any capacity, then model the 3 secret skills. The benefit is learning to use more powerful intrinsic motives to improve performance. This tends to increase your financial bottom line and build rapport with all your performers (workers)."

> **Chad E. Cooper**, Managing Director, Earth Wind Technologies http://www.chadecooper.com, http://www.twitter.com/cooper1801, https://www.facebook.com/ChadCooperAuthorSpeaker/

"I built my business and find it is no surprise to learn I follow the 3 secret skills of top performers to do so. The key is I treat my employees like family as the book content teaches. I care about their personal needs and values, and in return they are loyal, self-motivated, and I don't have to manage or supervise their performance. We're both happy."

> **Waiss Kader**, www.PrefabGraniteDepot.com, Businessman Founder and CEO, San Diego, CA

"I've seen many top performers in my experience, and Dr. Pete Andersen has correctly identified the three main qualities anyone would be wise to model. If you want to shorten your learning curve, then invest in the book and training course. This will help you to be a better leader."

> **Raymond Loewe**, www.TheLuckiestGuyInTheWorld.com, Business Owner, Podcaster "Changing the Rules."

"For years I've recommended books for my clients to read and enjoy. This is one of those must reads because you can learn how to improve your performance in less time for any job, task, skill, or relationship. And who wouldn't want to have more friends or feel job satisfaction helping others? Go to Amazon, a bookstore, or the website and order your copy today!"

> **Michael Wolf**, GRI & Author "*The First Time Homebuyer Book*" and "*The First Time Home Investor Book*"; National "30 under 30" REALTOR® honored by the NATIONAL ASSOCIATION OF REALTORS®; San Diego's Best REALTOR – San Diego Union Tribune; DRE#01709065;Wolf Real Estate Team Coldwell Banker West 410 Kalmia St – San Diego CA 92101 858-722-6847; Our LATEST VIDEO: https://youtu.be/-IqJ0dwHX-k

THE 3 SECRET SKILLS OF TOP PERFORMERS

Powerful Lessons in Transformational Leadership to Improve Performance in Less Time

PETER ANDERSEN, Ph.D.

TRIUS PUBLISHING
SAN DIEGO

THE 3 SECRET SKILLS OF TOP PERFORMERS

Copyright © 2020 by Dr. Peter Andersen

Published and printed in the United States of America

Trius Publishing, 6382 Lake Dora Ave., San Diego, CA 92119
https://TriusPublishing.com I https://The3SecretSkillsofTopPerformers.com

ISBN: 978-0-9986357-3-6 (paperback)
ISBN: 978-0-9986357-5-0 (hardcover)
ISBN: 978-0-9986357-4-3 (ebook)
ISBN: 978-0-9986357-6-7 (audiobook)

FREE BONUS OFFERS

Forward your Amazon receipt for this book to support@The3SecretSkillsof TopPerformers.com and get 50% off coupon code to apply for the affordable GENERAL 7-module course. So you can begin to see rapid performance improvements for jobs, tasks, skills, and relationships leading to a higher quality of life and income.

Download full-page survey in printable PDF format with spacing for recording your responses to identify your personal needs, abilities, and skills in six sections:
> https://the3secretskillsoftopperformers.com/wp-content/uploads/2021/02/
> Personal-Survey.pdf

> Part I: Talents, Abilities, and Skills
> Part II: Attitudes, Values, and Beliefs
> Part III: Activities, Preferences, and Goals
> Part IV: Performances, Achievements, and Planning
> Part V: Personality
> Part VI: Needs, Drives, and Motives

Download a FREE chapter to send to your friends:
> https://the3secretskillsoftopperformers.com/wp-content/uploads/2021/02/
> Free-Chapter.pdf

Review endorsements for Internet marketing resource links:
> https://the3secretskillsoftopperformers.com/wp-content/uploads/2021/02/
> Book-endorsements-page.pdf

To obtain specific course training for you and your family, or your business, education, and athletics use the drop-down window to make your selection:
> https://the3secretskillsoftopperformers.com/index.php/7-module-courses/

To order copies, contact, schedule an interview or FREE consult:
> https://The3SecretSkillsofTopPerformers.com

Follow us on social media...

Join our Facebook group tribe of readers to share how The Triad Performance Improvement System has benefitted your quality of life and those you lead for a job, task, skill, or relationship.
https://Facebook.com/The3SecretSkillsOfTopPerformers

LinkedIn Business page
https://linkedin.com/company/the-3-secret-skills-of-top-performers

YouTube Channel
https://youtube.com/channel/UCdAkxEyGxMd_tRc5jDF42DQ

Twitter
https://twitter.com/3Performers

Instagram
https://instagram.com/3SecretSkillsTopPerformers

CONTENTS

PART THREE
THE THIRD SECRET SKILL:
CONNECT REWARD WITH REINFORCEMENT

ACKNOWLEDGMENTS

I am grateful for all the top performers I have observed, taught, and been associated with over the past fifty years to learn what has made them so successful.

My interior graphic artist was Vinus van Baalen, Edmonton, Alberta, Canada, who passed away in 2012. Vinus was a remarkable late 20th Century Dutch modern art painter and sold his oil and watercolor paintings to wealthy Europeans. His artwork is now being discovered and introduces each secret skill of The Triad.

After he died, I obtained the rest of his original work to preserve the priceless value over time to share. http://vanBaalenArtOriginals.com. Vinus was a top performer, athlete and member of the 1964 Dutch Olympic swimming team. We became close friends setting Masters' Swimming Relay World Records for our age-group.

Jonatan Azpilcueta has designed my book covers for the last ten years. I highly recommend his talents to design your next book cover, brochure, poster, banner, ad, or any graphic design. Jonatan.Azpilcueta@Gmail.com

PREFACE

Authors are advised to avoid writing about politics or religion to improve book sales. However, how my book was created is my backstory.

I am a true believer. I believe there is something bigger than us in the universe. I believe we are all messengers of some kind to each other, or how would God speak to us?

In my experience, 95% of the people who are given a messenger to answer a problem they have been thinking about blow off the message. The rationale is "I don't know you. How could you know my problem? Why should I trust you?"

I am about to provide you with a message how to improve performance in less time for any job, task, skill, or relationship.

I am a behaviorist and transformational speaker. My doctoral study has been in behavioral, educational, and personality psychology. I am NOT a licensed clinical psychologist. I do not need to learn what is between your ears. If I do not get the correct output, I change the input cue or method, and once correct reinforce that behavior or skill.

I will teach you how to be self-motivated using your feedback to understand and modify your behaviors to be accountable and keep improving to become a top performer. What I teach you in this brief work will help you improve the quality of your life and those around you for the rest of your life.

Like most people, I do not pray and give thanks on a daily routine. I do feel blessed to have acquired my knowledge and skills to be a top performer and share with you now. Whether you choose to accept or reject my teaching is your right. I am a messenger none-the-less.

Twenty-five years prior to publishing Purposeful Intent my first book in 2009 I was depressed. I had two failed marriages and five sons. I love my kids, but I could not be with them like a normal father.

My mother was the spiritual leader of our family. She instilled in me and my brother the values of family. She called it acting like the three musketeers—"All for one and one for all." All she wanted was for her two sons to become good citizens. She taught us values, and belief in God was one of them.

I was about to turn 40. I had recently left my teaching and coaching position to enter business as a medical distributor sales rep calling on hospitals and clinics. I knew medical terms having been a health education teacher and swimming coach.

Like any depressed son I went to visit my parents who had retired to northern Wisconsin. My lament to my mom was who would even want to date me? I may have well put a big "L" for loser on my forehead.

Her advice was to explain who I was and had become. I was a good father, an All-American in swimming, and I had a good job and Ph.D. My problem was not being patient. Her comment was, "How can the good Lord keep up with you? If plan A does not work immediately you go to plan B, then plan C." Then she advised, "You go into your bedroom and pray alone like I taught you. And if you want to know more read all of Matthew 6." What she said next really got my attention.

My dad grew up in Chicago. I had heard every cuss word before I was 10, but mom rarely said a cross word. But this time she said, "Be prepared to wait a year for your answer and keep your eyes and ears open. Only this time, you get the HELL OUT OF THE WAY!" It was as if she had slapped my face.

Three days later I came home to my empty apartment in a suburb west of Chicago, and I broke down. I missed my sons. I wanted to be a family. I did not have much time to date, and the unwritten rule in sales is you never date anyone you call upon. That narrows your search a lot.

I went into my bedroom and shut the door and unloaded my pain. It was not pretty on my knees bent over my bed, my face in my hands tearfully asking God for help. But I had my shopping list because the old me was thinking I was still in charge.

Then halfway through my list of what I wanted—a blonde with blue eyes and nice figure—I stopped. I remembered that God is loving and all-knowing. Who was I to demand anything? So, I ended with a final request for God to help me find the woman and partner whom I could spend the rest of my life with and grow old together. I reasoned that God showed us miracles and Noah to go through life two by two as partners.

It did not take a year! Eighteen-days later I met my wife. We have been married for 35 years! And, finally after five sons we have our daughter. So, now fast forward. I was out of education for twenty years but went back to school in 2000 to get my school administrator's endorsement to become a principal. After additional graduate courses and two years as a principal I became a licensed K-12 school superintendent.

I grew up with a work ethic and improved large aquatic programs and winning teams. For twenty years in business I advanced from a national sales trainer to rep and regional manager and CEO of my own rep company. I went back to school because I was motivated to make a difference as a school leader.

After four more years as a school superintendent I retired in 2008 to complete my first book Purposeful Intent I had started in 2004. Unfortunately, I wrote it like a textbook few people like to read after school. The design was to show teachers how to self-motivate—intrinsically motivate—their students to higher achievement. I had the book 65% completed when I realized my huge mistake.

From 400 personality and psychological variables I singled out 14. I thought if I could teach you these 14, you could be self-motivated. What I failed to see was all the variable interaction effects. For example, 6 with 9 or 10 with 12 and others. It was impossible to explain 14 to the 13th power.

Again, I was depressed and upset. I was driven to find an answer how we could best teach people to be self-motivated. I was frustrated and mad having spent a year of my life trying to create the right message. I made three stacks of papers on my dining room table and shut down my computer. I was done.

Then I sat in my chair and cried for a half hour. In that time, like Job in the Bible, I had some harsh words for God. I was really trying hard to do the right thing to help people. As an educator and administrator and former coach I saw methods how coaches motivate their athletes, but teachers were missing that skill. So, are most parents, managers, and leaders off the mark.

But as it was twenty some years earlier in the beginning, I again realized I was not the one in charge. So, my final request was, "God, I need your help. I can't do this on my own. I am a health and physical education teacher. We use visual, verbal, and kinesthetic cues to teach how to perform physical skills and take care of your health. Why can't we come up with a simple strategy to teach people how to be self-motivated?"

I did not think of my request as a prayer in my bedroom with the door shut, but God must have heard my emotional plea for help. It was 4:30 in the afternoon, and eleven hours later at 3:30 in the morning not 18 days later like before, I awoke and started to jot down some trigger words on a note pad next to my bed.

I use trigger pad notes to recall what I had been thinking and put those thoughts into action the next morning. Only this time, I was writing pages with sentences! I realized I was getting my answer NOW! So, I ran downstairs and got eight pages out of my printer.

For the next three hours I wrote the foundation for "The Triad Performance Improvement System." These are the three secret skills of top performers. They are teachable and learnable and transformational.

I kept an open mind and no sooner sat down was told, "Increase Awareness." I thought about how to teach that and roughed out an outline. Ninety minutes later I felt I had grasped that, so I sat quietly. In only a few minutes, I was told, "Enhance Self-Evaluation."

I remember printing and underlining that header at the top of the page. Then, I created an outline for pre, during, and post-performance evaluation chapter headings. Again, I sat quietly a lot longer this time, and was told, "Connect Reward with Reinforcement."

God answered my prayer. I am just the messenger. In the next eight to ten hours reading and absorbing this book you can make personal conclusions and decide to transform your life, improve your performance in less time, and become the top performer that is within you.

1

OVERVIEW

"Your education and personality identify you for a lifetime."

Andrew Christian

The Applied Transformational Leadership Design

The 3 Secret Skills of Top Performers is self or intrinsic motivation leadership designed to improve your performance in less time. I refer to these three teachable and learnable skills as The Triad Performance Improvement System, a.k.a. The Triad.

Theory and Hypothesis

The theory is when you are aware of a conscious cognitive motive to value and satisfy a personal need or goal you experience repeatable success and gratification. Personal needs, values, and goal setting behaviors will be reviewed.

The hypothesis is valued information is more readily stored and retrieved in the brain through the development of cognitive associational neurons that connect positive, pleasurable, and successful stimulus-response activities.

The theoretical construct for The Triad is that you can more readily recognize, receive, organize, store, and retrieve (RROSR) information you learn to cognitively choose as valuable, meaningful, and relevant from your familiar past experience and your unfamiliar future predicted experience.

Top performers take immediate action while other performers lose time considering what to do or wait to be directed by others. Top performers are motivated by satisfying personal needs and valued goals. When those needs are identified and goals are met, they activate pleasure centers in the brain to repeat those kinds of behaviors.

The Big Four Applications

The benefit of learning The Triad is applying these skills to improve your performance in less time to "The Big Four": a job, task, skill, or relationship. Like riding a bicycle once you learn The Triad you do not forget it. Few applications fall outside of those "Big Four" to be reviewed later in more detail.

The cornerstone of all motivational behavior is your desire to see continuous improvement in your performance to enhance your "quality of life." This begins with satisfying your personal needs and goals consistent with your values.

With awareness of continuous improvement, you activate and reinforce the pleasure centers in your brain. You connect the reward with reinforcement. This builds your confidence and motive to experience more pleasurable success repeating like behaviors.

Assumptions

1. Leadership is applied to groups and individual performance.
2. Knowledge from reading about top performers will transfer to the individual.
3. Learning The Triad improves performance in less time and takes fast action.
4. The Triad shortens the learning curve.
5. The 3 secret skills will transform leaders and performers.
6. All top performers do not make good role models.
7. Top performers' work ethic and strategies are worth copying.
8. Intrinsic comes from within and extrinsic comes from outside.
9. Quality of life is the underlying driving force in all motivation.
10. Leaders are assumed for the purposes of this book to be company CEO's, managers, supervisors, directors, teachers, coaches, and parents.
11. Performers are employees, workers, students, athletes, and people.

Premise

The intent of this book is to transform leadership using The Triad Performance Improvement System.

Most of us are conditioned to think of motivation as something someone does to us or someone else, or a pep talk from so called "experts" with variable credibility. I believe we are born with an innate drive to improve. Observing top performers in all fields, they consistently report a need to keep improving their knowledge and skills.

The primary motivation for personal performance improvement is to enhance the overall quality of life. There is little motivation to work hard to achieve anything with low value. The value of hard work is to enjoy the rewards rather than be victims deciding there is no hope or future.

Many motivational speakers use the same clichés, persistence, commitment, and others—you have heard them. The message of inspirational speakers is, "If I can do it, you can do it." Both offer enthusiastic sometimes celebrity entertainment but reflect on what your behavior was like 72 hours later. Did you create permanent personal performance improvement beyond 72 hours?

Both are extrinsic and less valuable. Intrinsic motives are always stronger than extrinsic motives. Telling someone how to do it like they did is a lot different from a transformational talk that teaches you methods and strategies to permanently improve your performance.

Learning the three secret skills is transformational. These leadership skills are modeled from top performers to create permanent changes in your behaviors and improve your performance over time. Like riding a bicycle, you will not forget how to apply those secret skills because they work. You can be the judge.

This is a study teaching powerful lessons in transformational leadership to improve performance in less time. Intrinsic motivation is a personal leadership skill taught with "The Triad Performance Improvement System."

The oldest method to improve performance is trial and error. You make a mistake and keep correcting your performances. But this takes time you may not have to succeed. A better old-time method is to model and copy top performers. Over the years, I have observed top performers everywhere. They unconsciously follow these three secret skills.

Stephen Covey used this same observational approach as described in his best-selling book The 7 Habits of Highly Effective People 1989. That work was transformational. People were happy to say they were a "Covey guy" because they could already do two or three of the seven habits. And they told all their friends about the book.

In my observations, top performers are successful usually doing two of the three secret skills, but not all three. There is a reason why they do not emphasize the third secret skill. Are you curious?

In human behavior, people quit activities when they continually fail and feel pain. Or, as the case with mal-adaptive behaviors, they may cover up the pain using drugs. When you learn The Triad, you gain pleasurable success to repeat and keep improving.

Primary Benefits and Aids to Learning

The Triad are three secret skills used to benefit learning and improve your performance in less time. Self-motivated people identify and provide for their own needs to keep improving their skills. Do you know any top performer who is not self-motivated?

Shortening the Learning Curve

To acquire an education and learn skills to meet your own needs there is a premium placed on "shortening the learning curve." W. Edwards Deming stated years ago, "Knowledge is king." Those who acquire The Triad skills early value the knowledge and information and make it more meaningful and relevant.

The main idea for learning The Triad is to improve performance in less time for any job, task, skill, or relationship. Generally, with greater knowledge and skills you have a performance advantage over your competitors.

Definitions and Use of Terms

The Triad – refers to the 3 secret skills of top performers. It is the system to learn performance improvement in less time applied to any purposeful job, task, skill, or relationship.

Needs – are factors that affect your behavior, education, and personality in the environments you choose to live in. Maturity is your ability to provide for your own needs.

Drives – are innate built-in on a subconscious level you are unaware of their operation affecting your behaviors.

Motives – are the conscious awareness of a drive stimulus to purposefully satisfy a personal need or goal. Motives are associated with your intent and behavior patterns. A strategy to increase your motive strength is to be more consciously aware of your needs, values, and goals, and hold yourself accountable to achieve them.

Motivation – is the defined strategy you use to satisfy a personal need or goal. Two performers can have the same personal need or goal, but the stronger motivation will come from the performer who makes a conscious awareness effort to value their achievement. The strength of your motivation is hard to improve when you have no satisfaction of an underlying personal need or goal.

Intrinsic motivation is the performer's internal desire to satisfy a personal need or goal.

Extrinsic motivation is another person's need or goal imposed on an individual or group.

Bias is the unreasonable personal judgment or prejudice of an expected outcome prior to the performance or events.

RROSR is an increase awareness strategy I introduce as a meme to easily remember its use. Each letter represents a word—Recognize, Receive, Organize, Store, and Retrieve information.

The Value Concept

Value is the cornerstone of The Triad. There is a big difference between what someone tells you to value (extrinsic), and what you consciously decide to value (intrinsic). A leader, manager, parent, teacher, or coach can tell you the value of a bit of knowledge by creating a need to learn. The trick is making the new information meaningful and relevant to your current level of understanding. This uses your prior knowledge and familiarity with each task so you will intrinsically value and remember how the new information can be applied for your benefit.

Hypothetically when you do not intrinsically value new information, you store these data in less retrievable parts of your brain. This is like creating a word document file on your computer and placing it in a folder inside another folder. By the time you perform those three iterations to retrieve the document file, the timing of the performance to be successful may be lost. You can learn to organize and store valued information in a more readily retrievable structure via associational neurons and specific access parts of your brain at will on demand.

Brain mapping studies indicate visual patterns are stored and associated with like patterns in the occipital lobe. Verbal and kinesthetic feeling skills are stored in other lobes. This suggests information input must be as accurate as possible in demonstrations and explanations.

The Extrinsic-Intrinsic Controversy

Leaders must understand the difference between intrinsic and extrinsic motivation. An **extrinsic** motive is provided by someone else in the form of a tangible product or service with the expectation the one providing the extrinsic motive will gain something in return. This is a Quid Pro Quo. Examples are money, paid vacations, candy, gifts, jewelry, clothing, praise, special recognition, grades, plaques, bonuses, and so forth in return for more productive work, affection, better behavior, and leadership conformity. An extrinsic motive is another person's need or goal imposed on the individual or group.

An **intrinsic** motive is the performer's internal desire to satisfy a personal need or goal. An intrinsic motive comes from within the performer understanding their personal needs, values, and goals. Personal assessment of the physical and mental abilities, skills, and strengths to meet personal needs is required. The perceived performance value comes from *feelings* of success, self-worth, and image exhibited by enthusiasm and passion to produce quality results.

Value of Intrinsic Motivation

The Triad skills adapt to all your needs as they change over time. For example, my neighbor told me his story about quitting smoking. He said when he was a young man, if someone had told him smoking was bad for his health, he would have ushered the person out the door. His health needs were invincible then. Years later the need increased his awareness for quality of life and he quit.

Unfortunately, we all have a hard time projecting our future needs. We often wait until it is too late to see greater benefits from changing our behavior because without the skills to know how, we are not motivated to do so. As you mature and grow with experience your Triad skills help you to project future personal needs to a higher relevant value to control this notion.

You also use these skills to be a better consumer to apply critical thinking skills. Advertising works against The Triad skills. Ads seek to lure you into being part of a bigger more accepted group behavior instead of thinking through the best value for you.

When you focus on identifying and meeting your personal needs with The Triad, you achieve above average results. If you follow the masses and resist changing your behaviors putting stress on your personality, then little will change in your life. You are extrinsically motivated to meet the needs of others who manipulate your need for acceptance and will do what everyone else does. This is poor leadership.

The Triad Performance Improvement System

The book is organized into three parts with several chapters to suggest how to learn and teach each secret skill in The Triad. In only a few hours you can grasp The Triad and take immediate action to modify your behaviors and begin your journey of self-improvement when and where you choose to be a top performer.

 The three secret skills of top performers are learned independently but interrelated when applied. The skills overlap like the spheres in this figure. As you learn each teachable skill, a light bulb goes on. Like water boiling it gets excited and agitates or bumps into the other two skills. Then one of those gets excited and bumps into the other two and so on. This continuous improvement process goes on for the rest of your life. You choose to apply when you feel the need to improve your performance for any job, task, skill, or relationship.

In your process of learning The Triad, I will explain the importance of needs, values, goals, paradigm shifts and strategies. They are essential to understand how and why to make permanent behavioral modifications to become a top performer.

While reading, pause and try to visualize a mental movie using suggested strategies applying The Triad to specific jobs, tasks, skills, and relationships you are familiar with and need to improve performance.

Einstein imagined learning everything in multiple senses so he could create huge numbers of associational neurons. Then, if he couldn't recall a bit of information, he may have used a different sense to locate the knowledge in another drawer of his brain's filing cabinet. Top performers use this multi-sensory approach to make new information meaningful and relevant.

I introduce RROSR as part of that strategy and suggests increasing awareness can increase your intelligence. But remember intelligence is specific. You can be smart in one area and unknowledgeable in another.

The three parts of The Triad are the 3 secret skills: Increase Awareness, Enhance Self-evaluation, and Connect Reward with Reinforcement are the foundation for all motivation. Once learned you will never forget them. When events trigger your need to improve any of those Big Four—jobs, tasks, skills, or relationships, remind yourself with a mental image to practice applying the skills.

The first part secret skill is **Increase Awareness**. *To appreciably increase intelligence, you must learn how to increase your awareness at will on demand.* Top performers do not operate at 100% all the time. They sense when to increase their awareness to recognize essential cues, mobilize their energy, and raise their level of performance to be successful.

Four key words are: AT WILL ON DEMAND. You choose when and where to apply The Triad. Increasing your awareness also creates value to organize, store, and retrieve differentiated information you find meaningful and relevant to successful past performance experience.

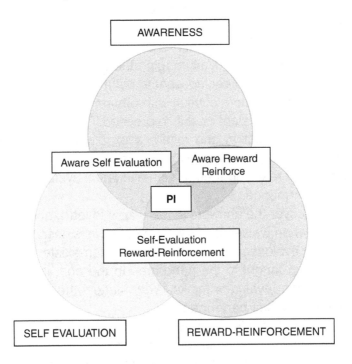

You perceive value from associating past familiar to new unfamiliar experiences. The frontal lobe behind your forehead does the thinking, predicting, and reasoning. The pre-frontal cortex immediately in front of the frontal lobe acts like the cache ram memory in your computer. As you acquire more knowledge and experience with specific tasks, you create an array of associational neurons linking the information stored in various parts of your brain.

When you learn to value information, you hypothetically store new information differently than non-valued information. But with more associational neurons you facilitate retrieval at will on demand to perform at higher optimum levels. Top performers use the pre-frontal cortex to retrieve valued information and hold in short term memory.

Then they modify and correct past performance mistakes by reviewing the sub routines or specific parts of the whole skill using mental practice and visualization strategies. These strategies create slow motion mental movie videos to fully rehearse the stimulus cues and response connections about to be performed in each part.

After the corrections have been made, the pre-frontal cortex executes the connected sub routines without having to think and interrupt the whole performance. Non-valued information is not as readily retrievable like a file stored in a closet instead of your brain's desktop. A long retrieval sequence hinders learning and performance. It is harder to associate pleasurable past experiences to self-evaluate past performance and improve your motivation to strive for a goal and connect to a reward.

The second part secret skill is **Enhance Self-Evaluation**. *No top performer ever waits for the approval of another.* Creative performers and leaders value their self-evaluation criteria and feedback more than to wait on their critic's opinion who is less familiar with the work. Can you imagine the great modern painter Picasso, waiting for the critic's opinion to decide what to paint?

Great leaders and performers consult with others, and they do not wait for the approval of a critic with less talent or skill to proceed. Our schools, organizational, and business systems condition and reinforce exactly the opposite. We explain to students, trainees, and performers what is meaningful, relevant, and valuable instead of showing and teaching them a self-evaluation system or rubric to objectively score their performance.

Learn how to discover the answers to learn how to learn and be self-sufficient. We all know quality when we see it, but we cannot always describe it or the reward we feel. Performance evaluations are often vague or non-existent because no feedback system has been taught to the performer. In the end, it is not the extrinsic evaluation the teacher or evaluator thinks. What matters the most is how performers intrinsically evaluate their performances.

The third part secret skill is **Connect Reward with Reinforcement**. Routine performances and familial relationships are subconsciously automated. They are unaware of a connection between reward and reinforcement to improve future performance. The strategy is to move from unconscious to conscious awareness and attach significant value for each performance.

Mundane tasks are routine and boring, so you are not as motivated to improve until you become consciously aware of small improvements to value enough to feel any reward. You cannot reinforce a reward you do not feel or value from exerting a conscious effort. By increasing awareness to work with your innate drives, you immediately enhance self-evaluation and self-reward.

This connection reinforces and increases your motivation to improve skilled performances with more purposeful training and effort. RROSR is the strategy to improve all parts of The Triad. It is your ability to properly recognize, receive, organize, store, and retrieve information to value as meaningful and relevant to improve any performance and feel rewarded.

Imagine your reward feelings in doing a task well. Now, imagine a task or event you did not do well. No one likes to fail. No one says, "Boy that was fun! Let's do it again!" The oldest behavioral notion is the tendency to repeat satisfying performances and avoid repeating painful ones.

To override routine subconscious behaviors and condition positive conscious behavioral responses, selectively focus on the correct cues to associate with purposeful correct responses. In other words, get clarity why you are performing what you do.

By enhancing your self-evaluation be aware of your personal feedback system to associate quality of effort with quality of reward. This builds value and a stronger personal reward system to overcome occasional failures. This is the best way to build your confidence and self-esteem. No one can convince you with words. It must occur by your own actions and intrinsic motivation.

The inner overlap (PI) is your purposeful intent. When you know your purpose for performing any job, task, skill, or relationship you improve your performances in less time. Compare this concept with lack of awareness simply going through the motions in your daily routines.

As you read these chapters stay focused on learning and applying these skills over time to put yourself in position to succeed. No great performance was ever created with a few trials. If you apply these principles and make them a part of your daily routine, you will see measurable consistent improvements in your performances and relationships over time. Use The Triad to learn your purpose and experience consistent improvement and success.

Without a purpose your odds for success are maybe 50-50 like flipping a coin to be heads or tails. This seldom motivates you to work hard to improve your performance and assure your success. If you subscribe to be a servant leader, and learn you are a messenger to others, I thank you for spreading the word.

Tenets of The Triad

Some scholars believe you cannot teach intrinsic or self-motivation. Based on my observations, personal research, and experience intrinsic motivation is a learned skill. As an All-American athlete, teacher, coach, sales trainer and regional manager, business owner, and school superintendent, I learned useful methods from my professors, coaches, and mentors who created an awareness of personal needs and values to motivate performance improvement.

Needs and values are the primary tenets. They evolve over time with the kinds of experiences you create in your environment—good or bad. How you choose to spend your time to gain useful feedback determines your outcomes.

Intrinsic or self-motivation revolves around satisfaction of personal needs. The problem is understanding needs are different from wants and be aware of their operation in your personal system. Some innate sub-conscious needs are powerful. You can learn to identify and discover how to bring those needs to a conscious level to enhance your motivation.

As you mature and gain experience you learn to value or discard new information. You do not waste your energy trying to store non useful information. The key is to be aware and show others you lead how to make new information meaningful and relevant to value and store as experience to apply to future events.

The secondary tenets are you choose when and where to apply The Triad to improve performance in less time for any job, task, skill, or relationship.

Using The Triad to Improve Your Performance Skills

As with any unfamiliar task, learning the process will seem confusing until you become more familiar with each task. The Triad concepts and skills you acquire will make more sense when you begin to apply them. You will become more aware of your subtle performance improvements to feel your success and enrich the quality of your life and those around you.

The Triad is a performance improvement system:

#1 A learned skill that must be practiced over time to achieve consistent results. Use it or lose it.

#2 Formed by the sum-total use of your personality, education, past performance, experiences, needs, values, and goals.

#3 Conditioned by your abilities, skills, attitudes, biased beliefs, and prejudices and motives in your responses.

#4 Not hard to learn but neither a quick fix nor opportune motivational system that lasts for 72 hours. Permanent changes take time and are motivated by knowledge and understanding of how intrinsic motivation works to improve performance in less time.

#5 Intrinsic motivation is based on proven psychological principles and observed behaviors common in top performers.

#6 The skills learning process can seem complex because many interrelated variables are difficult to control. Become conscious of the specific variable interactions to control and use their intrinsic motivational effect on performance improvement.

#7 The 3 secret skills are described in chapters under Part One, Two, and Three. These skills are learned independently but applied interdependently.

The following chart shows 7 steps to improve your performance with The Triad. Some personality adjustments will take time to condition and self-reinforce to make routine. You will notice these changes when you begin to master the awareness skills taught in Part One. As you read, practice applying these skills to yourself and those you lead.

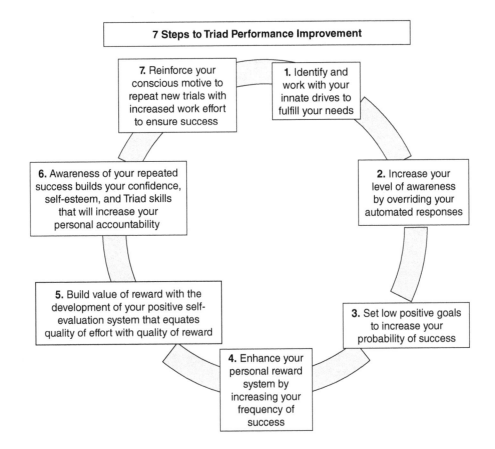

7 Steps to Triad Performance Improvement

7. Reinforce your conscious motive to repeat new trials with increased work effort to ensure success

1. Identify and work with your innate drives to fulfill your needs

2. Increase your level of awareness by overriding your automated responses

6. Awareness of your repeated success builds your confidence, self-esteem, and Triad skills that will increase your personal accountability

3. Set low positive goals to increase your probability of success

5. Build value of reward with the development of your positive self-evaluation system that equates quality of effort with quality of reward

4. Enhance your personal reward system by increasing your frequency of success

2
NEEDS

To be intrinsically motivated you must consciously identify your needs and how they operate to affect your performance. You can choose to create a positive environment and framework. All people color their world the way they want to see it. From your experience you gain beliefs about what works from your own performance feedback.

You can be influenced by others to model their behaviors or decide to learn personal leadership skills to guide your life. When you develop your personal need to learn you gain critical thinking skills to understand human behavior and avoid bias. You learn to make your own decisions and choices.

As a former public-school superintendent, I saw this happened dealing with many children and their parents in families. The more parents want to do for their children, the less the child learns to do for themselves to meet their basic needs. When a child would goof off, I would ask if they thought they could survive in the adult world with a 5th or 6th grade education? This would create a need in the student to focus on their current skills, behaviors, and attitudes toward learning to be more accountable to themselves.

Some children express, dress and groom themselves very differently when their basic needs are expected and provided by others. They lose the important awareness. This allows them to misbehave, to focus on satisfying what they want, and to blame others for poor performance. Parents and leaders would do better to not create an expectancy of reward without a personal work ethic.

Discriminating Needs and Wants to Improve Relationships

Some children seem to want everything when all their basic needs are provided by their parents. Parents naturally want their children to have and experience more than they had growing up. They forget work ethic creates value to satisfy the need. So, children may grow up not knowing what they really need to be adults.

I had a recent occasion to visit with one of my sons and his family. His two boys had specific assigned jobs. One had to empty the dishwasher. The other had to take out the trash. Other jobs were assigned as needed. I could see how the children were learning to value all the basic needs provided by the parents by contributing and learning a work ethic. I did not observe selfish spoiled self-interest.

Poor kinds of behaviors are learned from their peers whose parents seem to give them what they want so they will (you fill in the blank). It is natural to want more than you need to enhance the quality of your life. Some people want huge wardrobes while others only need the clothes on their back.

I have six kids, and I could tell when their friends had some new things. They wanted designer jeans, shoes, and spending money to go to the movies to keep up with their friends. I told them we can only afford to buy basic clothes. If they wanted designer clothes, they could get a job and buy those items with their own hard-earned money and value those items.

Today, high school students who qualify take dual-college credit. Several complete an entire year of college before they enroll! Those savings are huge. The Triad should be taught early in elementary schools, so students learn to provide for their future needs. Higher education is costly, but where there is a will there is a way.

I am observing two big benefits to students during the current virus pandemic and required on-line learning. First, students are becoming more aware of what they are putting on their hard drive—meaning their personal computer a.k.a. their brain. Second, they are learning to be better self-evaluators of their schoolwork and performance to help in the home.

If my children chose not to further their education, they had to find a roommate, move into an apartment, and secure a job to pay for their rent, food, car and insurance. I also mentioned I would not let them use our tent to live in the backyard with the squirrels.

Several years later after my triplet boys had graduated from college and had successful jobs from hard work. I asked Matt, "What made you work 14-hour days and sleep on the floor in your brother's apartment?" In less than five seconds he said, "Because you said we couldn't live with you." Tough love increases your awareness fast, but you cannot spring that upon them. Give them some advance notice so they can plan to identify and meet their needs or suffer painful consequences.

As leaders, parents, coaches, managers, and teachers often give in to what children whine to want not realizing you are doing a disservice for them to provide for their personal needs. It is natural behavior to value more what you work to satisfy a personal need. This always improves personal relationships.

Necessity is still the mother of invention. When you create the need using The Triad children learn to be self-reliant and self-starters without your constant oversight.

I advised all my children one question they could be asked in a job interview, "What was your earliest job?" Think how you would compare your answer to others answering this poorly competing for the same position. Who would your potential employer believe has the better work ethic to perform on the job?

Parents who extrinsically motivate children with gifts (bribes) for good behavior do not want to look like bad parents and suffer the consequences. When the child turns 16, they want the keys to the car more than getting the educational foundation to make it in higher learning. This lacks projection to acquire future needs. Immediate gratification is nice, but children who have parents who teach them discipline to delay the onset of rewards to satisfy greater future needs always perform better in the long run of life.

To plant the seed for needing to become educated beyond high school, my wife and I would wear our college sweatshirts and tee-shirts showing pride for our education. We encouraged our kids to socialize with friends who had similar aspirations. We created the expectations for higher learning early.

By increasing government and social programs we violate the behavioral rule: The more you do for people, the less they learn to do for themselves. Society becomes conditioned to expect "Big Brother" will take care of them. Instead, why not teach every performer to learn how to meet and be held accountable for their own needs?

The two most important needs I try to teach are:

1) The need to become educated is a lifelong process. No top performer trusts anyone who claims to know everything. Your education and personality identify you for a lifetime. These two basic life skills no one can take away from you— EVER! The job or need of every student is to work at becoming educated. Parents have a job to supply the basic needs for shelter and food by putting a roof over their heads and bread on the table, so their children can focus on learning to provide for their own needs.

2) The need to work on one's character development (personality). A quality character begins with integrity to oneself and others. You may get away with lying to others, but not to yourself. Your word must be a commitment that has meaning and value to hold yourself accountable, and so others you lead will trust you.

A quality character cares about helping others and shares their knowledge and skills. They strengthen the self-concept to feel pleasure rewarding and reinforcing valued behaviors. People are reinforced by an awareness of a personal feeling doing good deeds. These leaders build stronger organizations, systems, and communities to make a difference by their positive outlook and example.

Needs, Drives, and Motives

Top performers consistently increase awareness of the relationship between personal needs and drives to intrinsically motivate performance improvements. The #1 key is to find your abilities in a variety of experiences and keep improving them.

The best strategy top performers use is setting goals only one point better than their personal immediate past performance or average. This increases the probability for success meeting goals and enhances a personal reward system. The brain knows no excuse and puts forth more focused effort.

The natural innate drive is to seek pleasure with performance improvement. Frequent reward reinforces intrinsic motivation to continue pleasurable feelings. The drive is to work harder and keep improving.

Powerful drives are associated with unconscious primary needs like for food, clothing, and shelter. A secondary need would be to satisfy a personal need or goal higher in Maslow's pyramid. Drives rarely diminish in strength because you always need them. When deprived of primary needs, the drive level is high, but when satisfied is temporarily reduced.

By comparison, a motive is a conscious perception with intent and planning to satisfy a need. The drive is to satisfy your hunger. The motive is the intent and plan to get and prepare food to eat. Fearing loss of the next meal the unconscious drive may be acute and lead to overeating to store fat as needed future fuel.

The need to be loved and wanted has driven people to meet those needs by practicing crazy behaviors like stalking. You cannot easily question what drives an individual. But you can question their motives and intent that require perception and pre-planning thinking skills. The need may be the same, but the motive or process is wrong and must change to affect the performance outcome.

Motives, once satisfied, dissipate the drive strength until the need slowly increases again. Learn to consciously understand your needs and motives to control your behaviors to continuously improve your performance and hold yourself accountable. The interrelationship of your needs and drives and intent must create an awareness to condition whether you are improving or wasting your time going through the motions.

Top performers override feelings of satisfaction to delay the onset of rewards. Not so successful performances increase the motivation to refocus on the positive methods and cues that have led to success in the past. Use this example. You know you cannot operate at full throttle every play, every game, every performance. Focus on improving the quality of key performances at-will-on-demand to affect the outcome.

Professional athletes provide numerous examples. An NBA player can miss 9 of 12 shots early in a game, but with the game on the line can mobilize the energy at-will to get in the "zone" where the hoop appears larger and time goes into slow motion. In this zone of increased awareness, all the senses are working in concert. A few seconds seem like twenty seconds to provide time to get the body prepared to perform.

Maslow's Need Hierarchy

Abraham Maslow published in Psychological Review 50.4: 370-396, 1943 "A Theory of Human Motivation." He formed a "Need Hierarchy" in the shape of a pyramid. At the bottom are basic needs for food, clothing, and shelter. At the top is the need for self-actualization—to do something greater.

Maslow clarified you do not have to completely satisfy each level of needs before moving up the pyramid. When others meet your basic needs, of course you

Maslow's Hierarchy of Needs

can attend to higher order needs. But you may not become more aware of how to meet your personal needs over time.

Creating the Need in You

I create the need in you to learn "The Triad Performance Improvement System" by explaining the benefits. You shorten the learning curve and gain an advantage over the competition to experience the pleasure of more frequent success.

In my presentations to business leaders, teachers, coaches and managers, I always start standing on a chair at the back of the room. Perry Belcher, a well-known Internet marketer calls this psychology "pattern interrupt." Speaking behind a podium on a stage is same old boring delivery audiences have seen before.

To engage I start out with a simple enthusiastic question everyone can immediately identify with to demonstrate how we learn and keep improving a basic skill. This requires people to think and respond. "How many of you know how to ride a bicycle?" Of course, with adults all the hands go up. "How many of you know how to drive cars and maybe small trucks?" Again, adults know the system, the laws, and rules to prevent painful accidents.

As I walk between the tables and chairs, I ask everyone to get a coin to flip. On my command everyone flips their coin. You know there will be an even distribution of heads and tails. So, I remark, "Do you want to go through life with 50-50 odds for your success?" Do you know people who live their lives going through the motions? Is anyone ever a top performer going through the motions?

Personal Experience

I hear too many stories of college students getting wasted at parties doing drugs and mostly alcohol. I think in part because their parents are paying the bills. I do not believe drugs enhance anything except control symptoms of other poor health issues. When the drug wears off the pain is still there. Gaining knowledge and experiencing life is motivating enough.

Whenever your needs are provided by others, they are always extrinsic and less meaningful and relevant to you. You lose your sense of awareness as a human being. As you are helped to become educated the notion is you pass it on to help others in their quest for knowledge.

Authors do not want to take all the knowledge they have been blessed with to the grave. Authors are performers who need to share knowledge and help shorten the learning curve. Knowledge top performers have spent time and worked hard to acquire can make it easier to learn fast, grow and perform better.

I came from a middle-class family and grew up in a suburb northwest of Chicago. Neither parent nor any family relative had ever gone to college. I was the first. My parents were second generation Norwegian immigrants who instilled in me the value of an education.

My mother was in poor health but managed to take on a full-time position as a secretary. I was very aware of the sacrifices and sometimes pain she had keeping her position. She did this to pay for my college education needs so I did not have to get a job and could focus my energy on competing and learning how to coach. In my first years at Indiana University and member of our great swim team, I resisted temptations and harassment to party and drink. I could not dishonor my hard-working mother who was sacrificing so much to value for my benefit.

I would go to the movies by myself. I would rather be a loner than succumb to those poor behaviors I was aware would never help me become an All-American. Today people complain they are bullied and harassed on social media have simply lost their focus. As a kid we learned "sticks and stones may break my bones, but words can never hurt you." Learning to be tough-minded is good leadership quality. It shows personal discipline.

What does not kill you makes you stronger. The Triad teaches self-reliance, and not let others affect your performance. God gave you a purpose. You are unique and must try a variety to experience success and failure. Top performers focus on the outcomes and avoid negative distractions they cannot control.

My needs and motives were entirely different than some of my teammates. I wanted to be a teacher and swimming coach because I admired my coaches as mentors in my life and wanted to do the same to help others. I had to lead myself. In retrospect, none of those party fools ever became All-Americans, and that is something no one can ever take away from me. You must consciously be aware and stay true to your needs and values. Never take what you have for granted because someday that can and will be temporarily taken away to start all over again.

In high school I was a runt. When I graduated, I was only 5'6" tall and weighed 125 pounds. I was a late bloomer, so I got picked on a lot. But I had a great high school swim coach who instilled a strong desire to win by outworking your competitor.

I worked out hard in practices and had only fair meet times because of my small size. In my senior year it was doubtful I could score any points in our State Championship Meet. Coach asked me if he could swim a sophomore in my place so he could get some experience for next year to complete relays, and I said OK.

So, I never got to swim in a big meet. But I had a growing fire burning in me to be a good swimmer someday. It sometimes takes disappointments and failures you experience to motivate a stronger need to perform.

After practice I would catch a ride with our pool custodian on his way home. I would wait up in the bleachers of our new 1200 seat natatorium where we hosted State Championships. I recall breaking down praying to be a great swimmer and coach someday. I had a work ethic instilled in me by my parents and coaches. So, picture me being a walk-on of a great Indiana team laden with Olympic champions and World Record holders a runt and getting picked on by my teammates.

I had to prove myself every day. Workouts were tough, but I got to swim next to the world record holder in my events. Back then freshmen could not compete in the NCAA. You had to be a student first and athlete second. So, we could only compete in Amateur Athletic Union (AAU) meets at the time.

In ten months after graduation I had grown 5½" and 30 pounds! My first big meet was the AAU Championships. All the top college and high school swimmers came to compete. I took 3rd in the 220-yard breaststroke and never looked back. I also went on to coach All-American collegiate women and high school boys.

The point is your needs are different and personal to you. Do not compare your needs or values to others. Be your own person; be yourself. But never lose your awareness of your needs, values, and goals—maybe dreams. Never take for granted anything, and never go through the motions to acquire top performance. Be aware and thank those who provide for your basic needs so you can meet higher-order needs.

Intrinsic motivation comes from personal experience. When you are little your basic needs are met by others. As you mature, you should be taught how to provide for your own needs. Then when others no longer provide for your food, clothing, or shelter and you start to feel cold and hungry your motive is to learn ways to provide for those needs first.

The feedback you get from success or failure experience increases or decreases your motivation. Know that based on your needs being different from others also creates different motives in others.

For example, the needs of a homeless versus rich person are much different. The more you feel a need acquired from the feedback from your five senses increases your drive and motive to satisfy that need.

Thus, the more you do for people, the less they learn to do for themselves. You have removed their need and motives to provide for themselves.

More recently self-esteem psychology has been accepted to give unwarranted praise in hopes of motivating individuals to feel pleasure and repeat those experiences. But praise given by others is always extrinsic and less meaningful. In Maslow's Need Hierarchy self-esteem is high on the pyramid and implied to be intrinsic or the feelings you get from personal achievements, mastery, respect, and recognition.

Even a second grader knows false praise they have not earned. It may cause feelings of mistrust instead of teaching The Triad to improve performance. I feel that giving participation trophies is pointless because the personal comparative value of having earned the reward is lost.

3

VALUES

Value is the central hypothesis of The Triad. Value comes in many perceived forms, and behavior is motivated behind each underlying need. Some of those needs you are subconsciously unaware and others consciously aware. Value is learned by hard work and sacrifice of time, money, and pleasure to exceed expectations for something more desirable or needed.

Behaviorally people tend to not value anything they have been given for free. In most cases, the person in need will accept the free handout, but will not respect the giver or themselves. To value any performance some effort must be exchanged to accomplish the need or goal. Dependency does not create intrinsic motivation.

Different needs have different motivational values based on positive or negative feelings from previous experiences. Harder to acquire needs are valued more. Intrinsic motives are value centered frames of reference from unique past experiences. Performers know how much effort is expended to feel reward from those performances. A specific value expectation will vary for the same activity with different trials or performance of sub skills, and from less experienced ability performers.

This simple equation indicates how top performers perceive value for any performance.

$$V = R / E \quad \text{Value, V, is reward R divided by effort E}$$

Value is created by the amount of perceived reward divided by the amount of perceived effort. Value leads to stronger motivation over time. Therefore, any activity is assigned a relative value using the purely intrinsic equation. The motivation to improve performance and feel pleasure occurs with more frequent success.

R/E %	V
R60/E90	V .667
R70/E80	V .875
R80/E70	V 1.143
R90/E60	V 1.50
R90/E70	V 1.285
R90/E80	V 1.125
R90/E90	V 1.00
R80/E80	V 1.0

Immediate gratification table value range from .875 to 1.143 to indicate too hard or too easy.

Whenever the performer perceives the reward equal to the effort this yields an optimal 1.0 value. Performances rated below 1.0 are acceptable in value to a point about .875 where the effort exceeds the reward. When those numbers are exceeded, they start to feel painful and unrewarding. Too much effort must be expended.

Conversely, when the reward is much greater than the effort, performers feel less value in much higher than 1.143 and certainly at the 1.5 level and higher levels. Those performances are too easy and taken for granted. Top performers delay the onset of rewards and continue focused effort knowing from past experiences the rewards will be greater.

There was a time when I left teaching to go into business as the national sales trainer for a large medical distributor. Some of their reps were making more money than I was so I opted to leave and take a position as distributor rep with another company. As a competitive college swimmer, I was familiar with plateaus and valued my work ethic. When my sales seemed to plateau even though I felt I was working harder than ever to improve, one of our top-performing senior reps told me to just keep working and I would see a breakthrough. One month later several contracts came through. It reinforced my belief to delay the onset of rewards. Those who do value much greater rewards. In sports you see a winner breakdown and cry with emotion. You know they have put in the work to value the reward more. They sacrificed time, money, and pleasure in other areas of life to value one moment in time. Top performers associate quality of effort with quality of reward as a powerful motivating force.

By nature, activities requiring more effort place higher reward value on success. Every improvement or learning experience has reward value is not a failure. The brain is wired to desire positive pleasurable feelings and avoid negative painful experiences.

The following chart puts these notions into visual perspective.

Value Expectations

There are two kinds of values: expected value and actual value from the performance result. Top performers set realistic and achievable goals to obtain congruence or the same result for both values. The personality trait is realism.

Stronger needs create higher value. Your expectation to acquire something too hard or too easy has less intrinsic motivational value. It is that simple. Keep your expectations in line with reality to avoid negative frustration.

Expectation is your subjective assignment of probability for attainment. It is based on your familiarity with the task to improve performance with the criterion. You are not motivated to beat yourself up working hard only to experience failure more often than success. Perceived expectations are represented by a multiple regression analysis in the form of an equation. Each selected variable V has a perceived value.

$$V_1 + V_2 + V_3 + V_4 + V_5 = C$$

Activity Value Index

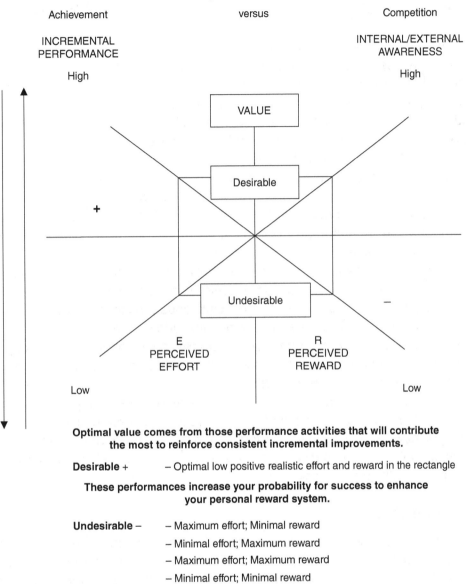

Achievement   versus   Competition

INCREMENTAL PERFORMANCE   INTERNAL/EXTERNAL AWARENESS

High   High

VALUE

Desirable

+

Undesirable

−

E PERCEIVED EFFORT   R PERCEIVED REWARD

Low   Low

Optimal value comes from those performance activities that will contribute the most to reinforce consistent incremental improvements.

Desirable +   – Optimal low positive realistic effort and reward in the rectangle

These performances increase your probability for success to enhance your personal reward system.

Undesirable −   – Maximum effort; Minimal reward

                     – Minimal effort; Maximum reward

                     – Maximum effort; Maximum reward

                     – Minimal effort; Minimal reward

The positive expectation or outcome is the criterion C to win the game or accomplish the goal. You project the most valued variables. The equation predicts variables with the most weight to spend more time to practice and perform.

When I was getting top 10 world rankings for my age-group events in Masters' Swimming, I kept a log of all my workout repeat times. This gave me a realistic variable of my progress to achieve criterion championship meet goals.

For example. Imagine your team in a competition. You must account for several variables. Each variable is beta weighted by your subjective priority of importance to focus on achieving the outcome. V_1 can be crowd size and noise; V_2 is officiating; V_3 is type of conditioning—mental and physical preparation; V_4 is your task familiarity; and V_5 is the health of your starters or as an individual your work-out log results.

There are variables you can control and some you cannot. As the leader your past experiences familiarize your performers with what to expect. This builds awareness of the skills and abilities performers need to practice and apply in competition. Top performers also bring a wealth of experience to share.

Identify ten key performance variables. As the leader or coach, you have experience to project 3 of the 10 variables add up to 60% of the variance. The other 7 only account for 20%. Due to the interaction affects you cannot account for 100% of the variance. What variables would you value spending more time to learn?

Top performing leaders figure out what and when to explain future task experience with a realistic expectation. This is the vision. If expectations exceed reality performers will be frustrated and lose their trust in you. Spend more time wisely on the higher predictive variables with larger subjective % beta weights.

Leadership experience is valuable to improve any organization. Pre-planned leadership builds value in the reward from satisfying the personal intrinsic needs of all your performers. Use pre-planned predictive equations to increase performer's awareness level to focus more intently in practice and on the job.

Narrow the focus to concentrate on the specific cues conditioned to recognize as input from past performances. This mental planning helps performers get peak performances with some level of confidence.

Valued activities are remembered and motivated to keep improving. If tasks are too hard or too easy the optimal reward value to reinforce continued attempts to improve may be lost on the top performer. If needs or goals are not satisfied frequently enough performers give up, get frustrated and stressed, and possibly take out negative feelings on others.

Perception of Value

Value for any activity must have a high positive correlation to Triad strength. A stronger awareness of your purpose and intent to improve increases value of any activity or performance. The predictive value of any activity will vary by performer. This prediction process occurs in two ways:

1. Focus the attention of your performers on what is personally at stake for a future performance to build a purpose to succeed.

    In sports a high level of performance motivation is when athletes feel they are representing their countries more than themselves. Although that is extrinsic overall, the specific focus must be on personal execution of skills from an intrinsic motive.

    Your motivation is to improve your personal best performance. Reflect on the personal value you felt rewarded for past efforts. Use the multiple-regression approach to plug in a host of personal variables such as your abilities and skills from past performances, and familiar outcomes.

Top performers create perceived amounts of reward and effort for every worthy activity to increase their motivation. As the leader, bigger performance events increase personal motivation. But if you start pep talks with extrinsic motives, they can over stress your performers and have negative consequences. Each performer needs to focus on specific cues to do their best. The intrinsic motivation is more powerful. The trick is to get everyone to peak perform at the same time.

2. Make performances worthy of reward to increase value achieved from effort.

You gotta pay the price. Nothing in life replaces learning a work ethic. You want every performer to associate quality of effort with quality of reward. When that is achieved give all the credit and rewards to your performers.

As the leader, you are more familiar with what to expect from past performances so you can offer performers what to expect. This reduces their anxiety from unfamiliar experience with the tasks and can build confidence for upcoming performances. Veteran performers also offer the same kind of quiet confidence and stability.

The awareness of rewards reinforces positive behaviors to create a synergetic effect and consistently improve future performances over time. But when you go through the motions of work with unconscious effort and no purpose, the reward value decreases.

Top performers constantly review personal immediate and past performances to evaluate pre-performances. Working in collaborative groups are seldom preferred. They cannot control the performances of others. This frustration often leads top performers criticizing those on the team who do not display the same work ethic.

The greatest value top performing companies have learned is to align company needs to earn a fair profit with meeting the personal needs for success of the people who do the work. Production and quality performance all improve as each member has a valued interest in the well-being of every performer.

Collaborative group members use group goals and needs to form their perceptual anchoring point or PAP about which they judge the value or worth of new pre-performance goals. From personal research in 1973 I found this to be the least effective drive stimulus to motivate performance improvement.

If you must work collaboratively to learn social skills or participate in a team performance, then it would be best to break the overall assignment into specific tasks and assign those tasks to group (team) members. Each performer is held accountable to do their part and set a specific goal to meet in a pre-performance evaluation. Leaders also benefit from successful performance feedback peers can share with other group members who need to do better.

Extrinsic Value

To improve performance in less time, move away from extrinsic motives like money, verbal praise, gold stars on helmets to more intrinsic performer values. Help your performers identify their personal needs for job satisfaction and align those to be congruent with the needs of the company or team. As a leader ask your performers questions. Get to know them personally so they know you care. Did you get your personal best? What did you do last time? Celebrate success together.

Be less specific in your job interviews. As the leader discuss the overall mission and your vision to set realistic achievable goals. Give your performers the freedom to use their personality and creativity to produce a quality process of intrinsic value. Everyone from the leaders and management at the top down to the people doing the work must be on the same page.

Focus on the positive outcomes, and let your performers define the process to achieve the outcome. They will feel job satisfaction from achieving daily success and look forward to coming to work. This worker freedom to do the work as they define the process and achieve the same outcome is one of the last freedoms to produce job satisfaction and lower employee turnover.

Building Value with Models

Modeling is external and inadequate to modify behaviors. Drug addicts may come from excellent family models, and successful athletes may come from poor family models. Modeling is not the answer. Top performers of all kinds can be role models, but personality and integrity are hard to duplicate. Learning and using The Triad is the answer.

The best model is for the individual to form a personal baseline. You must start somewhere. Then compare your current performances and behaviors to immediate past performances and behaviors.

Ask yourself, "Am I improving? If not, why not?" When you are continuously improving your performance skills and achieve success you connect rewards with reinforcement to repeat like behaviors. This creates awareness of work ethic behaviors.

No one can do your job for you. You must learn how to think, act, and do for yourself and eventually help others. You learn critical thinking skills and develop self-reliance to be independent. Your purpose is embedded in your personal needs and the motives and drives you control to achieve success and measured simply by how you feel value about each performance improvement.

As you acquire The Triad skills, you recognize consistent success over time. These frequent successes become your passion. This model never changes when you associate quality of effort with quality of reward. No one can tell you. You must feel it and know it. Then you will more often succeed than fail.

Two Steps to Increase Your Motivation:

The <u>first step</u> is to create awareness for improving your performance. This is an ability you improve through conscious awareness of your needs and values. Your purpose comes from understanding the overall component skill parts of the overall performance.

The <u>second step</u> is to increase the conscious value of your performance skills. Setting a value and purpose for your performances increases your reward opportunities.

Value is a relative term. Easy performance outcomes are not valuable. Easy come easy go will not increase personal value because the performance was not earned by some effort and is an external reward.

As a leader, understand the root cause of bad behaviors and poor performances. Are they intrinsically or extrinsically motivated? Create a personal connection for the value of the work accomplished and the quality of the reward to intrinsically motivate performance improvement.

To raise the conscious value of your performance skills, the best strategy is to articulate your intent to get clarity. Write your impressions down clearly and briefly. Your intent is pre-meditated from your larger vision of successful performance experiences.

Proper awareness cues can evaluate any performance with positive feedback. You work to correct your errors. You build character by how you respond to less than successful performances. Every top performer remarks they have plenty of failures and learned from those errors. Increase your conscious awareness to value improving your performances.

Steps to Increase Value:

1. Associate new to known information to make meaningful and relevant
2. Choose slightly more challenging tasks
3. Decide how you would like to feel after accomplishing a goal
4. Be more aware of your rewards for completing average tasks
5. Always try to perform better than your immediate past performance
6. Be more consistent
7. Say what you mean and mean what you say
8. Use more of your senses to accomplish tasks
9. Think positive
10. Look for the good in others as they may provide the solutions

4
GOALS

Top performers set realistic goals and consistently achieve them. Low achievers do not project goals and simply go through unchanging routine behaviors. Most of what you have been told about goal setting is not what top performers do! For example, you must set high goals to be a high achiever. Top performers may have ultimate goals but follow a different goal setting pattern.

How you set goals is a function of your personality and performance feedback. Over time your personality evolves as the sum-total of your experience. Successful performances activate pleasure centers in your brain. You are reinforced to want to repeat those pleasurable feelings. You avoid behaviors leading to painful losses. Top performers learn a work ethic early to gain valuable experience overcoming errors to ensure later success and pleasure more frequently.

What is Goal Setting?

Goal setting is a strategy performers used to improve motivation, performance, and validate personal abilities and achievements. Numerous factors affect the kind and strength of goals. Personal goals set by you are intrinsic. Goals set by others for you are always extrinsic and less powerful. A typical list of factors to consider setting goals are:

1. Use of immediate past performance or performance average
2. PAP – perceptual-anchoring point; a performance feedback tool
3. Personality type
4. Strength of need to satisfy
5. Amount of personal value
6. Social group influence
7. Verbal stating

Goal Setting Paradigm

From my personal research testing our 1972 U.S. Men's Olympic Swimming Team full of top performers I learned several key concepts. I gave each member an unfamiliar grip strength task setting goals for three trials each hand. I wanted to learn how they adjusted their new goals based on their immediate past performance or reported performance of other members.

I tried to manipulate their new goals by telling them higher scores from team-mates. To complete the testing, I gave each Cattell's 16PF a reliable sixteen personality factor inventory. From the raw data I used a factor design to correlate goal shifts with personality.

Every one of the top performers set a low positive goal only slightly better than their own immediate past performance. This is counter to being told to set high goals to be a high achiever. Top performers and Olympic team swimmers do exactly the opposite.

When you set a low positive goal only slightly better than your own immediate past performance you increase your probability for success. Success does breed success. Brain mapping shows pleasure centers become active when you feel success meeting a goal or need you value. Would you prefer pleasure meeting your goal, or pain for failing? What behaviors would you want to repeat? Winning or losing?

The factor analysis surprised me. I was aware of Type A and Type B personalities, and my personality factor data revealed three new personality types—Group, Verbal, and Self.

Group, Verbal, and Self Personality Types

No one knows you better than yourself except maybe your mother. Research indicates your brain subconsciously reviews your familiar past performance. This can be an immediate past performance, an average you have experienced, or the influence of a social group and their performances. Using your feedback preference, you form a PAP or perceptual-anchoring point about which to adjust your new goal up or down.

From testing our top performing Olympians and other subjects and correlating their unfamiliar novel task goal shift scores to the 16PF scores, I found these three predominant personality types based on the PAP they were observed using.

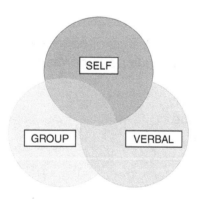

How you establish personal goal standards and use your performance feedback or social group influence is linked to personality factors. These three new personality types Group, Verbal, and Self emerged by observing the feedback preference and perceptual anchoring point (PAP) of these top performers for setting new goals on the novel unfamiliar grip strength task. The three personality preferences are: Group—past performances of groups of performers, Verbal—your spoken goal to others, and Self—your immediate past performance or average.

To categorize personalities as one type or another is not wise because of the interaction effects of personality variables. Top performers use specific types or combinations of performance feedback to set a preference for their perceptual anchoring point or PAP based on their personality.

The perceptual anchoring point is a hard to control dependent variable and why this subject has not been studied very well. The PAP is a perceived standard you use to compare to your familiar past performances to shift your personal goal up or down from that point.

The classic verbal sports examples are boxing champion Muhammed Ali predicting what round he would knock out his opponent and Willie Joe Namath predicting a super bowl win for his AFC team over a powerful NFL team. From my research, I found the least successful were the *Group* oriented performers. *Self* oriented performers were the most successful at consistent improvement by relying on their own immediate past performance or average feedback they could control.

Verbal oriented performers were somewhere in between. Since we are not completely one group or the other but a combined mixture or blend, the usual higher performers are those who are mostly *Self* and part *Verbal* blend of personality patterns. As a leader you must not get offended by the boasting of above average performers and put conceited or arrogant labels on them.

It is their goal setting personality preference to make verbal statements to increase their drive motivation to improve performance. It is important for each performer to be more aware of their valuable past performance feedback. Ask them to keep a personal log, journal, chart, or graph to encourage the *Self* personality type who display higher achievement results.

This *Self* personality type knows they cannot control the performances of others in groups, but they can control what they consciously choose to focus on as a goal to improve. When you record your work achieved, you build necessary value to increase your intrinsic motivation awareness and need to achieve.

When you are aware you have paid a price and worked hard to improve, you build a stronger need or intrinsic motivation to achieve results you can value for your efforts. Top coaches condition their teams mentally and physically to win. They outwork their competition to make them feel more deserving of the reward.

Winning is rarely a fluke or chance occurrence. Your job history or resume or schoolwork is your portfolio. This suggests cooperative group learning environments and teamwork do not necessarily create top performers or increase intrinsic motivation unless you define the role and achievement value for each performer.

The value of having top performers on your team is they demonstrate the intrinsic model to improve their own immediate past performance or average. They hold themselves and their teammates accountable for doing the same things to ensure performance improvement.

It is far better for leaders to teach the *self*-personality type model skills for performers to hold themselves personally accountable for their performance improvement. Once performers learn to equate quality of effort with quality of reward and you give them all the rewards, they will be more intrinsically motivated to improve on their own without having to berate them.

Boss management to be the "watch dog" and extrinsically motivate with threats to hold anyone accountable usually does not work. There is a need to know and understand how and why you are practicing and learning specific performance details. This practice increases the awareness level and purpose of all your performers. By teaching how to use performance feedback and natural drives, you create personal value and increase intrinsic motivation.

Goal Setting Strategies

The low positive goal strategy is preferred by top performers. If you think of any goal greater than one point better than your own immediate past performance, you condition a higher probability for failure. This creates pain you want to avoid and decreases your intrinsic motivation with less confidence.

When you increase your probability for success you can focus on the positive improvement over your own past performance. This reinforces the pleasure centers in your brain, so you will want to repeat those efforts.

When you follow this goal-set-performance improvement sequence, you condition good consistent performance. If you let others who are less familiar with your immediate and past performances evaluate and set your goals, you condition lower accountability and motivation to improve.

If you are only performing to please others, you will eventually fall short of your goals because your personal reward system is not reinforced. There are parents and coaches who want to vicariously see your performance as their performance. They can place extrinsic pressures to satisfy their needs and not yours. This leads to frustration and burnout until you quit to stop the pain or blame others for your poor performance.

Learn to keep your expectations in line with reality. This requires awareness of past performances, the methods, cues, and results that led to your success or failure. Set your own realistic goals. To not try is to fail. But before you perform know your purpose and why you are trying to improve.

Be aware there is a natural drive in you to improve. Use that as the benchmark to keep improving performances with focused practices on the methods and cues that brought you success and pleasure.

The top performer's goal strategy must be only slightly better than the immediate past performance. You cannot control what others think or do. You must learn to control what **you** think and do.

What is your purpose? To hold yourself accountable, ask yourself, "Are you improving? If not, why not?" Use your performance feedback to learn from your mistakes, adjust your goals, and keep trying. There are plateaus you can break through if you keep working to improve.

Be more aware of your small improvements to stay motivated from within to fulfill your goals. Use your personal feedback to increase your awareness and improve upon your next attempts to keep rewarding your effort. This reinforces your work ethic. Then when you improve your last result, you can feel success and pleasure more often.

This strategy boosts your confidence. There is no such thing as learning how to be a good loser or giving up by conditioning more responses to avoid than responses to succeed. Both take the same energy to perform, so choose a strategy to succeed. Your motive to achieve success must be greater than your motive to avoid failure MaS>MaF.

You can make excuses rationalizing your behaviors by lying to others, but you cannot lie to yourself. The personal intrinsic goals you set for yourself are always more powerful than extrinsic goals set for you by others to meet their needs and values.

Set Realistic Goals

Top performers focus on each intermediate goal leading up to achieving the main goal. Low positive component goals increase your probability for success. You can attend to specific cues to improve each part of the whole performance better than focusing on all the whole performance cues to add confusion to your brain. Then, as a rule, the more frequently you feel rewarded you are more likely to be motivated to improve your performance to keep that good feeling.

For example, imagine a friend who is learning to play golf. Rather than have his brain focus on his grip, stance, ball address, swing, and follow through to confuse him, I remind him to slow down his backswing. This one cue gives his brain time to focus on the correct swing path of the down swing and follow through to hit the ball straight. His performance is easy to self-evaluate the immediate feedback. He either hit it straight or pushed or pulled the ball by not keeping his stance to swing correctly.

Average performers compare their past performance to the performances of group members they associate with their activities. Top performers prefer to use their own immediate past performance or average as the PAP or perceptual anchoring point about which to value a new goal.

The Role of Personality in Goal Setting

It is equally important to know the role of personality in the kinds of goals selected. For example, performers who set very high goals or negative goals display an unrealistic personality pattern and have less intrinsic drive motivation. This allows them to build an excuse. This can be corrected by setting low positive goals only one point higher than your own immediate past performance or performance average. This goal strategy provides the highest intrinsic drive motivation as your brain knows would have no excuse for not achieving the goal.

You also add power to your motivation to achieve when you …

- first, understand your purpose for performing and trying to improve,
- second, focus on the cues to recognize and connect with correct responses to perform specific parts of a performance skill, and
- third, self-evaluate each performance part using your performance feedback output to adjust input cues and improve each new attempt.

Self-evaluation skills uses your performance feedback to show consistent improvement and reinforce reward. Start keeping a workout log. Record your practices and the methods and cues you attend to and improve competitive results. Without improving that awareness, you never know when or how much you are improving to feel pleasure and stay increasingly more motivated to keep improving.

Another common goal setting strategy is a mnemonic known as the SMART method. A paper by George T. Doran, "There's a S.M.A.R.T. way to write management's goals and objectives" was published in <u>Management Review</u>, November 1981.

- **S**pecific – the goal is defined
- **M**easurable – in number term objectives
- **A**chievable – for your abilities
- **R**elevant – to fulfill a personal need
- **T**imely – close to the performance

It would be wise to use a combination of your own immediate past performance and the SMART method to motivate performance improvement.

Leadership for Goals Management

As the leader help your performers break complex tasks and skills into smaller component parts. Then help them define and quantify their benchmarks to improve their personal bests despite what others on the team may perform. When the parts are improved chain them all together in sequence for the total performance. Use each performer's immediate past performance to let them set the new realistic goal only slightly better. Then stress the need to hold themselves accountable to consistently improve in measurable increments to feel rewarded. Then when they improve, give all the reward to your performers. This reinforces positive intrinsic motivation to satisfy personal needs and values. When your performers understand how to perform each skill part and keep their immediate past performance in their short term memory, you will see highly motivated performances, people showing up for work on time, report fewer sick days, and offer more creative ideas and energy to improve team performance.

Besides keeping a log or journal to record your immediate and past performances to increase the value of your work to improve your performance, you also need to be aware how you compare to higher performers and set realistic bench-marks. It would serve no purpose to feel good about your performance scoring well in local competition, and then learn you do not compare to others well nationally.

When I was a school superintendent in a small rural community I noted our top students were in the top 5% of their graduating class compared to other students in our school. When they went off to the university, they were only average students and suffered a let-down in their motivation and several quit school rather than com-pete to improve.

Survey a variety of factors to select your perceptual anchoring point (PAP). Your own immediate past performance provides the greatest intrinsic motivation to work with a purpose to improve. Leaders wisely make this intrinsic feedback comparison process important. Great coaches know the personality traits of their performers. They manipulate positive goals in the mode (*group, verbal, self*) their athletes prefer to motivate performance improvement.

If a player is verbal goal oriented gather several teammates and start a discus-sion of each performer's capable goals. Then for athletes with verbal personalities suggest a bit higher or sometimes slightly lower goal than the athlete stated goal. This would manipulate or adjust the goal to increase the drive motivation and pur-pose of the player.

Leaders need to be aware how top performers in specific roles display similar personality patterns to suggest higher performance standards. The top performer can be critical of management especially when performances of others are not improving. The usual result is management fires or trades those top performers to avoid scrutiny.

Raising Performance Expectations

This is a form of conflict resolution. If the leader or coach is respected and puts the performer in the doghouse for falling below expectations, the performer will resolve the conflict by changing their personality pattern to perform what the leader/coach expects. Great leaders/coaches/teachers know the needs and abilities of their performers and hold them accountable to reach their potential—provided those demands are realistic.

At the same time, leaders must explain how to improve the skills needed to per-form. More importantly, good leaders create the need to learn and value the work required to improve those skills. The benefits come from learning to delay the onset of the reward. Personal feedback requires awareness comparing past performance to an improved performance to feel success and stay motivated.

The trick is getting each performer to see the benefits of work to achieve their goal and take personal accountability. Feelings of reward follow to reinforce the work ethic.

What kills morale is when leaders take credit for the valued work of their per-formers instead of giving them all the credit. Take a step back and examine what you are doing. Who gets all the credit? Do your performers feel you really care to help them improve?

Goal Setting Strategy Review:

1. The motive to achieve a personal goal is highest when the goal is set only slightly better than the immediate past performance or average.
2. Merely setting a goal in writing increases the motive to achieve success (MaS) over having no set goal.
3. The motive to achieve a goal gets stronger closer to the achievement.
4. Low positive goals only slightly better than the PAP have stronger motivation than high positive goals well above the PAP.
5. The immediate past performance and performance average form the personal "self" perceptual-anchoring point.
6. Past performance feedback is essential to set realistic new goals.
7. Keeping performance logs or graphs with recorded strategies and cues, practice and trial results and efforts enhance the conscious awareness to set realistic and achievable new goals.
8. Experienced performers are more familiar with tasks and set realistic achievable goals.
9. Performers who think they are better than a reported average score from a lesser intelligent social or physically skilled group respond with positive goal shifts.
10. Intrinsic personal goals set by performers are more powerful motivators than extrinsic goals set by others.
11. Immediate short-term goals are stronger motivators than long term and ultimate goals.
12. Realistic high probability of achievement (PoA) goals provide stronger motives than unrealistic or low probability of achievement goals.
13. Early success with high probability of achievement (PoA) goals build a personal reward system that reinforces work ethic behaviors to achieve future goals.
14. A worthy personal goal has more value to work toward achieving.

Behaviorally, you cannot finish what you do not start. The longest journey begins with the first step. The sooner you commit to start begins to transform your behavior. It is not where you start but where you finish that counts.

Place more emphasis on consistent improvement with a conscious purpose to set low positive goals to increase the probability for success. Frequent success reinforces the connection to a personal reward system. This increases the motivation to improve each new performance to feel pleasure. Top performers control a greater purpose, and do not wait for the approval of others.

Telling performers to set high goals is extrinsic and not the strongest motivator you can reinforce. Performers who set personal intrinsic goals to satisfy needs are more powerful.

The premise for high goals is to set your sights high to achieve high. My research with Olympic swimmers suggests the opposite. Ultimate goals are more a wishful dream than reality, but better than having no goal. To dream is healthy, but the drive motivation is strongest to achieve focused goals only slightly better than personal immediate past performances.

The low positive goal is a predictable practice of top performers. A purpose with a positive intent to slightly improve skills and performance provides the brain with no excuse. The focus is consciously stronger to increase the probability for success. More frequent success reinforces and conditions working harder and purposeful to ensure successful feelings on the next performance.

Good goals come from the ability to self-evaluate, create value in work accomplished, and set realistic achievable goals for personal abilities, skills, and experience. The ideal is performance evaluations confirmed by significant and knowledgeable others who are skilled top performers to validate correct work. This is congruence or an agreement between a projected goal and actual result. Or, a performance self-evaluation in agreement with another evaluator's opinion.

Congruence is a comparison process strategy used to establish the necessary personality trait of realism that produces self-esteem and self-confidence. Increase the probability for success and the brain has no excuse. The commitment to perform above the low set standard greatly stimulates the motive to achieve success.

Leaders create the personal need for achievement using awareness of immediate and long-term needs. Performers consciously choose to focus on intelligent academic and physical study skills with known predictable strategies and cues.

Personality in the Workplace Affects Goals

The drive to improve is innate in all human beings. No one purposefully seeks to fail and feel miserable. Readily available free things provided by others are valued less. Effective leaders educate performers about strategies for learning how to be self-motivated and make personality adjustments using the innate motive to improve.

The personal value and reward-reinforcement system is not often conditioned by the educational system or in the home. My 13-year-old neighbor David was patiently waiting in the car for his mom to take him to school. I walked over to say hello and asked him how he was doing in school.

He said, "Yah, I'm doing OK, but I hate school; it's boring." His reply did not shock me. It is a typical response to public education. Perhaps this is a verbal conditioned response from the playground. More likely, students are not taught a self-evaluation system to learn self-approval and improve their conscious sensory awareness to take in more information and make it meaningful to value it.

The playground response becomes a "water-cooler response" by working adults who express job dissatisfaction daily to co-workers. This practice reduces personal initiative and creativity, company morale, and job performance. A "why bother" syndrome sets in. To get by, employees and students only perform the boss's way of doing tasks.

This is familiar and less upsetting to the boss or evaluator's personality. Suggestions intimidate the thinking process even when performers are encouraged to think outside the box. When talented performers make positive suggestions for improvement and are not given credit, it kills morale and professional growth throughout the company. Companies struggle to improve stagnant professional growth without knowing why. Performers do not care to improve when unable to connect personal reward with reinforcement to be intrinsically motivated.

Great Expectations and Goals

You cannot expect to lead yourself or others basing criteria on the average performance of a group or what critics may say. Do not make predictions based on perceptions of what you think will happen. Use personal past performance history for feedback guide.

Top performers set personal criteria for satisfying performance improvement. They do not wait for the approval of others. Performers may choose to increase the drive level by verbally stating goals with positive self-talk. This motivates performance to avoid bruising the ego.

The greatest predictor of success during a pre-performance evaluation is setting realistic achievable low positive goals only slightly better than personal immediate past performance or performance average. No other variable increases the drive level to succeed better than this goal strategy.

Increasing the probability for success adhering to a purpose enhances personal reward system. Rewarding pleasurable feelings creates value. This conditions pleasurable feelings to work hard and repeat those behaviors to experience more rewards.

The great advantage this goal strategy has is the personal standard to improve constantly adjusts with every improvement to be a new immediate past performance. This simple low positive goal setting strategy applies to intermediate goals. The expectation to perform at a championship or ultimate goal level all season long has low probability.

Learning curves look like lazy "S" shapes. As performance improves plateaus occur with introduction of new cues. Learning is still taking place to make sense of the new information.

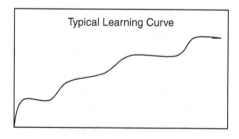

Typical Learning Curve

5

PARADIGM SHIFTS

These paradigm shifts benefit learning The Triad.

MaS>MaF Paradigm

Your motive "M" to a (achieve) success "S" must be greater than your motive "M" to a (avoid) failure "F."

Some athletic teams with a lead in the game start to play a "prevent" defense or slow down the game's pace of play to let the clock run. This shifts the intent and focus away from what the players did for success.

Some successful businesses fail forgetting the purpose and what they did to achieve success. Company management goals may not be congruent with the personal needs of the performers doing the work and the customers.

Focus on performing with a realistic positive intent to benefit the customers and performers. Define expectations to succeed. To focus on how to avoid failure creates coercive extrinsic motives and inconsistent results.

Change the perception and learning strategy. Setting proper goals is one strategy. Understanding needs and values is the other strategy to improve.

Homework and job training are practices designed to reinforce learning outside of school. The feedback is the assessment of the rate and progress of learning. Assigning zeros for incomplete homework or berating employees reinforces a negative motive to avoid failure and decreases intrinsic motivation.

Do overs provide additional credit for correct work accomplished. This reinforces a positive motive to achieve success and increases intrinsic motivation to keep improving performance.

Quality of Effort = Quality of Reward Paradigm

Top performers equate quality of effort with quality of reward. This shift occurs early when modeled by parents and others who display a work ethic and give credit to performers who do the work.

If at first you don't succeed, keep trying. To delay the onset of rewards is a hard lesson to learn. Performances that come easy are not as valued and decrease the motivation to focus on improving. Every great reward has its price. Top performers sacrifice some small short-lived rewards to get needed and valued greater rewards more.

Value Centered Hypothesis Paradigm

The Triad hypothesis assumes more valued information is stored in the brain as readily accessible knowledge. The paradigm shift is to make a conscious decision to equate *value* to new meaningful and relevant information and skills.

What separates top performers from average performers is their ability to store meaningful, relevant, and valued information directly on their brain's desktop. This information is retrieved in only one step to save time and provide a faster response leading to greater success.

Leaders, parents, teachers, and managers of all kinds can stress how valuable new knowledge and quality performance may be and have little effect on motivating performance improvement. Extrinsic communication from others means little until performers increase awareness of the intrinsic value and need to feel some pleasurable reward from the performance outcome.

Leaders need to articulate their conversations, so all performers personally identify and relate the new information to be meaningful and relevant by several kinds of examples. The easiest way is to ask questions so the wheels inside the brain must think of the personal effect on performers. Stress how and why the new knowledge benefits them to improve.

If performers set the goal, do the work, then they must get all the reward! When valued performers want to repeat the actions.

Extrinsic to Intrinsic Paradigm

When leaders rely on extrinsic motivation in the form of praise, grades, or some form of judgment of the performer's work creates a dependent approval system that requires more management for higher cost. Goals set by others are always extrinsic and less powerful.

Top performers are intrinsically motivated to perform quality work when the boss is not looking. The quality of work matters most to exceed personal standards. Observable and realistic goals identify and meet personal needs and values define top performers and leaders.

Performers who are accountable for achieving personal goals get all the credit to feel rewarded. Leaders must be more aware of what goals are being satisfied to reinforce work ethic. The intrinsic motivation comes from understanding the value of an education and need to share knowledge with other performers as a team player.

Sensations to Perceptions Paradigm

Multi-Sensory learning is powerful because it is resistant to forgetting. Albert Einstein was a genius. Upon his death, his brain was stolen and studied. They found he had a massive number of associational neurons.

To recall information to solve problems, Einstein would associate to his other senses. If he could not recall what an object looked or sounded like, he might recall what it smelled or felt like. From that knowledge he could perceive what a potential performance outcome may occur.

Choosing Pleasure over Pain Paradigm

A possible paradigm shift is choosing pleasure over pain and one of the oldest psychological motives. No one gets a good electrical shock, jumps up and says, "Wow, that was fun, let's do it again!" You smash your thumb with a hammer and next time you are more careful to hit the nail on the head.

Rather than go through the motions, how do you increase your odds for success in your favor? Once you learn how to do that for any job, task, skill, or relationship you are on your way to keep improving your performances over time. This is what top performers do to feel pleasure and avoid pain. This is what The Triad can do for you.

Other Desirable Paradigm Shifts

A benefit from using The Triad to improve your performance in less time are these other desirable paradigm shift points. These important shifts relate to moving from:

1) extrinsic motives to more powerful intrinsic motives,
2) unconscious sensory awareness to conscious perceptual awareness,
3) non-valued to valued knowledge acquisition, and
4) from being outer directed by others to being inner directed and holding yourself accountable for personal behaviors and performance.

The most realistic performer knows they can choose to change their behavior to perform better over time.

Practicing The Triad skills creates two major shifts:

1) You equate *quality of effort with quality of reward*. You get out of life what you put into it by becoming less dependent on others to meet your personal needs. This realization comes with maturity and may lead to a better quality of life.
2) The model for education has shifted from *"receptacles of knowledge"* to *"facilitators of knowledge."* This is driven by vast amounts of knowledge readily available through the Internet. As the performer acquiring knowledge, you decide what is meaningful and relevant by choice.

Summary

When you learn The Triad there are no guarantees you will experience 100% success. But you certainly increase the odds in your favor. Top performers learn from correcting mistakes. With greater awareness, even when you fail, 95% of the time you learn something positive to keep improving. That is far better than flipping a coin before you start to perform.

Most all successful performers unconsciously do one or two skills from The Triad, but generally not all three. There are reasons why and how you can learn to overcome that mistake.

6

TOP PERFORMERS

Are You a Top Performer?

A key question I ask is, "Do you know any top performer that ever waits for the approval of another performer, leader, manager, coach, or parent?" After the 2019 college football championship game, Joe Burrow, the winning quarterback with a perfect 15-0 season and Heisman Award Winner was asked if the coaches had anything to say when his team fell behind in the score. He replied, "No, we all knew what we had to do."

Top performers intrinsically know from success or failure feedback what it takes to keep improving. Hal Prince, a notable Broadway Musicals Producer/Director who died at age 91 said, "I've been more often correct listening to myself than listening to other people."

You cannot build accountability in a micromanagement system. Seriously, do you know of any top performer that ever waited for the approval of another person? Then why do you wait for others to judge you when you already know quality performance when you see it in yourself and others?

School systems, business management, and often society conditions us to wait for the judgment of our performance. But top performers develop a personal set of standards based on their personal immediate and past performance history. This provides immediate feedback to judge the relative value of any performance. For a new performance, a positive goal shift occurs slightly better to feel pleasurable improvement. This is intrinsic motivation.

Top Performers Often Set up Tougher Standard Performance Comparisons

Standards compare observed past performances with new expected performance results. I have observed top performing athletes and coaches for a long time. They set models for continuous performance improvement. The premise is they cannot control what other performers are going to do, but they can control what to focus on and try to improve.

As a rule, top performers hold themselves accountable for achieving their performances. They tend to be harder on themselves than leaders who would judge their performance. In more ways they take what they do for granted, and often do not seek the attention afforded them.

Top performing athletes may seem flamboyant to gain attention. I believe this is another method to enhance their motivation to live up to the hype they have created. Trash talk during the game is one more example. This puts them in the verbal type personality.

When I coached All-American swimmers, I stressed keeping outspoken views about opponents quiet. News articles posted in the opponent's locker room increase their motivation to beat you. For that I got in trouble with the Chicago press for restricting my swimmers from talking to news reporters. I made a clear policy for reporters to talk to me, the head coach, and not bother my swimmers.

No one, including yourself, should criticize improving a personal best perfor-mance. Michael Jordan or Tiger Woods got better because they kept evaluating their performance against a personal standard they created. That basic standard is/was to improve their own immediate past performance or average.

For any job, task, skill, or relationship choose a baseline starting point. Your annual physical test results are compared to your baselines and medical history so you can predict good or bad trends. That is the easy part.

The hard part is devoting more concentrated purposeful effort to value your work, improve your health, and ensure performance improvement. In the 2008 Beijing Olympic Games, Michael Phelps was totally devoted to an unprecedented swimming achievement to win eight Gold Medals in a single Olympic Games. He limited the distractions to stay focused on a singular goal. The immense value lives on forever. Any personal achievement you make no one can take that away either.

To be a top performer decide what you are willing to sacrifice that you want to get something of more value later. Top performers manage their time and focused effort. They identify their needs from wants and know their purpose. Some become anti-social and give up dating even marriages and other kinds of relationships to stay focused on their goals.

Learning to Improve Performance Begins with Attitude

As the leader you must ask, "What will you teach your performers who are not learning how to improve?" There are skills and process strategies that have been described. They take time to learn and become familiar with each new task.

One hallmark of many great leaders is they have a proven personal perfor-mance record. Many great coaches today were All-American athletes who played for the great coaches in their day. These leaders know from personal experience the correct methods, cues, and work ethic it takes to win.

My attitude for my achievements is I consider myself an average person who tries to do a better than average job. I have applied The Triad skills to every job, task, skill, or relationship to improve performance in less time.

Top performing leaders can shorten the learning curve. This gives you a leg up on your competition competing for the same position.

Good teachers and mentors apply the same learning process to their performance to know how and when to expect their performers to improve. If these expectations exceed reality, there will be frustration on both sides.

When the probability for achievement is high, you have no excuse. Your drive motivation is higher. When the probability to achieve a goal is very low, performers build in numerous excuses to protect the ego and the drive motivation to achieve is lower.

Performers do not care to improve when painful high frustration impedes learning. The process of learning is to demonstrate improvement in the application of knowledge. Change to a positive behavior by working on parts of performance skill to feel success and reward. This improves the personality, positive outlook, and attitude.

Training programs spend more time evaluating performance (extrinsic) than teaching performers how to self-evaluate personal performances with rubrics and do overs (intrinsic). Research indicates intrinsic motivation using self-evaluation is more powerful than extrinsic evaluation by others to improve learning.

Progressive companies ask employees to self-evaluate their performance prior to discussing the manager's evaluation. This is to determine congruence. If the congruence is high matching, performers are more likely to be intrinsically motivated and continue to improve when you are not looking. It is that simple.

Another helpful standard for transforming leaders is W. Edwards Deming's (1982) 14 principles of Total Quality Management (TQM). Deming used these principles to help rebuild Japan after World War II, and later published them in Out Of The Crisis. If you study Deming's 14 principles, they still apply today to motivate management performance improvement.

These 14 points have been paraphrased to shorten and provide the intent of the work. These points indicate the importance Deming placed on management to intrinsically motivate performers. The very first point is a constant purpose for continuous improvement I have stressed.

1. **Constancy of purpose.**
   This is the continual improvement of products and services by allocating resources for long range needs rather than short term profitability. The plan is to become competitive, stay in business, and provide jobs.
2. **The new philosophy.**
   In a new economic age, you cannot live in the past, accept delays, mistakes, defective materials, and workmanship. Adopt the new philosophy for transformation to Western management style and halt the continued decline of business and industry.
3. **Cease dependence on mass inspection.**
   If you build quality into the product, you eliminate the need for mass inspection to achieve quality after the fact of production. Require statistical evidence of quality materials and manufacturing practices.

4. End lowest tender contracts.

Stop awarding contracts solely on lowest price and require meaningful measures as proof of quality along with the price. Qualify and reduce the number of suppliers for any one item to minimize initial and total cost and variation from your standard of quality. Move toward loyal single suppliers you can trust.

5. Improve every process.

Continuously review and improve every process for planning, production, and service. Identify problems to efficient quality production to reduce costs. Work to innovate and improve every product, service, or product. Insist that management focus on improving the system for the design, purchasing, maintenance, improvement of machines, supervision, job training and retraining.

6. Institute on the job training.

Be certain that every employee is trained to perform their specific job well and offer suggestions for improvement as changes occur.

7. Institute leadership.

Provide leadership aimed at helping each worker improve by changing the thinking from mass production to quality production. Quality automatically improves productivity as workers take pride in their work. Management must immediately respond to reports of defects, poor maintenance, inconsistent operations, and all detrimental conditions to quality.

8. Drive out fear.

Encourage every employee to communicate concerns for quality production without fear of retaliation or retribution to work effectively and productively.

9. Break down barriers.

Eliminate titles to improve communication between departments and staff in order to work in teams with a common objective to improve.

10. Eliminate exhortations.

Remove posters and slogans demanding zero defects and new levels of production without first providing training and materials to produce them. Eliminate the blame game and other adversarial relationships between management and the production work force as low quality and productivity belong to a system that needs to change.

11. Eliminate arbitrary numerical targets.

Eliminate prescribed quotas and standards for the work force, and number goals for management. Instead, focus on helpful aids and leadership to continually improve the quality of the product or service.

12. Permit pride of workmanship.

Remove the annual merit rating of performance and management by objectives in order to provide every employee to reflect and have pride and value in the final outcome of the product or service that they played a role.

13. **Encourage education.**

Encourage self-improvement for every employee with a vigorous educational training program. Educated employees feel a greater sense of trust and loyalty knowing their knowledge is valued and transferred to other employees.

14. **Top management commitment and action.**

Clearly define top management's commitment to improving quality and production through an obligation to implement all the principles. Each must know their specific role in the systematic process to improve and commit to being held accountable for their work and actions to implement the necessary changes.

Performance Criteria System

All throughout your life others have been imposing their performance criteria and goals upon you. These are extrinsic until you learn to select and apply personal intrinsic performance goals. Select your leaders and mentors and their experiential knowledge carefully to learn from them.

Some leaders may have the success credits to coach you, but more probably the criteria imposed by others can never be as powerful a motivator as those self-evaluated criteria you learn to impose upon yourself. As a leader you must be careful in the criteria you impose.

Consult with your performers to devise realistic and achievable criteria to impose a mutually agreed upon quality standard to challenge every performer to improve. When you go away, your performers need to understand how to develop the skills to continuously improve for a lifetime.

Top performers create a personal self-evaluation system with self-imposed benchmarks and hold themselves accountable for reaching their goals. The great basketball player, Michael Jordan, was cut from the varsity high school team as a sophomore. His North Carolina college coach, Dean Smith, rated Michael a good basketball player among the many he had coached.

But no one, including Michael, ever predicted he had within him the purpose, and intent to keep improving his skills to perfection. Using a set of criteria only known to him he kept perfecting his fundamental skills in every aspect to demand more of his ability and become a complete player.

Michael Jordan acquired his criteria through an educational process learned in the home with strong discipline imposed by his mother. The standards of excellence continuously challenged his fundamental skills set by his older brother, coaches, and teachers. Michael Jordan elevated his vision to test his limits and be a complete player. With his fame and work ethic to improve, he felt an obligation to give fans a show to value the ticket price. This improved the entire NBA.

As his performance exceeded his immediate past performance it automatically created a new standard to improve. Use this same goal setting strategy to become a top performer over time. Jordan's pre-performance self-evaluation proved a quality standard with a need to improve that set his positive attitude for each new performance.

He desired and created the need to pay the price for success through learning an intense value system to try and do his best. My hope is you will carry over this idea to all your performances and be your personal leader.

Learning value and respect usually starts in the home with the mother. This enabled Michael to be in control and take accountability for performance improvement. The more he succeeded in small rewarding increments, the greater rewards he could feel to reinforce his work ethic.

Tiger Woods in interviews also reported similar experiences at home with his mother. His father served in the military and everyone thought he instilled military discipline. But Tiger commented he could not go play golf until he proved to his mother the homework was done well first. Education was valued, and golf was secondary.

The Quality of Individuality

Schools use school improvement criteria to improve student and teacher performance. The stakeholders—teachers and students—regard these efforts for change a waste of time. Teachers and building administrators routinely forget the mission statement, vision, values, beliefs, goals, and objectives of the district.

In the 1950's many Americans thought 'Rock-n'-Roll' music was sinful. The free expression in dancing to these tunes suggested moral decadence. In the 1980's two men named Gates and Job dropped out of Stanford University to work in a garage and create the personal computer. They had the vision to see a need and became billionaires!

How do you know if you will be the next leader? How do you know who will be the next Picasso, Jordan, Phelps, Gates, Einstein, or Edison?

These top performers learned how to think, act, and do for themselves and eventually others. They envisioned a different life from the traditional expectations of other performers. The environments created a purpose from increased awareness, self-evaluation, and reward-reinforcement in The Triad and not copying others.

Reporters tried to compare Michael Phelps to the previous great Olympic swimmer Mark Spitz. Michael replied he was not Mark Spitz. He was Michael Phelps.

You can never be creative if all you learn to do is copy other performers. Model top performers, yes, but take time to identify your personal needs and values to match up with your God-given abilities to make a difference.

There are specific skills to learn with your abilities and lead yourself and others to perform them as unique individuals. You are created for a unique purpose. Your main goal in life is to learn what you are gifted in talent and ability. Then develop those skills to eventually share and teach others to follow in your footsteps, not as copies but as uniquely talented individuals.

The beauty of being a young performer is you do not know what you are not supposed to know. Every top performer reports they were told they could not achieve what they dreamed of doing. I recently attended an age-group swim meet to watch my two granddaughters compete. I am amazed at how fast young swimmers' times have become. But my granddaughters do not know the history. They are expected to swim at a certain level, and nothing holds them back.

Extrinsic Motives as a Zero-Sum Incentive

The essence of zero-sum is for me to win you must lose. This is not a win-win situation. In competition you want to emphasize your strengths and capitalize on your opponent's weaknesses. For teams and groups working together, this approach may not be good for all participants.

Weak-minded performers can become bullies to intimidate teammates. They do not want to work as hard to achieve what you as a top performer have achieved. When you achieve great success, it makes them look bad. Top performing students suffer the same problem. The best approach is to avoid those confrontations and be yourself. Spend time with others who have like-minded needs and values.

Top performers consistently control what they think, the choices they make, and how they set and work to achieve low positive goals. Working together in groups with unmotivated performers can be highly frustrating for top performers.

Predicting Outstanding Performers

One of the great qualities of leaders is their ability to judge talent and predict when individuals will perform at a peak. Many factors influence this judgement. Personality and goal setting have already been identified. Work ethic, attitude, use of personal feedback, listening and communicating skills, coachability are among those to consider.

Top performing athletes use their immediate or past performance as a perceptual anchoring point (PAP) to evaluate the worth or value of a new goal. They become their own control group, and do not compare their performances with other performers they cannot control. These factors are easily observed in practice and competition.

You cannot affect what another person thinks or performs. You can control what you do to improve your performance. By setting low positive goals only slightly better than your own immediate past performance you create the strongest motivation to improve. Your brain has no excuse.

Satisfying more frequent goals also improves your personal reward system and confidence. If you break up complex skills or tasks into smaller component sub routines, you provide more opportunities to experience success with small improvements.

Frequent success conditions and reinforces the need to keep feeling good about the next performance. This drives positive motivation to ensure success with a little more focused effort and purpose. The value hypothesis is fulfilled by readily storing and retrieving valued information to perform complex skills.

Increasing awareness creates more associational neurons to assist in the speed of sensory data transmission. Top performers you respond faster to anticipatory cues. Good coaching teaches early recognition of correct cues in skilled performance.

Top performers know how and when to mobilize all their talents, abilities, and energy for a single moment in time. Average performers have not mastered this skill. They do not know how to use personal performance feedback.

Top performers see the big picture and base their vision on their individual diverse set of experiences. They are familiar with various tasks and jobs. All behavior is driven to improve quality of life and imagine how success will change them. Fulfillment of your needs is what drives all your behaviors and a function of the environment you create.

I like to believe and express to others there is no such thing as failure. However, there are varying degrees of success. Top performers know their purpose and rely on their familiar experience to get results. They accept failures as part of the learning process to improve, and do not give up.

Top performers consistently use logs or journals to track consistent improvement and create the need to improve. Inconsistent performers do not focus on their immediate past performance to create a personal need to improve.

Performance inconsistency encourages micromanagement by others, and the more performers are micromanaged the less they learn to do for themselves. This does not build good leadership or personal accountability.

In this era of everything now or do something else, top performers stay the course. The phrase, "Quitters never win, and winners never quit" comes to mind.

It takes the same effort to fail so why not choose a better performance improvement system like The Triad to improve your odds for success? When you put forth a little more focused effort to succeed with a purpose using The Triad, you greatly improve your odds for success, gain pleasure and want to repeat those performances and keep improving.

Top performers continually evaluate their performance feedback and change the input cues and methods to get better results. Feedback awareness is critical to learn what needs to change to improve performance. Otherwise you get the same old results. Be aware of personal needs and goals you are trying to satisfy. Over time associate your work ethic and paying the price with results to value performance improvements.

What makes a top performer over time is how to deal with the pain of failure. Greater pain is a greater motive to work with more purposeful effort to ensure success.

You may think a top performer is the star athlete or salesman. The top performer could be the best local bank teller at the or school custodian. It is any performer who understands their needs and abilities and is motivated to perform increasingly better over time. They are not a one-and-done performer.

Top performers increase awareness to focus on specific cues that contribute most to their success. The ability to identify and apply specific cues to predict learning correct skills faster improves performance.

Top performers are not unique. They eat, sweat, sleep, bathe, breathe, and brush their teeth like you do. The hallmark of top performers is they are aware when to increase their level of performance (LOP) at critical times. The increased awareness keeps pace to readily mobilize their energy. Average performers have fewer awareness skills to create value and miss meaningful and relevant cues.

Top performers use the personal immediate past performance as the perceptual anchoring point to set the next low positive goal. This skill is taught using portfolios, graphs, workout logs, diaries, etc. This feedback reminds you what your immediate past performance was, reflect on how you achieved it, and know what cues and skills to focus on to keep improving.

Complex tasks must be broken down into smaller parts to create specific sub routines to focus on improving and increase opportunities for reward. When each part is perfected you chain the parts together for entire skilled performance.

Each sub routine has a set of specific S-R connections. Each S-R is a specific stimulus cue, and response. Practice the identical elements you expect to see in the actual performance to condition the response speed. Faster responses yield better results.

To support this skill development, top performers use mental rehearsal, visual imagery, positive self-talk, and pre-competitive routines to mobilize energy when it counts the most. Try creating a subjective multiple regression equation and beta weight the most important cues to focus on learning correct responses to perform any criterion skill.

In education this is called best practices, but not everyone uses them. All throughout the first part of The Triad there are suggested steps to increase your awareness for specific concepts like needs, values, and goal setting.

Top Performers Know How to Focus

Value created from performance intensity raises intrinsic motivation. Your ability to focus on any given activity for any length of time to improve your performance begins with your "why" or purpose to get clarity. All Internet marketers and life coaches stress clarity of purpose.

Top performer's performances appear to be fluid in motion and look easy. A variety of performance experiences, and specific practice are conditioned to instantly recognize the best predictive cues (stimuli) to focus on and connect the correct response for best results.

Here are several strategies top performers use to improve focus:

- Recognize when to raise the level of performance when it counts the most value. Pro basketball legend, Michael Jordan, was not "on fire" every minute of every game but had the awareness to elevate his performance when it counted the most.

- Focus on key elements to consistently produce quality results. Practice enough to readily recognize stimulus cues and reinforce with specific response connections in concentrated periods of time. Top performers increase focus on specific elements or parts of performances in manageable increments in the sequence performed.
- Use more of your senses on a conscious level to bring purpose of tasks into clear focus.
- Use performance output to provide valuable feedback about what senses provided the best results. Then modify practices to focus on the new input cues to improve performance. See the B.F. Skinner black box feedback loop diagram.

B.F. Skinner Black Box

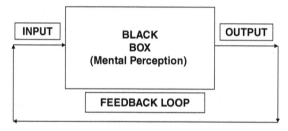

- Keep working on performance improvement even though no change may be seen learning is still taking place. These are called plateaus or in athletics "slumps." This diagram was shown earlier in a different format shows a lazy "S" type curve in learning and performance.

Typical Learning Curve

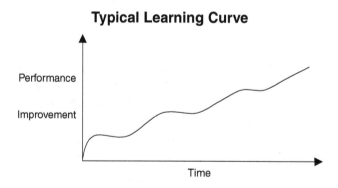

- Work on your personality. Top performers use past experienced feedback to associate correct cues with familiar response patterns for various tasks. Then compare them to an expected performance. They are high in the personality trait of realism to predict the next trial or performance. Poor performers are low in realism with expectations exceeding reality or logically possible. Congruence results when your goals and performances are the same.

- Top performers have a clear purpose to match their abilities and plan specific practice for specific results, and not on luck. This is specificity of training.
- Task familiarity. As you become more familiar and experienced with tasks, your personality traits of confidence and security to take risks increase.
- Use a keyhole strategy to imagine looking through a small keyhole and picking out specific objects in the background to see more details.
- Another useful strategy is the third eye to visualize an image of your performance from behind.
- Practice immediate refocus. It is not possible to take back a mistake. If you have difficulty in the beginning, middle or end of a performance, refocus on correct cues rather than reinforce the negative feelings or remorse over something you can no longer control.
- Displace – replace. You hit a bad shot in golf or basketball and play must continue so refocus on the positives and extinct the negatives. Your brain is a micro-processor. It does not know right from wrong so it can be programed to focus on performing the correct cues and responses.
- Visualization. Create the perfect mental movie of the performance you realistically expect. Be specific with your cues and positive outcomes in the sequence you will perform. This is what I look like prior to a big swim race.

If you lead or manage groups of individuals who cannot concentrate for longer periods, try these strategies to increase their perceptual awareness:

1) Help them identify their needs and abilities to create a purpose for performing smaller parts of an activity well.
2) Explain each performer's role in the quality of the finished product or service. Then ask them to reflect and visualize more value for the work they accomplish.

Old behaviors are hard to shake. If the attention span decreases, provide smaller incremental time periods to help refocus on only one or two specific cues. For example, if a reader suffers from attention deficit disorder, instead of reading an entire page before taking a break, suggest a paragraph or a certain number of sentences to read before getting up to stretch or get a drink.

Do a quick review of older familiar knowledge to transfer to new unfamiliar information and allow time to associate and organize the new information. This kind of achievement and reward system disciplines the mind to complete small tasks focusing on retention of information for future applications.

Steps to increase your focus:

1. attach significant value to the work you accomplish
2. take ownership and hold yourself accountable for your behaviors
3. remove prejudice and personal bias thinking what you or a performer cannot learn or learn

4. think positive; restate negative thoughts into positive terms
5. use the emotion of caring and loving thoughts to help others succeed
6. whatever you think your brain will translate into your body language for people to read
7. add realism for reinforcement value
8. set realistic achievable goals
9. keep your expectations in line with reality to avoid negative reinforcement
10. understand your needs and abilities before you do anything
11. know your purpose for what and why you choose to perform
12. lead yourself before you expect to lead others
13. learn skills you can master and teach others
14. set low positive goals to frequently achieve and enhance your personal reward system
15. master the important cues and forget the rest

Selective Attention

Selective attention is the ability to focus on specific cues to predict the best process to learn a skilled pattern. This conditioning process happens when you override your unconscious sensory system.

Create a conscious cognitive perceptual awareness to make more valued information meaningful and relevant. The Triad increases sensory awareness for recognizing selected biological cues to improve performance. This paradigm shifts awareness from unconscious to conscious sensation known as biofeedback.

For example, if you are aware of your body and strain a muscle performing, you may risk greater injury failing to recognize the possibility. Top performers are acutely aware of their surroundings, crowd noise, and other distractions to remain focused. Fans try to distract a foul shot with moving visual objects behind the basket. But the focus is only on the rim and pre-shot routine.

The value created with a work ethic and preparation increases the need to succeed and be rewarded. Hard-working top performers are seldom denied rewards for a long period of time. Begin to connect your success to valued work and preparation and increase your intrinsic motivation.

Use diaries, logs, or portfolios of your work to increase awareness and recall of immediate past performance. Then recognize the performance success cues to reinforce your personal accountability.

Top performers are motivated by satisfying personal needs, awareness of what they value, and a positive belief they can achieve their goals. All behaviors are driven by a subconscious need to improve quality of life.

The Triad makes you aware of your subconscious sometimes innate needs and shift them to a conscious level. Your personal needs and values define your purpose. And understanding your personality to set realistic goals increases your reward system and motivates you to continue improving your performances in less time.

As a side bar. How do you define success or failure? Every top performer accepts failure as a learning opportunity to keep improving. Others may quit because they cannot accept the pain of losing. I do not see failure. I see varying degrees of success. Success is not whether the team wins or loses a match or game. It is your contribution to exceed your immediate past performance or average to do your personal best. No one can ever criticize you. Your critics cannot do what you do.

Top performers perceive the relation of the performances of others far less important and use their own past performance as benchmarks to improve. Students and athletes choose mentors, schools, athletic programs, teachers, and coaches who help them shorten the learning curve to become better top performers faster. This provides an advantage over your competition vying for the same position or result.

PART ONE

THE FIRST SECRET SKILL

INCREASE AWARENESS

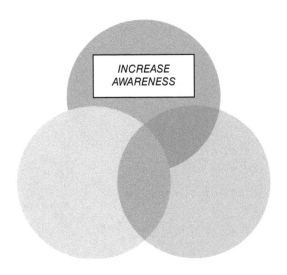

There are over 1001 different ways to increase your awareness. Part One focuses on these main ideas: Structure, Ability, Intelligence, Accountability, and Strategies to increase your awareness.

7

PART ONE OF THE TRIAD TO INCREASE AWARENESS

Top Performer Forward Thinking

You cannot change the past. Focus on your future to be a top performer. Use awareness of the environment and needs you create to keep improving practice performance in small increments to feel rewarded.

By constantly improving your awareness skills, you appreciate mentors, teachers, coaches, friends, and family helping you. In conversations project what is meaningful and relevant to add value. People help people when they value the worth of every performer. No one performer is more important than another when you increase your awareness of others as messengers sent to help you.

A positive attitude provides intent and purpose to your life. According to the 80–20 rule, 20% of the people account for 80% of the objections in your life! Focus on the majority and body of your work in small successes. Think positively and critics are less worthy of your time and negative focus. Use the power of your faith to lead yourself and others. With awareness skills and practice, you perform and achieve more positive good to benefit you and those you lead.

I had a discussion with our daughter who is a successful events planner for an international company. She is a leader in her company but feels the need to manage people, too. My fatherly advice was, "If you lead, plan to learn what the needs and values are of those you lead. Then align the needs and values of the company to coincide to meet those needs." That is what creates intrinsically motivated employees.

I also mentioned the time-honored business philosophy of the great circus magnate P.T. Barnum. P.T. chose to hire what others thought were freaks such as the beaded lady, dwarfs, and very tall people. He gave them a job and a purpose so they could help themselves.

At the height of his success a fire destroyed his whole business. He had built millions and lost it all. He wanted to quit, but his performers demanded he rebuild. His loyalty to them was returned, and he made millions again. His business philosophy was simple.

1. You dream the biggest dream
2. You market the living hell out of it
3. You treat your workers like family

Successful top performing business leaders today use the same basic philosophy. No top performing employee wants to be considered as a commodity to be bought and sold. Although, no matter how successful you become, always remind yourself we are all replaceable. We do not live forever, and others need to take our place to continue our legacies.

Great leaders are visionaries, inventors, and artists. They display strong passions. They have projection skills acquired from experience and task familiarity to know what to expect. They use past performances and meaningful and relevant information to lead.

To be a top performer, your first awareness should be to model or copy what other top performers in your field are doing. Then, use your personality, experience, and intelligence to be your own brand. A variation of the same theme to shorten your learning curve and benefit over your competition.

Einstein used multi-sensory learning to create more meaningful associations from his environment in proven practices, methods, and cues. Your brain has the same capacity to store and retrieve a lot of information. Why waste time and energy packing it with non-essential data?

Be aware of your natural drives and needs. Then compare your performance behavior with top performers. Make a list of similar compatible awareness skills and results.

The average performer has lower awareness skills, purpose, and knowledge of needs versus wants. Simply wanting to perform better is not the same as needing to perform better. What wants will you sacrifice to gain something more valuable that you need or value?

How much time do you waste watching TV, listening to music, or playing video games? Top performers focus on increasing the awareness skills to get results from the work they put in. Motivation is to enjoy greater feelings of frequent reward. Those rewards enhance the pleasure centers in the brain and are longer lasting. Recall the paradigm shift, Quality of Effort = Quality of Reward.

Make yourself a unique performer. While leaders are more aware, whole societies are decreasing their awareness skills. You are unique. God gave you talents and abilities to improve and make a difference to help others.

Experience is still the best teacher. Practicing a positive focus reflects on your abilities, skills, needs, and goals you gain from past experiences increases your awareness. Learn to convert negative thoughts to positive thoughts by simply restating them in your mind.

RROSR

This meme or anachronism you must memorize to help you associate new to old information. This is what makes new information intrinsic by the amount you value. You cannot appreciably increase your intelligence until you learn to increase your awareness to recognize, receive, organize, store, and retrieve (RROSR). You decide what value new information is meaningful and relevant information to learn.

Parents, teachers, managers, coaches, and leaders can tell you what is meaningful and relevant to shorten your learning curve, but you ultimately decide how new information has value in your performance system.

Value makes new knowledge acquisition intrinsic and measurable. Based on your value system and philosophy you create your personal set of standards. I state this several times, "No top performer ever waits for the approval of another person." Your choices make or break you as a top performer over time. Give those some thought to choose wisely.

To begin this process, imagine your reward feelings in doing a task well. Now, imagine a task or event you did not do well. No one likes to fail and feel pain.

The oldest behavioral notion is to repeat pleasurable satisfying performances and avoid painful ones. Avoid routine "go through the motions" subconscious behaviors. Instead selectively focus on the correct cues to associate with correct responses to condition positive conscious behavioral responses.

Build value and a stronger personal reward system associating quality of effort with quality of reward using your personal feedback system. This overcomes occasional failures and learn from them to build your confidence and self-esteem. No one can convince you with words. It must occur by your own actions and intrinsic motivation. How badly do you need to be successful?

Hypothetically, your brain can more readily recognize, receive, organize, store, and retrieve knowledge you value. Non-valued information may be stored, but it is not readily retrievable because it lacks the positive intrinsic associations to other pleasurable successful activities.

The Triad is a performance improvement system in less time. Awareness is one of those skills, and RROSR is one of the strategies to increase your awareness and applies to all skill learning.

The Brain's Structure

The size of the circles does not depict relative importance.

RROSR—Circles of Interconnected Brain Lobes

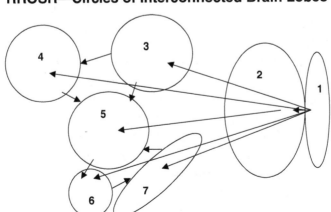

The pre-frontal cortex PFC takes in information from the senses and organizes it into tiny bit maps for faster storage and retrieval with similar associated patterns and data. Your PFC is not fully developed until you are 23–25 years old. When you make decisions or manage others can you understand why this is important?

With purposeful and valued experience, the brain is organized to respond and perform efficiently. The brain learns best by associating patterns and sequences to stored data.

1. Pre-Frontal Cortex- associated with planning, reasoning, and short-term memory to organize information into bit maps
2. Frontal Lobe- associated with thinking, reasoning, planning, parts of speech, movement, emotions, and problem solving
3. Parietal Lobe- associated with movement, orientation, recognition, perception of stimuli
4. Occipital Lobe- associated with visual processing
5. Temporal Lobe- associated with perception and recognition of auditory stimuli, memory, and speech
6. Cerebellum, or "little brain", is associated with regulation and coordination of movement, posture, and balance.
7. Brain Stem. This is your spinal cord where all the information to and from the brain travels through bundles of nerves.

Each lobe compresses information into bit maps and organizes them for easier storage with other like information or patterns to improve the storage efficiency. Capacity with billions of brain cells is not the problem. A child learns efficiently better and faster if taught RROSR and multi-sensory sequential learning.

The large number of correct stimulus-response connections are compressed into tiny bit maps to improve and condition performance and thinking capacity. This is necessary transmit large amounts of data fast to avoid confusion and delayed performance. This is well documented in the flight or fight mechanism.

Think of a long train of cars carrying loads of coal and how long it takes to move across a railroad crossing. Now think of a high-speed bullet train loaded with all the same contents shot across the same crossing. You may have a movie icon on your computer's desktop. In one click a two-hour long movie opens with millions of stimulus-response connections. Reflex neuronal transmission is in milliseconds.

Practicing repetitive skills whether athletic physical or academic math problems teaches efficient early sensory recognition of cues. The information is received from the five senses. Then similar associated patterns and data sequences are believed to be organized in the PFC as a temporary short-term memory file to select the proper brain lobe to zip the file and store it. Now you get to quickly retrieve the most relevant information once you become familiar with the tasks from practices.

As an early learner it may seem boring to perform the same kind of math problem 20–30 times when you already know how. More practice helps you recognize and correctly perform similar math problems faster. Physical skills practice aids in faster recognition of cues with a correct response provided you have the proper information stored from experience to make skilled top performances.

Top performers have a wealth of sensory information from prior experience already stored in their memory banks. Beginners make more mistakes because they do not have enough familiar experience with cue recognition to respond correctly.

Each lobe properly stores the information and the associations, so the brain is ready to retrieve all the information it needs to perform skills. As the information is passed through the brain, the PFC and other centers, make comparisons of past performance as stored knowledge with new performance knowledge to improve learning and performance.

Prior to an important performance or getting ready for a written test you review your notes. Similarly, you draw upon all your past stored information to visualize a top performance to beat your goal.

There are times when I need to get an answer to a problem and rest my eyes on my folded arms on my desktop. There are stories of Thomas Edison and Albert Einstein using this same process to draw upon their stored multi-sensory information to get solutions to try. Or, maybe they were searching for Divine Intervention.

Your brain is a micro-processor. It does not know right from wrong. It is designed to process sensory information sometimes reflexively looping through the spinal column and lower brain stem to provide an instantaneous response. To prevent severe injury, you withdraw your hand from a hot pan or blink when a speck of dirt hits your eye.

Your Brain as a Microprocessor

Be aware of what and how you are learning. Think of what you are putting on your personal hard drive (your brain). Once any event is on your brain it gets stored and compressed into tiny bitmaps. It cannot be totally erased even if you try to block out the memory.

The brain is an awesome organ made up of billions of cells linked by associational neurons. The central nervous system connects the body to the brain with nerve cells. Practicing repetitive skills creates nervous pathways and speeds up transmission through the nervous system network.

The brain is a micro-processor that responds to a continual barrage of stimuli by the second and minute. The body has built in synapse filters to prevent the brain from being overloaded with non-essential details, or man would have been an extinct species a long time ago. A built-in sensory flight or fight mechanism does not require thinking to delay action.

In the early 1900's, Korbinian Brodmann defined specific structures and functions of the cerebral cortex or human brain. Brodmann area 11 is defined as the prefrontal cortex, and is involved in planning, reasoning, and decision making. Persons who have had brain injuries to this area are not able to use these skills.

Theoretically the prefrontal cortex acts like the cache short-term memory on your computer. This short-term memory space is where you assign value, meaning and relevance to new information, compare patterns and sequences to associate with prior knowledge, and plan where to store the new information.

This calculative valuation process establishes the quality of your personal need to be satisfied and develops your intrinsic motivation. More importantly, this part of the brain is used to preplan a correct visual pattern sequence to perform complex skills at will on demand by recalling prior experiences specific to the program you create.

First create your personal pre-performance visual mental movie of your expected performance. Then set up a trigger cue like a race starting gun or pre-shot routine to execute your planned performance.

U.S. Olympic gold medalist Michael Phelps was a swimmer who set numerous world records in a variety of events. He created a pre-planned and mentally rehearsed strategy to perfect a subroutine to win all eight events in the 2008 Beijing Olympic Games. As a top performer he and others create a wealth of quality stored information to readily retrieve. To be a top performer requires the same effort.

As a performer set up similar executable files using mental imagery or visualization to see yourself performing a skill as if you were videotaping your performance. Through mental practice visualize and program the correct stimulus-response connections to perform in the proper sequence. Then set up a trigger sound or flash to start your program.

Then trust your experience and prior stored knowledge to execute the pre-planned program to the best of your ability. This a skill that gets better with practice.

To achieve the best results, learn the best strategies and cues to predict success. When the information you used in your stored files is more accurate to start with, and you have practiced and conditioned yourself for the task, you are more likely to be successful.

A common mistake all leaders make by not understanding how the brain functions as a microprocessor is to focus the performer's attention to negative cues and outcomes to avoid. Those negative verbal communications and non-verbal images condition the association to make the negative event more likely to happen.

I once overheard a gymnastics coach yell out instructions for the entire team to avoid mistakes today to prevent injuries. A sport psychologist tells the story about a pitching coach who came out to the mound with the bases loaded to tell his pitcher how to pitch to the next batter. "Whatever you do, don't pitch him anything low and inside. That's his wheelhouse."

You know the image this pitcher made. Your imagery creates an automated response and reinforces the behavioral connection. The pitcher's behavior was to replicate that image and the batter pounded a grand slam.

The 2008 U.S. Women's Olympic gymnasts made a huge blunder watching the performances and mistakes of the Chinese gymnasts immediately before their performance. Several made similar mistakes because this was what was last programmed in their mental movie subroutine. Tiger Woods never looks at another golfer's swing, and only programs his personal short visualization in his pre-shot routine to take dead aim.

If I yell a negative instruction loud enough to bridge the synapse for you NOT to think about oranges, you immediately create an image of 2–3 brightly colored oranges. This demonstrates your brain is a microprocessor that does not know right from wrong.

After you form the negative image, I tell you to think about a positive image of bananas. Those oranges fade out of view and the bananas appear. This supports why positive self-talk, mental rehearsal, and correct visualization of cues in sequence can improve your awareness and performance focus.

Perceptual-Motor Learning

Your brain also makes new information meaningful and relevant by taking sensations and turning them into organized information with a process called perception. How you learn to turn sensations into meaningful perceptions and improve your performance is better practiced by knowing your purpose to value the process. Leaders tend to not fully understand the need for this process and provide the correct cues and sensations in verbal instructions and demonstrations.

New information you intrinsically make meaningful and relevant to value you store as knowledge because you perceive the benefit to your learning and link or associate to your performance. RROSR is a simple way to recall the process for how the brain works to recognize, receive, organize, store, and retrieve information to learn and understand.

It is harder to unlearn a conditioned response than to have learned the correct conditioned S-R connection in the beginning. You must be conditioned to recognize the correct cues to correct responses or learning suffers immediately. Refocus skills can recondition a correct response to the same stimulus, but it takes more time.

A blatant example is when I was a swimming professional. The Red Cross advocated teaching side stroke before breaststroke because it was easier for inexperienced teachers in their system. Breaststroke may be complex but is easy to teach and learn when you chain together sub routines or parts of the kick or arm strokes.

But once a student is conditioned to perform a sidestroke scissors kick, the perceptual-motor panels that control the dorsi-flexion of the one foot is confused. The result is a scissors kick doing the breaststroke on their stomachs inefficiently. However, I teach breaststroke first in about one hour using my system of easy-to-master one-minute steps. After learning breaststroke, I can teach sidestroke in 5–10 minutes.

Use selective attention to recognize the correct sensory cues to readily receive the information into the brain. Multi-sensory learning has a distinct advantage over acquiring knowledge in only one sense modality. The dominant sense is vision, but performance is improved best by creating more associations using more senses to improve storage and retrieval.

In psychology paired-associate conditioning is when you use two different sense modalities to make new skills more resistant to forgetting. You have visual, verbal, and kinesthetic modalities. Visual is predominant, but you can also pair with a kinesthetic or feeling cue. Now you can see what you feel so when the visual is gone you can still create the image by the feel you associated with that image.

All new information is believed to be temporarily kept in short-term memory. The pre-frontal cortex or PFC in front of your frontal lobe where all your thinking takes place is believed to serve this function. The PFC organizes new information and funnels data to brain lobes associated with like patterns and sequences.

Visual patterns are probably compressed and stored as bit maps through the optic nerve in the occipital lobe. Each lobe has specific storage functions, and they are connected by brain cells and associational neurons.

As the "organizer" the PFC stores new information in temporary files and the cerebellum connects stored associations to compare with the new information. Visualization and mental rehearsal techniques create a mental movie of the spatial and temporal operations taken from the associated lobes of the brain.

Congruent RROSR Awareness

Increasing your awareness creates numerous multi-sensory associations to enhance the way you respond. You develop an efficient valuing system using your multiple senses to increase your motivation.

Intrinsic motivation conversely improves your awareness skills and increases your intelligence defined as your ability to recognize, receive, organize, store, and retrieve (RROSR) information to store as knowledge.

Perceptual awareness is a leadership skill. Leaders need to learn and practice correct teaching methods and demonstrate sensory cues to assign value and meaning relevant to past and future performances. This creates knowledge. Your past may be less important than your future, but your awareness applies the memory of feelings from past experiences to anticipated future goals. Your immediate past performance provides a valuable perceptual anchoring point about which to judge the value of your next goal.

How to Teach Intrinsic Motivation

You must closely align perceived value meaning with actual performance results. This reward connection reinforces and strengthens your motivation to repeat those behaviors. Reflecting on your past performances and associating a value to your new goal increases your probability for attainment to slightly improve with each new attempt and feel rewarded. Keep a log, diary, or journal to recall your past performance results and feelings.

Reflection and alignment are teachable and learnable intrinsic skills. As a leader or teacher tell and demonstrate to performers how to do a skill and explain the personal benefits. This makes new information meaningful and relevant in their learning system. Without the why would be extrinsic and less powerful motive.

Motivation, awareness, and intelligence have a complex interrelationship that builds synergy. As you work to improve one area, your performance affects the other two by the interrelated associations you create from your past experiences and task familiarity.

Several quality performers raise the awareness level for teammates. Opposing teams raise their awareness levels to motivate focused competitive behaviors against a better team. Top performing athletes get in a "zone" increasing their awareness during a performance.

Michael Jordan joined the Chicago Bulls and spent his first four years realizing as his talents grew, he could not win an NBA Championship by himself. He led team members and elevated their performances in practices and games by focusing on teaching them specific higher awareness skills relevant to the task. Sport psychologists call this the will to win or toughmindedness.

Success breeds success, although few top performers can tell you how this works. But they all know quality when they see it. The strength of your awareness comes from being able to identify and understand your personal needs, drives, motives and goals, and aligning them with actual performance outcomes.

To go through routine motions without a clear purpose, your success is haphazard and 50% probable at best. You may be lucky to occasionally succeed, but you cannot attribute your success to your skills. You need to process personal feedback.

Luck is when preparation meets opportunity. The Triad leadership training develops your intrinsic motivational skills to a conscious cognitive level to understand your motives. The acquisition of this knowledge consistently improves your performance and helps other performers.

Most performers use intrinsic motivation occasionally by chance. Top performers are consistently self-motivated to improve their performance in small increments. This enhances their personal reward system and work ethic to keep feeling the pleasure of success.

Leading with Intrinsic Motivation

How do leaders reach people who are failing and not self-motivated? Failure is a painful feeling to avoid. I believe boss leaders spend more time telling and less explaining how to benefit the personal needs of the workers.

A lead manager teaches self-reliance with a can-do attitude to build confidence and personal reward from a job well done. No matter how much work it takes to build the team to function together, the lead manager never takes credit for the team.

The problem is most people have not understood the difference between a want and a need. You can waste valuable time and effort wanting all kinds of things you do not need. Personal needs and values are the driving force of intrinsic motivation.

In affluent societies worldwide, children have learned an expectation for others to provide everything they want. Older generations had to get a work ethic to acquire what they wanted, and needs came first. As a behavioral rule I state several times, "The more you do for people, the less they learn to do for themselves."

When no one holds you accountable to meet your personal needs with a work ethic, you learn to expect others to provide for your needs and do the work for you. As the mentor, manager, teacher, coach, or parent leader you may think initial failures are harmful. You feel the pain sometimes worse than your performer, so you feel the need to ease the pain and help by doing the work to show them how.

The exact opposite effect occurs to enable more failing behaviors. The idea of self-improvement is remote because you did not teach an intrinsic motivation strategy. Getting failing performers to increase their awareness and take accountability for their learning, behavior, and performance is a huge task. There will be painful feelings, but you cannot let performers place the blame on the leaders.

The trick is getting performers to hold themselves accountable for their performance instead of evaluators like a teacher or parent threatening consequences. The process is not unlike getting someone who is in denial to recognize they have a problem.

Increasing awareness is an essential Part One of The Triad for teaching the skills to be intrinsically motivated and improve performance in less time. I use four chapters structure, ability, intelligence, and accountability to help you learn how to increase your awareness.

Structure

Your mind and body work together. Awareness of all your senses provides feedback about how you feel and perceive potential success and reward.

The structure of your nerves from your senses connect your mind with your body. The awareness of your biological processes from your senses is biofeedback. Top performers use biofeedback to know and plan when to increase energy to perform. They use more of their senses to gather performance knowledge under a variety of circumstances.

Besides the development of your physical skills, top performers also develop their mental skills. They use knowledge of past experiences from practice and competition to visualize and program ideal performances. RROSR is invaluable to learn how to improve performance. Cue recognition helps you anticipate actions to make faster positive responses.

Ability

Top performers improve their ability to process sensory information quickly so they can react with correct responses. Experience is your best teacher. However, good coaches and teachers with experience can tell you what methods and cues to shorten your learning curve.

Top performers use a comparator operator to measure a projected performance against past performances in similar familiar situations. They use anticipatory cues and "trigger" words to initiate faster responses. These examples demonstrate the complex structure of the connection between the mind and body. The body provides the structures to respond and move to perform. The brain provides the thinking or meta-cognitive ability for increasing the awareness to evaluate current with past performance, assign meaningful and relevant value, and learn to improve performance over time.

Intelligence

Intelligence is specific. You can be smart in one area and lost in another. Top performers make intelligent use of their skills and abilities. They are motivated to quickly identify and satisfy personal needs. They are relentless in acquiring more knowledge to keep improving their performance.

Accountability

This is a compilation of your feelings from past experiences. You know what it takes to succeed at a level you value compared to past performances. You feel guilty if you have not earned your reward, so you hold yourself accountable to do whatever it takes to succeed.

When you understand your structures and abilities you learn to set realistic goals and hold yourself accountable to reach them. This chapter is broken into two sections: Education and Learning to understand how training programs, school systems, teachers, and parents can teach intrinsic motivation as a leadership skill using The Triad.

Rather than just show and tell, take time to explain the benefits new information provides. The simplest strategy is to engage performers by asking questions. Asking questions requires the wheels in your performer's brain to turn and think of an answer. You will learn what your performers are thinking so you can modify your training.

You must not interrupt or worse offer the answer, but instead wait for the reply. If you interrupt, everything you say will be extrinsic and lose intrinsic value. Make the new information meaningful and relevant to value. No one can make you learn or do anything with quality until you see the personal value in performing. Top performers accept personal accountability for their performance and do not blame others for their lack of effort or poor performance.

Top performers are self-directed. If your parent, boss, manager, or coach yell at you, ask yourself why? Are you not aware how to self-evaluate your performances? That will be coming up in Part Two, Enhance Self-Evaluation.

8

MULTI-SENSORY LEARNING STRUCTURE

To increase an awareness of your structures are three sections:

Discover to identify, reflect, assess, and plan;
Define your needs, values, goals; and
Realize your purpose and potential using The Triad and RROSR to learn how
to learn.

Discovering your needs and abilities and defining how they are created and
formed is the key to realizing your purpose and potential. Otherwise, your aimless
direction is trial and error wasting valuable time, and more like trying to hit a moving target blindfolded.

Information Processing Model

Prior to 1980 your personal computer was and still is your brain. Compared to computer operations imagine a little switch at the base of your brain where the spinal
column brings the sensory information from all over your body to be processed and
turned into knowledge.

When you choose to think negative thoughts, your imaginary switch moves
to the "off" position. Little information will get on your "hard drive." Similarly, if you
allow your senses to receive and store inappropriate and needless information like
violent video games, they will make a permanent file in your brain and affect your
behavior.

The idea that violent information from movies and games does not harm you
comes from the marketers who have needs to make a profit. They choose to not
understand how the brain functions! As a behavioral rule you learn what you
focus on.

Your brain works like a computer to process information. It can be programmed
with a purpose to recognize value in meaningful and relevant information. Great
teachers and coaches use pre-cognitive cues and strategies in practice to familiarize you with the correct stimulus-response (S-R) connections.

Microprocessors in computers keep getting faster, and software programs
function better with more ram memory. Your RAM memory is your prefrontal cortex

that acts like a short-term bridge to your long-term memory file storage. The more experience and associational neurons you can link together like Einstein chose to do with multi-sensory learning, you will be more efficient at drawing upon the vast amount of your stored knowledge.

The British play write Shakespeare said, "Nothing is either good or bad, but thinking makes it so." This is your mind-body connection. It requires learning how to use your personal feedback from your senses while performing. When you understand how your brain functions you become aware of how to think to create improved performances. Paying attention to your senses provides valuable feedback to judge the value of each new performance compared to memorable past performances.

Your mind and body have structures to help you perform better once you understand how they function together. Your brain directs your body and all your behavior. You can get in touch with your body through your mind and vice versa. This involves both physical and mental activities.

Your body carries your brain around like an ever-present personal computer that needs no plug in for electric power. Your brain has its own generator when you learn how to turn it on and focus your performance at any given moment in time. Top performers display this as energy mobilization.

Periodically assessing what your needs and abilities are provides you with a road map for your life. Otherwise, it is hard to motivate yourself when you are not aware of your needs and abilities. Your needs change as you mature, and you must think about how to fulfill your personal needs with your abilities.

In China, children are assessed early. Those who meet the early predictors are given the opportunity to learn skills and train in government paid schools. How to develop predictors in a multiple regression equation was discussed earlier.

Contrast this system to the United States and other countries where children self-select their activity preferences by chance. A child could have perfect pitch and never sing a note or play a musical instrument because music and art are the first programs to be cut to conserve finances at struggling schools.

My guess is better than half the students who graduate from high school do not have a clue what their needs and abilities are. These are unmotivated students who complain of their boredom. Perhaps two-thirds of public-school students are underachievers. They do the least to get by with a passing grade to focus on their social skills. As adults, we are routinely caught up in our jobs and do not take time to ponder our needs or consider other abilities to try and improve.

Biofeedback Awareness

Biofeedback is the feedback you learn from the interaction of your environment with your biological senses. To develop your senses, use all of them. This is what multi-sensory learning attempts to achieve. You associate pain coming from your senses when you touch something hot, or your muscles feel sore from excessive activity, then your perception takes over.

Using your vision and projection skills—if I touch a hot stove, it will hurt. Using your touch and feeling resistance—if I lift these weights too much, I will be sore with pain. You get the same perception of pain when you feel anguish losing valued efforts.

You sense something is wrong with your biological system when a specific function is not working correctly. Or, you can raise your conscious awareness for your heart rate and check it during and after a bout of strenuous exercise. Athletes with physical skills frequently apply biofeedback to judge the worth of their next performance or practice based on how they feel while getting ready or performing.

You gain an expectation or value by how easy or hard the activity is to perform with your current skills and knowledge. If you allow your expectations to exceed reality, you will be frustrated, negatively motivated, and more likely to perform poorly. You have heard the phrase: Get Real! Every top performer has a valuing system to process their personal performance feedback.

Spatial awareness is a biofeedback feeling for how each body part performs in space in relation to the whole body. Great athletes test higher than regular athletes in spatial awareness. Think about how aware you are of the needs of your mind and body. When you are thirsty you drink; when hungry find food to eat.

Now transfer to academic feedback for equal importance. Do you value your education? Do you value your relationships? Do you value your spouse or significant other? With a purposeful you value your performances more and process the necessary feedback to develop and improve your mind and body by conscious control.

To increase your awareness skills, you must bring more sensory and perceptual information and knowledge to a conscious level to perform with a stronger motivation to continuously improve all your life. This is what The Triad Performance Improvement System is designed to do.

Your brain directs your body and all your behavior. You get in touch with your body through your mind and vice versa. This involves both physical and mental activities. For example, you have physical experiences performing skills. For mental activities you create a visualization performing those same skills correctly to practice. Then, you put your next performance on autopilot without having to think and slow down your performance.

Your body carries your brain around like an ever-present personal computer that needs no plug in for electric power. Your brain has its own generator when you learn how to turn it on and focus your performance at any given moment in time.

Like your computer it stores programs you put on its hard drive. Your operating system uses different software programs to do specific functions. Your senses act in similar ways.

Discover to Identify, Reflect, Assess, and Plan

Try creating a word document on your computer with your monitor off. Not much is going to go on your hard drive. Imagine your head with a satellite dish mounted to receive signals of information from a variety of sources. Or, growing antennae like a butterfly.

What information is most important? Who decides the meaningful and relevant value of new information? Is it others or you who decide? What information do you prioritize? What do you already know? What seems logical to compare to prior knowledge?

Take time to discover your personality. Your traits are largely set in the first years of life, but patterns evolve over time from those traits and can be altered to define and affect how you perform. The personality traits of persistence and realism are conditioned by success with repeated trial efforts and the actual performance closely approximates the goal. You can change your personality patterns to improve your performance. The easiest is to create a positive attitude toward relationships and performances.

Compare Past Performance

Make a list of your successful performances. What was your mind-set when you began and ended? Did you have a positive intent to improve? Did you clearly understand your purpose why you were working to improve your performance?

Conversely, list several times when you were just going through the motions in a job or task. What was your mind-set? What were the outcomes? Your mind and body must work together to motivate performance improvement.

No one is perfect but trying to improve is perfect. Keep your expectations in line with reality to avoid frustration and negatively motivate you. Instead, enhance your personal reward system with attainable low positive goals and be motivated to continue working hard to keep improving and feel pleasure.

Michael Freshley is a Masters' Swimming world record holder buddy of mine and a financial planner. We have been on several record setting relays together. A few years ago, he got my attention in a conversation about what drives top performers to succeed. He had these four points I want to share with you. To be successful financially or a physical skill he has observed these four planning steps:

1. Decide what you want. You cannot be confused about your needs and ability to work to get what you want.
2. Make-a-plan. Decide how to get what you want. This establishes your purpose and intent.
3. Decide what you are going to give up. Many performers want lots of things to distract from what they really need. Most are not willing to make the necessary sacrifices in time and relationships to focus on achieving their goals.

4. Never give up. Persistence is the key. Worthwhile activities take time to produce a return on your investment.

Mike also remarked that 25% of the performers drop off at each step and why 3% of the people own 90% of the world's wealth. To clarify this discussion, in a free market, performers purchase what pleases them, and discard what they perceive no longer has value. One man's junk is another man's treasure.

What may be stressful to someone is joy to another. "If you think you are beaten ...."—you know the rest of this prose. You have a choice to think positive or negative, be happy or sad, smart or dumb, but without discovering your needs identified with The Triad your performances will be hit or miss.

History is loaded with creative works once thought by critics as inappropriate for their time and later became precious works of art. When Picasso led the modern art revolution, there were legions of art critics who thought this new work was extremely distasteful. This is one more example of a top performer leading and discovering his personal path to success. Today his works sell for millions of dollars.

Here is an exercise for you. To identify your current needs and abilities, compare to reflect what they were in prior five-year increments. Make a list. Use Maslow's Need Hierarchy, and separate your abilities into physical, mental, social, and emotional categories. Compare and contrast your past with the present. Look for trends or patterns in your personality, too. Are you changing for the better or worse? What incidents changed you the most or least?

Assess your list objectively to be certain items are real needs separate from desires or wants. For example, you may think you need a car when you turn 16, but you can get to your job and school using the bus or get a ride to eliminate the expense and increase your net income. Now the car is a want or desired item for the convenience.

Download and take the needs and abilities survey in the Appendix.
go to http://The3SecretSkillsOfTopPerformers.com/Survey
It will be worth your time and effort.

After you have taken time to reflect your past with your present needs and abilities, start to project and plan for your future needs also in five-year incremental periods to note the changes you expect. Use the multiple regression analysis to plug in specific variables your needs and abilities define to predict the criterion of where you want to be and what you want to do. This is personal leadership.

This defines your purpose. A plan is nothing more than a long-range goal based on your past performance history. To assess and plan, learn to use your personal performance feedback presented in the next section of this chapter.

Keep in mind that you were given unique needs and abilities to fulfill your purpose. You do not have to copy some of the ridiculous role models people choose to follow in social media today. You are a unique individual, act and perform like it. Be yourself. Lead yourself.

Learn and do what you can do best and keep improving in as many abilities as you discover who you are. Treat early failures as opportunities to learn. Thomas Edison learned 1119 ways how not to build a battery before discovering the answer on the 1120th try.

If at first you do not succeed try try again. How many people do you know are that patient or persistent? Or do they expect immediate success or quit? Plan for success with a purpose. Do not leave your performance to chance. What are you willing to sacrifice?

Persistence and realism are learned personality traits. You cannot be some-body you are not designed to be. Discover your physical abilities. If your parents are both short and compact, you probably are not going to play basketball or vol-leyball but could play golf, tennis, or baseball with some power.

What emphasis have you placed on your mental abilities? Learning to learn is a lifelong skill to keep improving. Can you focus on any task for some time? How do you make new information meaningful and relevant to what you already know or want to know to motivate your memory? All this relates to your personality and planning to set realistic goals to achieve some purpose. You were given a brain, and if you condition it properly using the 3 secret skills in The Triad you can use it for all kinds of ways to improve upon your abilities and accomplish your needs.

Define Your Needs, Values, and Goals

Before you can define your needs, values, goals, abilities, and personality, you must use B.F. Skinner's 'Black Box' feedback model presented earlier and shown again because of its importance. You cannot control what other performers do, but you can control how you learn and plan to improve your performance with The Triad.

B.F. Skinner's Black Box

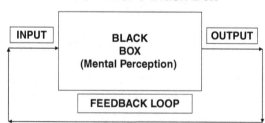

If you are not getting the correct performance output, the feedback identifies changing the input cues for your brain to process to get a better result. This feed-back model is essential to learn from your performance and experience. It will be used extensively in Part Two of The Triad, Enhance Self-Evaluation.

This information has been expressed in earlier chapters so give these topics more thought. Accept input cues as variables will constantly change over time. Be prepared to make input adjustments with different cues but never stop thinking how to apply performance feedback. This self-correction skill is a major tenet in top performers. They teach themselves how to keep improving.

Use all your senses to gain more performance experience for later use. If your output is poor, change your input cue or method. You cannot keep doing the same old and expect better results.

9

MIND-BODY CONNECTION ABILITY

A sign of intelligence and maturity is your ability to use information from your senses (sensations) to anticipate or perceive future performance (perceptions). Together these form your projection skills to predict future performance outcomes. When you understand your brain is structured, focus awareness on learning more of your abilities. You may be surprised to learn you have potential in other areas of your life.

Part of being smart is to know what you are dumb at. Bullies criticize others they think have lesser abilities so they can feel superior. Socially we all are different in many ways. I have found others much smarter than me in my weak areas.

I have never observed or met a top performer who claimed to know-it-all. They are more like perfectionists always trying to improve as life-long learners. I prefer life-long learners and avoid know-it-alls and consider myself an average guy who tries to do a better than average job. There is something we can learn from everyone we encounter if we open our minds and give them a chance.

Your mind-body connection is simply telling your mind what you expect your body to perform. Your past performance experience keeps your expectations in line with reality to perform your best in that given moment. This is confidence.

A question I like to ask is, "Do you own a laptop computer? What happens when you close the lid? It goes to sleep." Then when you lift the lid it wakes up. To make new information meaningful and relevant in your mind as opposed to your teacher trying to tell you how important that may be, it can be a simple suggestion.

Tell your brain to get out of sleep mode like lifting the lid up to awaken your laptop. Then use your mind to create value and need to know so your brain will store that information in its proper place to make it readily retrievable. This single point is what makes top performers!

Use the RROSR method to find and improve your abilities. The more information you take in, assign a purpose to value, and store properly improves your retrieval process. You associate new knowledge to stored knowledge using performance feedback (Black Box).

The key to consistent top performance is your ability to quickly retrieve valuable information necessary to perform a given task well at will on demand. You assign value by making what you learn meaningful and relevant.

A teacher can tell you the new knowledge is valuable, meaningful, and relevant, and extrinsic. Intrinsic is you telling your brain it is all those things. Top performers create the will to win by what they value to perform. And like leaders, they are made, not born.

Discover your abilities to find new activities you can excel in performing especially when you are young. Parents and coaches may see your abilities before you do so ask them if they agree with your personal assessment survey. Some activities have physical limitations to limit your choices. You can still participate but may not become a top performer.

Are you a concrete thinker and like to work with numbers to be an accountant and solve math problems? Or, are you an abstract thinker who likes to solve artistic layouts and design systems? Are you better with hands-on skills building or repairing things or better at writing and communicating about projects?

My great coach Doc Counsilman at Indiana University shortened my learning curve. I went on the be a five-time All-American. It helped to grow 5½ inches and 30 pounds in ten months my freshman year. I coached All-American collegiate women and high school boys, and earned my Ph.D.

The point I make is if you want to be a top performer you cannot always listen to what others tell you to do. Besides your mother only you know you as well as you do. You may not be an Einstein, but even he flunked early math and did not start to speak until he was four. The moral of the story is at an early age you do not know how you will turn out. But certainly nothing good will happen if you do not risk failure and try until you find success in what you are good at performing.

There are countless stories of top performers who suffered horrendous failures early in their careers. But they persisted to overcome their early errors. Your brain is funny that way. It knows the quality of effort and purpose you have and your sacrifices and emotional trauma from losing. Then the sweet smell of success is so much greater. You are hooked!

A friend sent me a power point about a guy who had trouble learning. He may have had ADD or attention deficit disorder when teachers did not know how to help these students. He failed at everything he tried including writing and sports, but he liked to doodle and draw characters. After graduation he was rejected from college because of poor grades, but he kept drawing.

He presented his drawings to the Disney Corporation, and they rejected him. He did not fit in, but he was persistent. Eventually a newspaper picked up his cartoon strip about a little boy who seemed to fail and was rejected. He had a pet dog he could confide in and tell his troubles.

The little boy was Charlie Brown and his dog was Snoopy. He signed his name, Charles Schultz. The comic strip became so popular because readers could identify with the characters whom Charles experienced. Stuffed animals, T-shirts, calendars, and even Christmas and Thanksgiving holiday specials have been created with the same message. Be persistent.

Imagine a tough winter. It has been cold and dreary for months on end. Then spring comes. Temperatures warm up and the trees leaf out in bright green vibrant colors and you feel alive inside. When you see a top performer break down after a huge win, you know they sacrificed a lot and worked hard to achieve that level of performance.

Ability is more than physical skills. It is also your mental toughness and ability to visualize quality performance in practice and competitions. You know quality when you see it if you cannot fully describe it.

So, take some time to be aware of your strengths and weaknesses. What are your abilities? What are your needs and goals? You can consult with others you respect like your mom or your coach to give you honest answers to compare with what you think of yourself.

Take your personal survey in the Appendix. It will help you discover what you are good at performing. It lets you ask significant others who know you to offer their opinion, too. Then compare what you think to what they think are your abilities.

When I was a high school principal speaking to all my students, I'd ask for a show of hands, "How many of you think Michael Jordan knew he'd become a great NBA basketball star when he was in high school?" No hands went up. What about other top performers like Thomas Edison, Henry Ford, Martin Luther-King?

The point is when you are young you do not know how you will turn out. What is certain is if you do not search for your purpose to improve your abilities you will not be a top performer.

In my case, I hung out with four guys in my peer group. We all had a need to improve instilled in us by our swim coach, Dobbie Burton. We were motivated to be somebody and make a difference. We were taught a work-ethic to outwork our competition and overcome any lack of skill to improve our abilities. We did not succumb to social pressures or bullying. We stayed focused on continuous improvement, and we all are still life-long learners.

MaS>MaF as Motivation

Use your mind to think. Your motive (M) to achieve (a) success (S) must be greater than your motive (M) to avoid (a) failure (F). This paradigm shift sounds complex but is the heart of The Triad. By converting to a positive focus strategy, you will have an affinity for positive and fortunate events.

As a leader look for the positive good to reinforce in your performers. Keep them motivated from within teaching how to use their personal feedback to self-evaluate performances for improvement. Begin every conversation with a complement and listen for a response to lead you.

Reinforcing a performer's faults does not reward them to want to repeat good behaviors. Performers create avoidance behaviors and motives to avoid failure more than focus on how to achieve success. Have you ever taken a different route to avoid meeting people you did not like? Maybe a boss or manager?

A fear of failure is conditioned by external forces in systems to meet the needs of others. Learn to identify and meet your personal needs in a successful strategy detailed in Chapter 11 Accountability *Your Responsibility*.

10

IMPROVING INTELLIGENCE

The four keys to intelligence are moving sensations to perceptions, taking sub conscious to conscious sensations, projecting a result or consequence of your actions, and learning to predict a future outcome. Increased intelligence is directly proportional to increased awareness. The best strategy is using multi-sensory learning.

The Triad is an intrinsic personal behavior modification and motivation system to improve performance in less time. B.F. Skinner is noted for use of operant conditioning to modify behavior. Today, modern behaviorism includes how needs, values, and goals affect motivation. Behaviors are still conditioned but also learned to improve intelligence and performance.

The difference between intrinsic and extrinsic motivation is what anyone tells, advises, or bribes you to do with a reward is extrinsic. You must keep increasing the reward to motivate performance. Intrinsic motivation is when you value meaningful and relevant new information and acquire knowledge to satisfy a personal need or goal to improve your performance.

Intelligence is specific. You can be an intelligent top performer in one or two areas specific to your performance. Then make a poor decision about your future. Many highly paid top professional athletes are poor money managers.

Top performers are self-motivated. They practice a work ethic earning a path to rewards with many valuable smaller achievements. Performers who give up easily set too high goals and do not increase the frequency of reward enough to condition repeating positive responses. Great achievements are seldom earned on the first trial. You get back in the game with gradual successes to fuel your confidence. Change your goal setting strategy to perceive success more frequently than failure.

Paired-Associate Conditioning

Increasing the number of associational neurons is essential for conditioning correct stimulus-response connections in performance sequences. Your brain compresses large amounts of sensory data into tiny bit maps. This process increases the speed of transmission of visual patterns, verbal instruction, and kinesthetic feeling cues to store and retrieve more efficiently in various brain lobes.

Each brain lobe stores similar patterns to associate with new information. Two different stimuli are paired up or associated with the same response. For example, an instructor teaching a skill may provide a visual demonstration and use verbal cues to describe how the action will feel in the muscles providing the movement.

This pairs up visual, verbal, and kinesthetic stimuli to provide a specific cue for every kind of learning preference. Some call this differentiated instruction. These kinds of associations are powerful motives more resistant to forgetting what to perform in the sequence.

Two of my granddaughters recently texted me a short video of a complex dance routine they were working on. The visual dance sequence and kinesthetic moves with the feet and arms in time with the music was impressive.

The brain learns best observing patterns and sequences. Similarly, top performers associate pleasure with conscious feelings of success in an activity. The reinforcement comes from increasing the motivation to continue those feelings in performances by putting forth more effort in practice to ensure success in small increments.

The genius Albert Einstein created more associational neurons with multi-sensory learning. Top performers create associations to transfer similar or identical elements from practice to their performance. Do you wonder how actors memorize so many lines for all the scenes? They practice learning by associating patterns and sequences in scenes or segments. They visualize cues or triggers when to perform.

Practicing skills focuses on specific multi-sensory cues or triggers to transfer to performance. Paired-associate conditioning uses two sensory stimuli to trigger a faster response. Performers have sensory preferences for learning new tasks and get familiar with the process. This changes personality patterns to build confidence and trust in the performance for a variety of performers.

Planer Thinking

Planer thinking implies as your intelligence improves you begin to think on higher and higher levels of thought or planes. Task familiarity and personality play a critical role.

Howard Gardner, a Harvard psychology professor, writes about multiple intelligences in his book, Intelligence Reframed (1999). My personal view of intelligence is the execution of small specific stimulus-response (S-R) connections to create awareness for higher acquisition of knowledge in task familiar planes. I call this Planer Thinking.

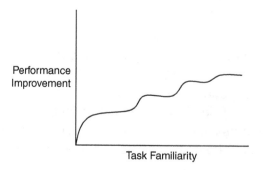

Performance Improvement

Task Familiarity

There are failures where observable performance improvement does not change, but learning is still taking place. Some call these slumps or plateaus you must keep working. Eventually a breakthrough occurs, and you are happy again. Using all your senses creates more associations and improves performance with the RROSR strategy.

Daniel Goleman published Emotional Intelligence: Why It Can Matter More Than IQ in 1995. The premise is there are many leaders who have developed emotional intelligence to be top performers in many avocations with average IQ. Intelligence Quotient or IQ with 100 as average has long been barometers of native intelligence.

Emotional Intelligence or EQ has become popular in leadership training using social psychology principles to improve interactive communication in groups. Have you encountered intelligent performers in their fields who lack common sense?

Top performers routinely access a variety of information to increase the storage and retrieval efficiency of the associational neurons connected in the brain. Good coaches and teachers provide more specific cues to selectively attend to (recognition) that improve the response time. As tasks become more familiar, the complex pattern with its host of cues (receive) is compressed (organized) into a "bit map" for faster (storage) and (retrieval) that anyone can learn (RROSR).

What bothers me is how available technology is being used and abused. I hate to see my grandchildren buried in video games on their "smart" phones 12" from their face. They cannot tell you the temperature or if the sun is shining or raining outside.

There are distractions with technology leading to terrible consequences. It used to be drinking and driving impaired your ability. Now it is texting and keeping your eyes on the road. Earlier I mentioned how your brain does not know right from wrong. And your PFC or pre-frontal cortex essential for processing incoming data to store in short-term memory is not fully developed until age 23–25.

The Increasing Awareness flow chart on the following pages creates a visual flow for how to increase your awareness. Intelligent top performers develop and use their sensory and perceptual awareness skills to efficiently recognize, receive, organize, store, and retrieve (RROSR) more information when they assign personal meaningful and relevant value. This is how you lead and teach others intrinsic motivation skills.

Take these factors into account when you lead others to improve their awareness and intelligence. You must provide the specific performance methods and cues proven from your prior experience to get faster longer-lasting results. The correct stimulus-response connections are associated with success to reinforce learning and increase motivation.

As a leader you simply cannot demonstrate and give a brief how-to explanation and expect your performers to be self-motivated to improve. Leaders as top performers have more experience to draw upon. Beginners have little or no experience in what to expect. They cannot project outcomes if they are unfamiliar with the task.

Increasing Awareness Flow Chart

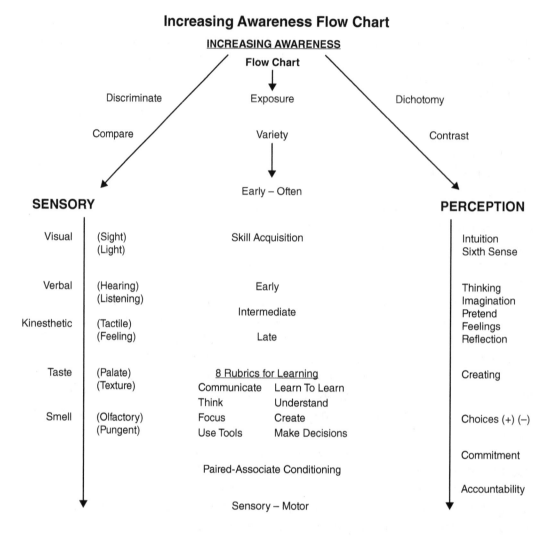

INCREASING AWARENESS

Flow Chart

Discriminate	Exposure	Dichotomy
Compare	Variety	Contrast
	Early – Often	

| **SENSORY** | | Skill Acquisition | **PERCEPTION** |

Visual	(Sight) (Light)	Skill Acquisition	Intuition Sixth Sense
Verbal	(Hearing) (Listening)	Early	Thinking Imagination Pretend
Kinesthetic	(Tactile) (Feeling)	Intermediate Late	Feelings Reflection
Taste	(Palate) (Texture)		Creating
Smell	(Olfactory) (Pungent)		Choices (+) (–)

8 Rubrics for Learning

Communicate	Learn To Learn
Think	Understand
Focus	Create
Use Tools	Make Decisions

Commitment

Accountability

Paired-Associate Conditioning

Sensory – Motor

I published <u>Teach Yourself to Swim</u> in 2012. In the introduction I created the safety needs and health benefits for knowing how to swim. I had been teaching swimming for over 50 years and saw a need to help people in rural and low-income areas where there was no pool or experienced swim instructors.

My thinking was I could teach using intelligent methods and cues I learned from years of experience to shorten the learning curve and fulfill a need for families to save time and money. My system is easy-to-master one-minute steps in patterns and sequences, so the brain learns faster and feels rewarded to continue learning.

I start at home without a pool using a kitchen or bath sink, dressing mirror, mattress and a bathtub to learn all the basic skills and overcome fears. I use six new methods and numerous cues proven to get faster longer-lasting results. All my content is based on never out-of-date applied physics and psychology of learning principles. My great coach, Ph.D. studies, and All-American competitive college years shortened my learning curve.

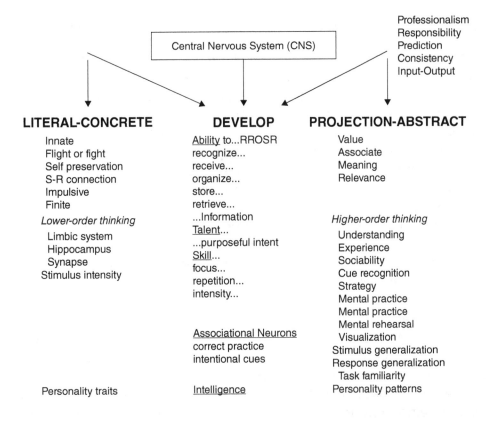

Here are the six teaching methods I use to increase intelligence:

1) Spatial Awareness – learning where your body parts are in space
2) Mind Control – of your body parts to relax and process new information
3) Sequential Learning – easy steps are chained together into strokes
4) Mastery Learning – each step is mastered to feel rewarded and confident
5) Feedback Information Processing – using goggles to correct your mechanics
6) Transfer of Identical Elements – copying the motor skills from land to water

Mastery and sequential learning are keys to stimulus-response (S-R) and paired-associate conditioning to improve performance. This simple step sequence creates frequent reward to motivate more learning. Chaining the steps together in sequence follows how the brain learns best in patterns and sequences I demonstrate with pictures.

The key intrinsic motivation is to create the need and value in the introductory chapters. The benefits are learning correct methods and cues from an experienced professional in visual, verbal (brief explanations of small steps), and kinesthetic (feeling the water pressure on the hands and forearms) learning styles to shorten the learning curve. This saves time and money teaching swimmers cue recognition and self-correction skills based on proven physics and psychology of learning principles.

As the leader familiarize your performers with what to expect prior to big events. This builds confidence. You have been there and know what to expect. Be specific to describe the environment, crowd noise, level of competition, timing, and preparation. Your expectations are always extrinsic and less meaningful to your performers. If they do not perform well, it is your fault. Can you see the value in teaching personal accountability for performance outcomes in practice with intrinsic motivation skills?

My Ph.D. dissertation found changes in personality patterns as you become more familiar with a task. Your personality patterns move from insecure to secure, less trusting to trusting, less confident to confident, and less apprehensive to reduce anxiety.

Rely on your intelligent performers. Communicate new methods or cues as meaningful and relevant benefits for performers to value. Remember needs and values are specific to each performer. You must know each to get them all on the same page and aligned with the needs and values of the team effort. That is the toughest leadership task.

The other day I had a lengthy discussion with a good friend who has a Ph.D. in social psychology. She is project manager for a company subcontracted with the government Environmental Protection Agency EPA. A portion of the project had been submitted and two performers were praised for their efforts.

She wanted to pass along this praise to the two performers but also copy the rest of the team to encourage their performance improvement. The gist of our conversation was she did not believe the other members could be intrinsically motivated. They had to be told a deadline and what to do.

This is a typical example of leaders who do not understand or trust workers how to be intrinsically motivated. This includes teachers, and parents, but coaches a little less—top coaches are great motivators.

The easiest method is to explain how to use RROSR, so performers quickly learn to recognize cues and explain why the correct response or process method works better than others. Top performing leaders ask questions to explain why chosen responses to specific cues (stimuli) work better. Then be quiet and wait for answers.

If your performers are going through the motions without thinking and understanding their why and purpose, you are not leading them. They will regard everything you tell them as extrinsic and feel no personal accountability for improving their performance. Parents appear to give fine directions, but their children do not know why except for the consequences.

The behavioral rule is if you show performers how to do a job more than once and do not ask for understanding questions, they will perform poorly so you will do the job for them. They learn no personal accountability and blame you when they fail.

As a leader show intelligent emotional and social communication. If you are unable to personally do a job you expect your performers to do, then use a top performer as your example. Then give them the praise and reward so others may socially want to model their performance.

This system works provided you make each performer aware of how to process their own feedback to judge the worth of their performance. Provide realistic benchmarks. When possible use each performer's past experiences or results as the starting point. This creates a dichotomy to compare where you started with where you are now in the performance improvement track.

All behavior is motivated by a desire to satisfy a personal need or goal. All performers have personal needs, but they are not usually brought to a conscious level. From my observations of top performers are unaware and much of their behavior operates at a sub conscious automated level.

Top performers generally do two of the three secret skills in The Triad, but not all three. They can be their own tough critic to self-evaluate performances. And they are usually aware of the key skills to perform to feel success. But they are not used to having a personal conversation in their brain to connect reward with reinforcement. Many top performers take for granted what they do and cannot understand why others could learn to perform at their level.

Consider these logical points of view:

1) Unintelligent performers block the need for a performance valuing process.
2) Do you know top performers with a high awareness during performance?
3) Do you know of any top performer waiting for the approval of others?
4) Top performers use prior and past performances as the personality "self" standard for the perceptual anchoring point to set realistic goals.
5) Top performers know what quality performance looks like but cannot describe the process strategies to be successful.
6) Average and successful performers do not generally develop leadership skills if conditioned to wait for the approval of others.
7) Top performers become stale or burned out who do not connect reward with reinforcement.

Moving Sensations to Perceptions

Thinking modifies a sensation into a perception of right and wrong, also known as your conscience. If you are improving, it is right. If you are not improving, something is wrong. The approval of others like teachers in schools, parents, or managers on the job is inherently conditioned in your daily life. These are powerful social motivators, but also external motivational traps creating inappropriate dependencies.

Performers who repeatedly fail sense pain to avoid. As the leader quickly convert sensation to perception showing your performers strategies for mastery of complex skills or tasks in smaller subroutines to feel rewarded. Demonstrate a positive performance sequence of smaller incremental steps to perceive success.

Pain associated with failure and success associated with reward are both perceptions in the mind of the performer. Leaders can explain failure is not real pain but a positive call for a stronger work ethic attitude to identify and value small performance improvements to feel rewarded.

Top performers regard pain as a positive motive to work smarter and ensure success to feel rewarded. Performers who feel they have not worked enough to earn the reward are not confident in performance. They do not perceive worthy of success. This self-awareness confidence is intrinsic. If you are not confident no one else will feel confident in your performance.

To be self-directed and not externally directed is the goal. Leaders cannot expect to externally motivate every performer every day in every setting. If parents fall into this trap, when their children get older, they seldom do anything that is not connected to a conditioned external reward.

When external rewards are not great enough in value, performers do not act to improve. Many wealthy people are unhappy because the extrinsic rewards are not great enough to satisfy their higher needs. Whereas self-actualization in Maslow's Need Hierarchy helping others to achieve is greater than accumulating money and wealth. To know that one life has improved because of your top performer efforts is to have succeeded.

Top performers perceive value in meaningful and relevant information to meet their personal needs. If new information is perceived to have little or no value it is stored in less readily accessible brain lobes. The brain does not waste energy to recall useless information.

Top performers are consciously driven with a learned process to identify, acquire, and fulfill specific needs. This lets them select even higher order needs to increase their motivation. They think on different planes, or 'think outside the box' as some prefer the term.

You have heard of the absent-minded professor. This is more than forgetting where you placed your car keys. You can be good with your hands, or a problem solver using your brains. You can be good with numbers but cannot draw a straight line. Or, you can paint a picture but cannot write a story.

Sometimes it takes common sense to be aware of your surroundings and the environment you created. Can you see the "big picture" or do you like to color your world the way you would like it to be? Some call this bias. Almost everything you do revolves around quality of life issues. Some leaders believe this gives them the right to tell you how to live your life. They enact laws to control your freedom to choose and hold yourself accountable for behaviors. But you cannot legislate morality.

Part of being smart is knowing what you are dumb at. You do not have to be a genius to figure out what works for you. Over time, experience teaches you success or failure. Success gives you pleasure, and failure gives you pain. The problem is most people do not know their personal strengths or weaknesses to learn how or what to improve in their personal lives. There is so much potential that goes to waste.

I like the lyrics from an Eagles song. "Often times we put ourselves in chains never knowing we got the key." Does this sound like an identification problem? The Triad teaches you skills to improve your performance in less time for any job, task, skill, or relationship. But you must be aware to identify and apply these new secret skills to see your improvements.

Mental Shifts

The Triad and RROSR teach several skills for increasing awareness. The most important one is to take unconscious automated routines and bring them up to a conscious level of performance. You can do this with selective attention to specific stimulus cues (S) and response (R) associations to perform RROSR.

The objective is to be more consciously aware of your sensations at specific times and convert them to positive perceptions. When you sense a certain key cue or method, you connect the pre thought out response to improve performance. That design comes from plugging in the key variables in a subjective multiple regression equation to project and predict your outcome.

Sensation to Perception

Awareness implies using all your senses. They provide valuable feedback if you pay attention. The feedback from your sensations provide you with a perception of what to expect in future performances.

The perception or feeling of success or failure resides with the performer. Self-esteem psychology does not work. You can lead and tell performers they are successful. But if they know they have not earned the reward, the perception is you are lying. Performers may not want to trust anything you tell them. A performer may lie to others but not to themselves. The brain knows the real truth.

You have an innate drive to want to learn and improve. Leaders must use innate drives and bring to a conscious awareness level. Extrinsic rewards to bribe performance are not necessary. Performers must refocus on their personal immediate past performance and set a new goal only slightly higher to frequently improve upon that performance. This kind of reward has more personal value.

Portfolios, logs, and diaries are one way to provide a reflective comparison of actual past performance to expected future performances to increase value. Graphs also visualize improvements by tracking performance results. These form the "self" personality trait and PAP or perceptual anchoring point for setting new realistic goals. For students, homework is another essential feedback tool equating quality of effort with quality of reward and indicating learning progress.

Value as a Perception

Value was defined in chapter three as the perceived amount of Reward divided by the perceived amount of Effort usually expressed as a per cent. The equation is $V=R/E$. Value is in the perceived eye of the beholder. Meaningful and relevant value is based on prior knowledge and past performance. Hypothetically, the assignment of value determines the strength of your motivation to achieve success.

Taking Subconscious Sensations to a Conscious Level

If you allow your mind to work in the subconscious level, your behaviors will be impulsive, spur-of-the-moment-quick-fix, and inconsistent with less value. This decreases your probability to feel success and reward used to store meaningful and relevant knowledge you value to readily retrieve when you need it.

Taking sensations from a subconscious to conscious level of awareness increases your intelligence to perform specific tasks. Setting realistic goals does that for you. Impulsive and chance subconscious behavior is like trying to hit a moving target blindfolded. They have limited value to make rewards temporarily seem greater and more reinforcing to chance again.

Subconscious to Conscious

Most basic needs are driven by your subconscious mind. People in affluent cultures seldom worry about basic needs for food, clothing, or shelter. However, once higher order needs are identified you move them to a conscience level to act on them.

A compulsive gambler falsely believes subconsciously they can make up for losses on the next trial. To be a top performer, you do not gamble with your life's experiences. You acquire purposeful behaviors focused on specific cues to produce consistent responses. Wise choices with purposeful behaviors are better made on a conscious level.

Learning to Learn Strategies Improve Intelligence

You can teach yourself many kinds of skills if you know your need and the value of new information to make that personally meaningful and relevant. Use all your senses to create numerous associational neurons to aid your memory.

When you sat in a classroom to listen to your teacher, hopefully you took notes. The teacher speaks words—the verbal part. Then you use your kinesthetic feeling to write notes on your paper. To write clearly you use your vision to see the words go on the paper. Typing notes on a laptop works the same way.

You read the textbook and underline key words to remember what was taught in that section. This process requires you to make new information meaningful and relevant. Hypothetically, the more you perceive value new information will be stored and readily accessible in your brain and resistant to forgetting. Be aware of value-based curriculums so you can gain more useful knowledge to apply in your world today and tomorrow.

Stimulus-Response (S-R) Conditioning

Great leader/coaches use a displace-replace refocus strategy to condition correct responses to selected cues. They replace the incorrect with the correct cue, and verbally explain or visually demonstrate an image to increase the performer's awareness and improve the response.

This selective stimulus cue recognition is a learned awareness skill. It displaces the incorrect stimulus and replaces it with the correct stimulus to improve the desired response. This refocus strategy is used for smaller more manageable specific positive outcomes to increase probability for success and build confidence.

Practice makes you more familiar with performing tasks so you can readily retrieve stored associated knowledge and skills. Albert Einstein was intelligent to accommodate and assimilate new information with more numerous associational neurons adding to his body of knowledge.

To increase your sensory awareness, you need to consciously value any input, and link the new to stored information using associational neurons to compare patterns and sequences. Use the RROSR strategy to recognize, receive, organize, store, and retrieve information faster. This is what separates top performers from others.

Automated Routines: The Biological Autopilot

When activities become too routine, your brain switches to autopilot and the activity value decreases. Routine automated experiences are less meaningful and relevant, and hypothetically are stored in slower retrievable sequences.

Typical sensory responses are routinely automated to reduce conflicting messages to the brain in potential life-threatening flight or fight situations. Automation does reduce stress which partly explains why change is difficult and no improvement occurs. Not all routines are bad, but you must be aware of them to guard against errors, stagnation, and boredom.

W.D. Cannon (1964) presented a biological theory of homeostatic equilibrium in 1943 that explains how heart rate, respiration, hormones, and other physiological functions are automated to achieve balance or equilibrium. You would go nuts trying to keep track of your heart beating or lungs breathing.

The brain can override automated impulses to increase awareness or block pain to attend to more important cues and perform purposeful tasks *at will on demand*. Great marathon runners and other athletes routinely block pain when they "hit the wall" to go beyond normal performance. Jeff Farrell is a good friend of mine and was a 1960 Olympian. One week before he Olympic Trials to make the team he had an emergency appendectomy. In those days only sutures could close the incision.

At the time Jeff was the fastest sprint freestyle swimmer in the world and a lock on winning both the 100 and 200-meter freestyle events. Incisions have pain to manage for several days. Jeff told me how he blocked out the pain by focusing on his start, turns, split pace, and mechanics. He was only able to qualify for a 200-meter leg of the 800-meter freestyle relay. There are countless stories of professional athletes who play with pain by staying focused on performance cues and goals.

Similarly, unconscious environmental conditioning shows how poverty affects social and emotional learning. The motivation to change an environment to acquire knowledge, learn a value system, and seek hope to improve the quality of life is secondary to providing for basic needs. Performers are trapped in a painful routine cycle that is hard to break.

The best hope for impoverished communities or performers is to rely on a faith-based system. Empower every member with a purpose to contribute and make the necessary changes in their life. Alcoholics Anonymous is a perfect example for using faith to inspire a purpose that intrinsically motivates individuals to hold themselves accountable for their daily behaviors.

Mundane Tasks, Emotion, and Learning

Highly familiar tasks become routine and have only mundane value. These common tasks like doing the laundry or washing the dishes are automated to a subconscious level. As you learn routine behaviors you also lose conscious control of your needs and abilities to meet them. You must learn to override this built in response.

I used to live in a Chicago suburb. In the hot summer I had to mow my lawn. In the fall I had to clean leaves out of my gutters. In the winter I had to shovel snow off my driveway. Of course, I did not care to do any of those chores. But to motivate myself I created a pet phrase, "Well those (blank) are not going to do themselves." And I would be motivated enough to start the task. You cannot finish a task you do not start.

To effect a change in a learning pattern requires greater emotion such as shouting new instructions or suggest information to be retained. Positive self-talk is a strategy to direct new information to a higher awareness or conscious state. Tell your brain the new information is important to value, and maybe picture a positive result. Or, review the old information—what was and was not working—and set a value for a low positive goal improvement and tell your brain to remember it.

Remember your brain is a microprocessor to process information from your senses and does not know right from wrong. You achieve what you focus your efforts on by bringing your thinking to a conscious level, and like binoculars only work when you focus them.

Understanding Your Needs on a Conscious Level

Top performers understand their needs on a conscious level and get more familiar with tasks to constantly increase their motivation. The process to increase your awareness and understand your personal needs must be purposeful or the changes you desire in your overall performance cannot occur as readily.

To continuously improve your performance, tune in to your environment and connect the "awareness of mind" strategy to direct your body's response. Biofeedback is taking sensations from your body and converting them to feelings stored in your mind. You can choose to condition or associate a positive or negative feeling.

Identifying your needs is an on-going process of self-evaluation. Needs drive your behaviors. To understand your behaviors and what strongly motivates you to act begins with your needs. You must know your needs to quantify their strength and value you gain from satisfying them.

When your needs are routinely satisfied, you take them for granted and no longer value them until they are removed. A homeless man will still value all his worldly possessions. Our survival skills are lost in the comfort of a home and being loved and wanted. Yet relationships continue to suffer through divorce seeking a more perfect partner or boss and job to meet our needs.

Under-performers are less able to identify their needs because others have been conditioned to meet those needs. Perceptual awareness skills are low, and work is haphazard and aimless without a goal to satisfy. Conversely, top performers have high perceptual awareness skills. Every behavior is consciously performed and evaluated for value to enhance self-improvement and feel rewarded.

Top performers know why they perform in purposeful ways. They have learned to identify and provide for their personal needs and be independent. Make identifying and satisfying your personal needs a conscious activity and you will more likely change your behavior to take accountability and improve your performance.

Value the work you perform to meet your personal needs, and readily retrieve the valued information stored in your brain to help you perform on a higher level. To increase the value of your work, occasionally remind yourself why you are doing work few others will perform today. Top performers do not value easy success.

Projecting a Result or Consequence of Your Actions

Projection is a skill using your experiences to imagine a future performance.

Use your mind to turn negative behaviors into positive behaviors. You feel successful increasing your odds with slightly better goals than your last personal performance. Give yourself permission to feel rewarded. Frequency of success in small improvements keeps you motivated to put forth more effort to enjoy feeling rewarded. Increasingly more effort is required to better each goal and project a feeling of greater reward.

Whatever you think as a leader is expressed and communicated by your body language. Recall results of communications when you had bad thoughts about a person. If not in person, your tone is different and sensed on the phone.

Negative to Positive Conversion Strategy for Learning

Normal Vincent Peale wrote The Power of Positive Thinking in 1952. Positive Mental Attitude or PMA as it became known to explain how your attitudes affect your performance. Your thinking capacity for learning can greatly improve your skilled performances over time with a positive attitude toward correct practice.

Try this exercise strategy. On a sheet of paper draw a line down the middle and across the top for a header. In the left header write negative thinking behaviors and positive thinking behaviors in the right header.

Next, reflect on several of your latter performances and record your negative and positive thoughts under each header with an event description in the middle across the line. A Δ delta symbol indicates change. For each positive thought that resulted in an improved performance, place a + symbol to mark it. For each negative thought that resulted in a lesser performance, place a—symbol to mark it.

This awareness exercise should quickly demonstrate how your positive or negative thoughts impact your performance. My mother used to say, "Turn lemons into lemonade." Take a positive attitude to change your thinking skills. This strategy is also choice psychology. Begin to rewrite every negative thought you stated in the left column into a positive statement in the right-hand column in the form of "I can" or "I will" statements. This completes the written exercise and increases your awareness of a positive mental attitude.

Another strategy to project positive results is a *mental exercise*. Trigger positive responses to stop and convert every negative thought pattern. First, create an image of a traffic stop sign, red flashing stop light, or flat hand palm out extended at arms-length to stop a dog. Second, condition a paired response to the visual image and say to yourself, "Stop!" This increases awareness of negative thoughts on performance behaviors.

Third and fourth, if you are emotionally charged up, take a breath exhale slowly, and condition slow silent number count-down 10 to 1 or 0. This diverts and neutralizes emotion to easily focus converting to positive thoughts in the heat of frustration. Use your diaphragm to control stress and anxiety by deeply inhaling and exhaling slowly.

Mentally rehearse the positive physical outcomes of your present and future expected performance. Think positive!

Mastery Learning

Practice makes perfect is not true. Perfect practice with correct methods and cues proven to get faster results is true. Top performing experienced leaders know and communicate best practices to get better results. Why choose a top performing coach or school or workplace over other lesser options?

If you adopt, "Failure is NOT an Option," then let your performers do over their work using self-evaluation rubrics until they get it correct. In the adult world, a marketing brochure gets a dozen reviews before being printed. The ultimate outcome is LEARNING to improve!

Mastery learning from do-overs provides for early and frequent success to build confidence. Confidence and familiarity with tasks lend to realistic predictions of your future success.

Learning to Predict a Future Outcome

Prediction

Personal past performance experiences predict future performance. The personality trait of realism plays a key role to be honest with yourself. The predictive equation is simple. Know your personal needs and values to motivate positive behaviors and accomplish consistent results over time.

How you approach difficult tasks is important. Break down hard complex tasks into smaller incremental tasks accomplished in a sequence. Your frequent success responses provide feedback to predict a success pattern. You learn what methods and cues predict success and reward value.

How would you feel standing at the base of a small mountain you need to climb? The first day of a new semester long class you predict all the work to get a grade and credits toward graduation with a degree. You start a new position in an unfamiliar place with a new manager who expects you to master in a few short weeks. You just got married with a shared lifetime ahead.

Remind yourself, "Rome wasn't built in a day." The longest journey begins with the first step. I tell myself, "You cannot finish what you don't start." Do you know performers who procrastinate? But if they had just started, they would have finished the job in the same time it took to think of all the excuses. This occurs from a negative prediction of work instead of the rewards value. This is why tough tasks need to be broken into smaller more manageable parts to set low positive goals and increase frequency of success and reward.

Predict a suitable reward to value satisfying your need or goal and your motivation to achieve success increases. Your work ethic becomes manageable in smaller incremental efforts. If you look at the overall task you are overwhelmed and hesitate to improve or condition a fear of failure.

You cannot learn all about art or science in a day, week, month, or even a year. Mastery of any skill takes time. Break down skills into no more than five components at a time to focus on the sequence of cues and responses.

Create Dichotomies to Predict Future Performance

A dichotomy forces you to recognize both ends of a larger spectrum so you can readily choose correct methods and cues. Dichotomies are right or wrong, positive or negative, yes or no, and pleasure or pain. When you feel frequent success the reward value reinforces your motivation to continue to work hard and ensure more success.

Dichotomies are an awareness strategy to convert negative to positive images or feelings. For any outcome, the obvious correct choice is positive over negative. No one purposefully seeks failure.

Performers can become conditioned by failure and react as victims instead of learning how to be proactive and positive. No one purposefully wants to repeat an accidental electric shock from a wire, or cattle fence. That negative unpleasant sensory feeling is avoided.

A dichotomy lets your brain compare past with expected future performances. It is a microprocessor and autoresponder and predictor all rolled into one. And within reason your brain does what you program it to do.

Julian Rotter (1954) a professor at The Ohio State University researched the personality dichotomy of being inner or outer directed. Essentially the theory suggests performers who are inner directed take personal accountability for performances. Performers who are externally directed blame others and make excuses for poor performance outside of their control.

Earlier I asked if people are always telling you what to do, and why? Are you self-directed? Do you follow directions and know what your needs and goals are to be self-directed? These are the kinds of dichotomies you create. Can you or cannot perform? Can you feel pleasure from assured success or pain from failure to perform difficult tasks?

Hypothetically, new valued information is associated as rewarding and stored in pleasure centers directly on your brain's desktop. The dichotomy pain is avoided, and pleasure is associated with reward. Pleasure is conditioned to repeat those behaviors and the cues and methods associated with the results are immediately available in one click. Some call this "top of mind awareness." It is what separates top performers from average and poor performers.

The pain of performing poorly only reinforces negative feelings and more avoidance behaviors. Failing students are externally directed to make excuses and disrupt classrooms to shift the focus from their poor performance, or worse self-medicate with drugs. To lead explain how to stop the pain of failure and shift the focus to set low positive goals with a purpose to predict higher probability of success for future performances. Then observe how this improves a positive mental outlook and personal accountability.

Alfie Kohn published Punished by Rewards (1993). Self-improvement implies feeling good about any kind of improvement over your last performance. But what Kohn implies is schools create too many extrinsic rewards with grading systems and awards. The real value of reward is the personal feeling of self-improvement or intrinsic motivation. Good grades mean little if you forget how to apply what you learn after the test.

Personal Prediction Skills

Your human computer constantly makes unconscious comparisons and iterations to predict potential outcomes based on your life experience. Some performers call this common sense. Safety awareness is designed to save your life by predicting unfavorable results of bad behaviors. For example, texting while driving is a highly probable cause of accidental deaths and bodily harm. Personal profiling is another example based on your past experiences.

With any kind of experience, you visualize an image or make a mental movie of cause and effect relationships. Mental practice is closing your eyes and visualizing yourself successfully performing the way you want to perform in every detail.

You want to build a positive self-evaluation system using your own performance feedback to create a stronger personal reward system. You factor in bias to be aware of its effect on your thinking to make reasonable choices. Top performers are less concerned with critics than improving their personal past performance.

Mentally visualize a sequence of skill components in pre-performance routines. This reviews your work to motivate accomplishing your goal. If you have done the work, then you deserve the reward.

Take time to reflect on all the work you have accomplished in practice and displayed in your workout log. Decide to be successful. You have earned the right to be in position to compete successfully. You compare your work ethic to other performers. Repeat to yourself, "Someone has to win, and it may as well be me."

Have you done the work? Have you set a realistic goal? Have your outworked your competition? Do you deserve to win or succeed and feel rewarded? Top performers use strategy asking these kinds of questions to build confidence and self-esteem leading to consistently higher quality achievements over time.

Predictive Value and Triad Strength

There are two highly predictable strategies to build value strength:

1) Increase awareness to a conscious level, and
2) Predict how your abilities match the performance task and probability for success.

In your mind, create a predictive equation estimating what key variables (cues) to perform the task well. Then weight each variable but not to exceed a total of 100%. Subjectively evaluate your performance on each variable to compare how top performers in those tasks would rate. Both personal value and The Triad skills increase with knowledge and task familiarity. Great coaching leaders with a wealth of knowledge from their past top performers shorten the learning curve to build familiarity, value, and purpose with The Triad for impending competitions.

Correlation Value and Triad Strength

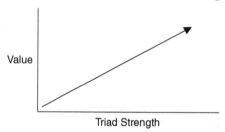

11

ACCOUNTABILITY IS YOUR RESPONSIBILITY

Accountability has long been a subject of systems management. Accountability is defined as responsible, liable, or explainable. In the traditional sense, accountable is what someone else expects of another performer. The thought process is associated with external forces outside the performer. Personal accountability is a tough lesson to learn.

Performers who are taught how to self-evaluate and self-reward their purpose setting proper goals, hold themselves accountable for improving their performance, and become independent of extrinsic motivators provided by others. Top performers as a rule learn early discipline in the home effected by the mother. They hold the children accountable for their behaviors.

What has changed is the social family unit and social media relationships. More children are being raised by single parents. The children have easier access to social media to compare notes about others who describe what they have and how they got it. At the same time parents felt a need to protect their children from wandering around connecting with wrong elements.

Children did not ride around on bikes to hang out with friends or create sports play. Unless it was an organized and supervised sport, children did not self-organize and play sports. In play your performance was judged by your friends and peers who held you accountable to play better. Organized sports had rules so every child would get equal play time. Parents encouraged children to play and rewarded poor performance in hopes of encouraging improvement. Self-evaluation and peer socialization fell aside.

The Triad is a performance improvement system. Increasing awareness of your needs and values for any activity teaches personal accountability. Satisfaction of personal needs by setting and meeting a goal is rewarding. You connect an accountable work ethic to be proud of.

You found a need, set a goal, performed the work, and you deserve all the reward. It is easier to learn accountability through success than failure. Success is pleasure motivated to repeat and feel accountable. Failure is pain motivated to avoid and hold yourself accountable.

It is natural human behavior to deny responsibility and accountability for maladaptive behaviors. This is a defense mechanism. Do you know of any successful top performer who denies personal accountability for their performance? Do top performers deny accountability in unsuccessful behaviors? Of course.

Performers who learn and practice The Triad are more engaged and accountable for personal performance improvement. The 3 secret skills are teachable and learnable early in the home and a school system. Then the probability for success improves. These are powerful lessons in transformational leadership.

A dichotomy compares observations of boss and lead management styles. Boss managers view management as their way or the highway—meaning you are fired if you vary from what the boss tells you to perform. Lead managers use an empowerment approach to improve performance with intrinsic motivation principles in The Triad.

As a behavioral rule, you cannot build accountability in a micromanagement system. Micromanaged performers easily blame others for poor performance. They seldom suffer the consequences of poor decisions leading to poor performance behaviors. They do not learn to identify needs, learn values, set goals, and experience success or failure. Observing, do you know of any top performers who wait for the approval of another?

Do you know people who always blame others for their poor performance? Or, do they make excuses to rationalize why they did so poorly? These are defense mechanisms to buffer the pain of poor performance. Top performers are aware of excuses and do not use them. They hold themselves accountable to satisfy personal needs and goal standards and feel those rewards.

This chapter has two components: Education and Learning, and Leadership Management. How you learn and manage today is determined by how you were conditioned for performance accountability from your system experience. The older less progressive system was boss management. Employees could not be trusted to make decisions. Only management could set policy, performance standards, and process methods.

Education and Learning Accountability

Training programs were regimented with specific methods and process skills. After World War II this kind of system produced results. Then education and learning began to take over training systems and shift to lead management styles. This empowered employees to participate in the process and motivated performance improvement. Companies saw the need to make employees partners and have a stake with profit sharing benefits. In several cases, employee owned companies emerged.

How accountability is taught and conditioned in schools, homes, or on the job are important issues. The Triad Performance Improvement System offers strategies to increase personal awareness and accountability from self-evaluation performance feedback. When more rules and regulations are created to coerce performance improvement there is no comparison to individually motivated performers working as a team.

A leader in this movement was behaviorist Robert Gagné (1916–2002) who published The Nine Events of Instruction to assist training U.S. Air Force personnel in 1949. He is best known for authoring "Conditions of Learning" and served as a Professor of Education and Research at Florida State University from 1969. His nine events are listed below and are a hallmark for teaching and learning.

Robert Gagné's Nine Events of Instruction

Gain Attention	A quotation; opening sentence; or thought-provoking question
Learner Objective	A statement about what you should know and do
Recall Prior Knowledge	A brief sentence or two about the previous chapter(s).
Present Material	The written body of work about the chapter topic
Provide Guided Learning	Thought provoking questions on your personal performance feedback
Elicit Performance	Take a survey or quiz, practice a specific strategy to condition correct responses, or reflect on past performances
Provide Feedback	Evaluate your current performance to past performance
Assess Performance	Measurable steps to improve your immediate past performance
Enhance Retention and Transfer	You will repeat what works and apply those strategies to other performances

The Triad conditions your mind to hold yourself accountable rather than expecting others to make you do something based on their expectations. Take a moment to recall how you learned success and held yourself accountable for your behaviors, and performances.

For starters, think of school grading systems and handbooks with behavioral rules and consequences. Most likely you were not taught a self-evaluation system. Teachers evaluated your performances, but coaches taught you to set performance goals and hold yourself accountable for achieving them.

On your first job you were given an interview and discussion of the company mission and vision. Then you were handed a job description and a sales quota to meet. You had 90 days to perform or be fired without cause. I guarantee your focus was not on how the company would benefit you but how you would benefit the company.

Those are typical but not how to teach personal accountability. The key variable is success. Quantify and be aware of small improvements from your immediate past performance to feel rewarded and stay motivated. This reward is more than the paycheck. Failures do not lead to improving accountability. They are painful and naturally avoided to blame others or uncontrollable outside factors.

Top performers are successful and proud to hold themselves accountable and take credit for their performances. They do not need to blame others for poor performances. They take responsibility. External forces still exist. Others, fans, and critics who are unable to perform at your level boo and whistle. You have ruined their pleasurable feeling enjoying your success or made your manager look bad.

When a highly motivated hard-working top performer wants to win and shows their displeasure, management takes it personally to discipline or trade them. But top coaches and managers know how to redirect that anger into positive self-improvement. Those performers become team leaders putting social pressure on everyone to improve their personal performance.

One of the training outcomes to create a culture of self-improvement is for organizations to evaluate personnel into three kinds of groups. The top group are self-motivated empowered and valued participants in the decision-making process to improve the organization. The middle group are average performers who do not complain to others and enjoy their work environment. The bottom group are complainers who seem unhappy with their lives and carry that over into the work environment.

The bottom group socializes during breaks and lunches with the middle group to create or taint their dissatisfaction outlook. No amount of training would change that personality. The bottom line was to replace performers in the bottom group by identifying and hiring average or top performers.

I cannot get into all the details for how that process of change would work. But the process for teaching and learning personal accountability begins with transforming the leaders. To create top performers, identify what management style the leaders were conditioned to learn. Or, as Gagné describes "conditions of learning."

Were you conditioned by external forces or conditioned yourself by internal forces to hold yourself accountable for your performance? We already know intrinsic motivation is more powerful than extrinsic motivation.

To transform your leadership skills be aware of how you were conditioned to manage performers. What are your personal needs and values now? Do you have a sound philosophy that drives your positive behavior? Do you take time to learn the personal needs and values of performers you manage and lead?

The Accountability Paradigm chart that follows offers a contrast between micromanagement and empowerment leadership. Reflect on how you were educated and permitted to perform by your teachers and then compare to on-the-job training by company management.

Empowerment increases intrinsic motivation with management's expectation of performance improvement. Micromanagement uses extrinsic motives to coerce compliance with the company mission. You decide which company or organization you would like to work for.

Accountability Paradigm

Micromanagement	Empowerment
No choice	Many choices
Loss of control to paranoid control freaks	Control of your ideas
Loss of creativity for ideas, methods, processes	Creative freely sharing of ideas, methods, processes
Boss managers	Professional learning community culture
– Little coaching	Lead managers
– Perform or be fired	– Strong coaching to build knowledge, skills, and teamwork
Extrinsic motives	– Recognition of personal needs of the performers
– Needs of the boss or corporation to be met Non-caring	Intrinsic motives
– Cold; impersonal; no fun atmosphere/culture	– Personal needs satisfied of the people doing the work
– Work, job, non-satisfying	Caring
	– Warm; personal; fun helping others atmosphere/culture
Excuse	– Family values; work, job, satisfying personal needs
– Can blame others for poor performance	Personal efforts recognized by co-workers
– Can spread false rumors and beliefs	No excuse
No personal accountability	– Blame yourself for poor performance
Lower morale	Hold yourself accountable
– "Why bother syndrome"	Higher morale
– Learned helplessness	– Can take personal credit
– Leader steals your ideas	– Can equate quality of effort to quality of reward
– Leader takes the credit for good;	– Positive continuous incremental performance improvements are recognized and celebrated
– Leader blames workers for poor performance	
Employees finger point and blame others for weak performance outcomes	Personal reward system is reinforced to repeat positive behaviors
No regard for what worker thinks	Desire to care what worker is thinking
Employees do not care what co-workers think	
Collection of individual performers doing their own thing	Take personal responsibility to achieve outcomes to support team effort
Lost sight of company mission	

Micromanagement	Empowerment
Dysfunctional teams—no cohesiveness Inconsistent policy toward personal skill development; and lack of performance recognition	Aware of company mission and vision Teamwork, good communication
	– Workers care about what co-workers are thinking and doing that reflect on overall group performance
Ignorance and bias = bliss	Focus on outcomes more than process
Focus more on process and rules	Consistent, stable approach to continuously improve personal skills, Policy decisions reflect best practice and overall performance
Resistance to change keeps personality and stress management in check for short term	Performances are recognized outcomes
Poor planning, no vision, nobody cares	Adapt to change recognizing temporary state of stress to manage for the short term
No joy in performing	Communicate vision to produce long term personal growth and satisfaction
Go through the motions daily	You keep pace with your profession and competition by setting goals and planning positive and rewarding outcomes
Fly by the seat of your pants	

To teach others how to hold themselves accountable, instead of passing judgment for a performance, ask questions to get performers to reflect on and judge their performance. Did you do the best that you could? Did you try to do your best? What did you have to do to get that grade, score, or evaluation? Did you improve? Are you happy with your performance? There are all kinds of questions designed to get performers to reflect on and review personal performance. If any effort was made leaders must recognize and reinforce those moderate successes to build pride and motive to improve accountable personal performance.

Accountable implies a standard to apply to current performance. Is that standard expectation known to all performers prior to performing? Do all performers know who is credited with improvements? What is the performance expectation? Is the expectation based on the realistic abilities of the performers? The expectation must account for a performer's ability level and a realistic low-positive standard to meet given the circumstances to ensure probability of success.

It was already noted how top performers set private goals based on a "self" personality type. The perceptual anchoring point is their personal immediate past performance or past performance average. If you are going to use standards and have expectations, then use the goal-setting patterns of top performers and condition those kinds of stimulus-response connections. This is a powerful transformational leadership lesson.

To condition personal accountability, whether at home, school, or on the job provide a realistic expectation prior to the performance. Support your case with evidence. However, if you are the evaluator parent, teacher, coach or manager, refrain from stating the expectation until you can determine what the performer feels is realistic for their ability. This is how you build intrinsic motivation.

Each performer identifies their personal performance baseline control or starting point. Baseline expectations and standards are based on the immediate past performance or average of each performer and what they are individually capable of performing given their abilities. Leaders build confidence making their performers aware of their talents and abilities to raise personal expectations. Average performers are usually unaware of their talent and ability until a trusted advisor, teacher or coach creates a discussion with past performance improvement proof.

This process takes you back to creating dichotomies. All performers do not spend time reflecting on where they started to improve. The dichotomy is the comparison of where you started to where you are now. The notable difference creates a positive work ethic.

Keep a workout log or diary to be aware of all those small measurable improvements. Note how the work effort has been rewarded and the positive feelings. This increases personal intrinsic motivation more than external praise from others.

The nice concept about kids and performers with inexperience is they do not know what they are not supposed to know. They condition correct personal behaviors when you teach them to self-evaluate their performances. Use B.F. Skinner's "Black Box" feedback model to compare input and output. Ask what cues work, and what do not.

I guarantee this strategy works for children or adults. Neither cares whether the neighbor kid or co-worker improves at anything. What matters is feeling reward for seeing improved personal baseline performance. Therefore, objectify performance in smaller parts of the total performance (maybe only their part) to condition frequent success.

After performers have some experience with tasks ask them what feedback (input-output) they are processing from their performance. Then condition them to the low-positive goal strategy to slightly keep improving the immediate past performance.

This requires personal or intrinsic control the make the process meaningful and relevant to value and increase intrinsic motivation. This is another powerful leadership transformational lesson.

Children and other performers who are fearful of trying or make exaggerated expectations or goals have been conditioned to behave this way by external forces in the home, school, or on the job. Normal human behavior is trial and error. Using The Triad Performance Improvement System leaders transform performer's behaviors, so they learn to hold themselves accountable for learning and performance improvement.

Condition performers to observe performance improvement and feel pleasure from their success. They will hold themselves accountable for improving performance. And correct personality patterns of realism, persistence, and will-power will occur. This is the path of top performers.

Realism is when the goal expectation is closely aligned with the actual observed performance. This feedback behavior teaches realism keeping your expectations in line with your abilities to avoid serious frustrations.

Anxious frustrated learners disrupt classrooms and teams, display bad behaviors, and reduce their capacity to learn how to learn. Usually when performers make mistakes, others want to manage their behavior instead of teaching them self-evaluation feedback skills to take accountability for their performance and behavior. This is one more powerful transformational leadership lesson.

Leadership Suggestions

Hold yourself accountable for your leadership performance before you set expectations for your performers. You must teach others the strategies and skills to hold themselves accountable for their performances.

Our society and political correctness are quick to judge and hold others accountable. More often the critics and media take messages out of context to fit a different narrative. Crowd size and polling statistics are skewed to make it seem the opinions and beliefs of the citizen majority.

I recently invited a friend over for coffee and conversation. He said something that got my attention. His comment was, "I may not know the truth, but I surely know a lie when I hear it." Every story has two sides, but lately we only get to hear a one-sided view. Perhaps if we heard both sides to a story, we could be trusted to make our own conclusions.

Then there is blatant hypocrisy. Politicians do and say anything to get elected. Why? Do you wonder how an elected candidate's net worth grows ten-fold on their salary and benefits? Political positions change with the wind, or as one performer said whoever makes a lasting impression like a sat-upon pillow.

Proven results and positive track records of performance speak volumes. The basis for consistent words and actions flow from a positive philosophy. "We hold these truths to be self-evident."

Top performing leaders are consistent in their words and actions getting proven results. Leaders are human and prone to mistakes. Consistency is the key. As my friend said, knowing and withholding the truth to fit a false narrative and then to lie about it is sinful.

Lately I have noted performers who cannot support their positions get frustrated and resort to name calling and yelling obscenities. You begin to understand these performers have not learned The Triad to lead personal performance improvement any better or hold themselves accountable for their performances. As the leader be reluctant to cast negative evaluations until you get your own house in order. Hold yourself accountable. It is your job.

You have a choice to feel pleasure over pain. You construct your attitudes, beliefs and values and personality to socially interact in your chosen environment. The breakdown of the family to learn these lessons in the home appear lost. The value of learning an intrinsic motivational system in The Triad is to help you understand and manage what information you choose meaningful and relevant to value and remember.

Parents are the first line of leadership. Teach your children is a virtue. My experience in education as a teacher and school superintendent is more parents demand others teach and discipline their children. Parents have abdicated this job and are first to demand and hold others accountable for their child's behaviors. Evidence is the growth of free and reduced meals to provide not only lunch but breakfasts, too. And then there are afterschool programs for working parents.

The choices you make determine how you are behaviorally conditioned by systems. The nature of your personal drives and motives you work to improve are often pitted against those imposed by the organization and leaders.

Nature versus nurture also creates intrinsic motives to satisfy subconscious needs. With certainty performers must learn to identify personal needs and understand how they change with maturity and knowledge. This is an awareness skill that can be reinforced to produce accountability.

As a leader I am older and wiser. It is apparent the opinions and values of younger generations who have been conditioned to feel entitled with free everything. They have not lived or worked long enough to value the work and sacrifices of previous generations. My parents taught me to respect the knowledge of my elders and law and order as a good citizen, and to vote my opinion.

History tends to repeat itself. Historical reference offers future predictions of pain or pleasure to motivate a better quality of life. To put this into context, I observed the mistakes of an older brother so I could avoid them.

A personal performance feedback system creates a personal need for achievement. Success equals pleasure and failure equals pain. What do you prefer? Pleasure or pain? Increasing your awareness of feelings of satisfaction and reward are self-reinforced to motivate more like behaviors and continuously improve your performance.

Top performers are highly aware if new information is meaningful and relevant to improve their skills and performance, they follow the leader. Transformational leaders are aware of the effect of bias and beliefs imposed by others. They are forthright in words and actions. To lead you must have followers who believe in you. Evaluations from others are always extrinsic and never as valuable as what you learn to self-evaluate and compare performances against a realistic personal intrinsic standard. Do you hear both sides of stories to compare and learn the truth?

You are successful improving performance. No one can argue unless you are grossly underperforming for your ability level. Learning to self-evaluate your personal performance feedback is essential. You must know your capabilities and limitations better than others including your parents and spouse.

You may lie to others but not to yourself. Only a sociopath believes what they lied about is the truth. The parental leadership advice to your children must be true or they will no longer follow you.

Parents, teachers, and school systems can point you in the right direction, but you must educate yourself to value new information as meaningful and relevant. This increases your motivation and ability to store more useful information. Learn how to learn. Understand your purpose and intent with manageable goals to meet your personal needs and increase your reward system.

In school systems it is what you intend to learn from your curriculum of study. In management and business, it is what you can do to benefit your personnel and customer. No one can make you learn or do anything with quality until you see the personal value in performing. Accept personal accountability for your performance and do not blame others for their lack of effort or poor leadership.

Continuum of Performance Improvement

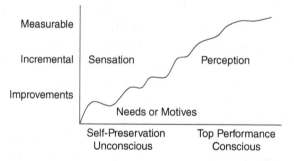

The continuum gives you a visual idea how performance gradually improves. Slumps or plateaus can be frustrating. But learning is still taking place. To keep improving figure out your needs, drives and motives. Then make conscious cognitive decisions with your perception of future performance based on past experiences. You cannot control what others think or do, but you can control what you think and do to affect a change in your performance and environment.

What behaviors, current and past, do you now associate meeting your needs at the time, and are they still operating? What needs do you associate to performance improvement? For example, do you need to make independent goals and earn all the rewards for doing all the work?

Your unconscious drives are on the sensory self-preservation end of the continuum of performance improvement. Your conscious drives are on the perceptual top performance end.

Behavioral Accountability

The Triad is a leadership training method to achieve personal behavioral accountability and performance improvement. It is a leadership style interwoven in all training, teaching, coaching, and evaluation. As a learned skill it can be applied to all forms of teaching and training.

The Triad is not a simple learned lesson or unit. It is the foundation for all motivation. The Triad is the 3 secret skills and promotes powerful lessons in transformational leadership. It represents a major paradigm shift in how to evaluate and improve performance behaviors and lead other performers. It is a commitment to teach how to reflect, evaluate and structure a positive deliberate plan to efficiently improve upon performance for any job, task, skill, or relationship.

In sport psychology we advocate being your own best friend. Top performers tend to tear themselves down and get mad at poor performances. Some throw temper tantrums. I recommend you must keep your emotions under control to learn from your mistakes.

When you are "overamped" your brain is not operating correctly to process information. There is a point where you enhance your performance if you are slightly nervous or anxious. But when you exceed that level your performance worsens. This is called the Yerkes-Dodson Law and resembles an upside-down letter U.

Yerkes-Dodson Law

It would be wrong to think a complex performance improvement system in The Triad or the RROSR skills can be learned overnight. For any process, knowing how and what to practice are key to improving your performance.

You cannot be a top performer with one trial, but you can apply what you learn to continuously motivate your improvement in small increments so that over time you can look back and see your success. The truest measure of success is the continuous improvement of your personal performance over time.

What follows is a schematic diagram of what happens to create consistently motivated and successful performance. If you expect to lead, you must empower others to succeed more often than fail. This requires appealing to the personal intrinsic needs of individuals as opposed to extrinsic group management needs.

Identify and frequently acquire your needs and hold yourself accountable for achieving an increasingly higher standard of performance. What matters the most is not what others think of your performance, but what you learn to value from the standards you hold yourself accountable for achieving.

The Triad Skills Development Model

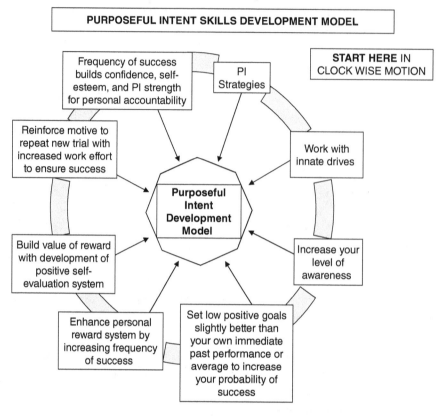

PURPOSEFUL INTENT SKILLS DEVELOPMENT MODEL

Frequency of success builds confidence, self-esteem, and PI strength for personal accountability

PI Strategies

START HERE IN CLOCK WISE MOTION

Reinforce motive to repeat new trial with increased work effort to ensure success

Work with innate drives

Purposeful Intent Development Model

Build value of reward with development of positive self-evaluation system

Increase your level of awareness

Enhance personal reward system by increasing frequency of success

Set low positive goals slightly better than your own immediate past performance or average to increase your probability of success

The Triad Skills Development Model shows the organic nature of these skills. Each skill leads into the next to continuously improve. The first step is PI strategies or understanding your purpose and intent for any performance. You identify all the component skills for any activity or task and the personal need motivating you to achieve performance improvement.

The second step is to identify and work with your natural innate drives. Maslow's Hierarchy provides a good start. The third step is to increase your levels of awareness using RROSR by learning to attend to the most important selected and predictable cues to aid your performance.

The fourth step is to set low positive goals to increase your probability of success. This process enhances the fifth step to develop your personal reward system by increasing your frequency of success. In the sixth step the value of your perceived reward serves to develop a positive self-evaluation system.

By the seventh step, your motives are reinforced by your success to increase your work effort to ensure your continued success. Finally, the eighth step leads to the development of your confidence, self-esteem, purposeful intent strength, and personal accountability. As the cycle is repeated your skills improve, get stronger, and your personal success continuously motivates you to greater achievements.

Caring Builds Accountability

The ultimate theme of caring is leaders teaching "accountable independence" in each performer. This includes everyone from the CEO on down. Needs and values are the key components to intrinsic motivation. Systems and corporate training programs must transform leadership to motivate their performers to achieve more.

Caring builds accountability and creativity. Creating more coercive rules to get performance conformity does the opposite.

We are in a new age of modern behaviorism. Traditional training programs to benefit the company yield poor performance with the bias belief performers are incapable of processing information to improve.

The purpose of this book is to provide powerful lessons in transformational leadership so leaders learn new strategies, and methods to teach and expect intrinsic motivation from their performers to improve performance in less time.

The old traditional motivation has been to offer extrinsic rewards. That solution fosters a two-fold problem. Extrinsic rewards are far less powerful than intrinsic rewards for doing a job well. And, you must keep increasing the reward value. Perhaps a third problem is only a few can vie for and achieve the reward. Who cares?

New employees (performers) who subscribe to the motives of the company or manager survive. Those propose better ideas get fired and look for another job. This turnover is costly. A science has evolved to hire the best employees based on their personality, work ethic, history, and other past performance criteria.

These variables are hard to spot until leaders learn The Triad to apply to their personal performance before evaluating others and overall group performance. Intrinsically motivated performers need creative leaders who have vision to understand how to identify the needs and values of their performers. Then align with the needs and values of the company mission.

This is most evident in successful professional sports organizations. Top performing coaches are who have played the game and better at selecting and coaching new talent. They provide their performers with knowledge of specific successful strategies and cues to RROSR—recognize, receive, organize, store, and retrieve information for top performance.

12

STRATEGIES TO INCREASE AWARENESS

A variety of concept strategies described throughout this book suggest how leadership transformation applies the value of intrinsic motivation to benefit performance improvement.

1. The Triad theorizes the conscious cognitive motive to satisfy a personal need or goal intrinsically motivates performance improvement to feel pleasure.
2. The Triad hypothesizes valued information is more readily stored and retrieved in the brain through the development of cognitive associational neurons that connect positive, pleasurable, and successful activities.
3. The Triad is three knowledge skills learned independently but applied interdependently. They are the foundation for all motivation. Increase Awareness, Enhance Self-Evaluation, and Connect Reward with Reinforcement.
4. The Triad moves unconscious sensations to conscious perceptions to increase awareness of meaningful and relevant value associations to enhance self-evaluation and connect reward to reinforce activities that improve performance.
5. Needs and values are central to the The Triad theory and hypothesis. Needs and values are associated to prior success knowledge and connected by neuronal pathways to pleasure centers in the brain.
6. RROSR is the anachronism for processing information Recognizing, Receiving, Organizing, Storing, and Retrieving valuable knowledge to improve skilled performance.
7. Mobilization of Energy is to get in the "zone" to perform at your highest level. Top performers use prior knowledge to visualize optimal performance prior to performing.
8. Congruence is when the goal expectation and actual performance approximate each other to affect the personality trait of Realism. Similarly, a performer's self-evaluation has more intrinsic motivational value when it approximates the manager's performance evaluation.
9. Task familiarity is how personality patterns are modified as performers become increasingly familiar with a task. Be patient with new performers. As performers become more familiar with tasks personality patterns change from insecurity to security, apprehensive to confident, and distrustful to trusting.

10. Planer Thinking is when performers become highly familiar with specialized tasks to think on higher and higher planes of thought processes using more knowledge from specific previous experiences.

11. Associate quality of effort with quality of reward. Performers value rewards more with effort and increase the need for achievement motivation.

12. Multiple regression task analysis is a prediction equation to subjectively select and weight specific variables by relative importance. Cues, methods, strategies, patterns or traits are identified to efficiently learn and perform a criterion skill.

Multiple Regression Prediction Equation

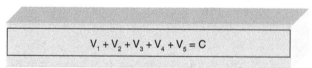

$$V_1 + V_2 + V_3 + V_4 + V_5 = C$$

13. MaS>MaF means your motive to achieve success must be greater than your motive to avoid failure. Focus on the positive over the negative to perform better.

14. Group, Verbal, and Self personality types like Type A and Type B are used to describe how performers prefer to set goals, motivate behavior and performance. Each type shows a perceptual anchoring point preference using performance data to judge the worth of each new personal performance goal.

15. Receptacles of Knowledge to Facilitators of Knowledge means the model for education has changed. No one has a lock on the door. To increase intelligence, learn to facilitate knowledge acquisition. According to W. Edwards Deming, knowledge is the key to all performance improvement.

16. You cannot build accountability in a micromanagement system. The needs of the people performing the work empowers an accountable feeling of success to reward their performance and be intrinsically motivated.

17. Affluent cultures produce literal societies. Performers become less aware of their personal needs and abilities met by others. They are less likely to be motivated to improve personal performance and prefer to have others fulfill their needs. Problems arise when free goods and services are no longer valued but expected. A work ethic to provide for personal needs is lost.

18. Displace/Replace or trick your brain. Your brain is a complex microprocessor and does not know right from wrong. You can displace a negative thought, image, or pattern, and replace with the correct visual and verbal cues to perform.

19. Set low positive goals only one point or slightly better than your own immediate past performance or average. This increases the probability for success and enhances a reward system. Success motivates a work ethic to repeat like behaviors to gain pleasure and reward.

Strategies for Discriminating Extrinsic from Intrinsic Motives

A leadership mistake is believing extrinsic motives build personal performance accountability. If a need or goal comes from outside the performer, there is no control over reducing or increasing the goal. The value attached to an extrinsic motive cannot be as great as an intrinsic motive.

Performers are less motivated to be accountable or take ownership of the performances demanded by others. The biggest leadership trap is to believe more micro-management of poor performance increases personal accountability.

A wise leader, teacher, or parent strategy first asks performers how they felt about their performances before offering an evaluation or opinion. This creates a reflection of the work accomplished by the performer to value the effort and reward and learn personal performance accountability.

The strategy evaluates performance effort and reward value and creates a self-evaluation paradigm shift to associate quality of effort with quality of reward. Leaders who overly manage and make accountable decisions for their performers, are more likely to be blamed for their poor performance and not learn personal accountability.

A second strategy focuses on creating an immediate positive feedback system to self-evaluate and critique personal performances over time. The gaming industry is built on this notion. The game may win big or more often bust but does not deter the player's motive to succeed on the next trial.

Similarly, top performers have built-in intrinsic needs and values motivating future achievement rewards. They are not deterred by an occasional poor performance.

The Triad focuses on your purpose with conscious intent. Your brain reflects on your immediate past performance and creates a new benchmark to better and reward the pleasure centers.

Purpose Versus Intent Provide Strategies for Change

Awareness levels focus on learning to move from a natural, automated, unconscious sensory state, to a more conscious purposeful perceptual level in your capacity to think, learn, and make choices. Typical responses to stimulus cues result in a behavioral pattern and gives you some idea of your purpose. Purpose is your vision to project or perceive a future benefit or result of your behavior.

Your intent is your basic behavioral response to common stimuli. For example, while driving you put on your turn signal. Your intent is to turn left or right to warn other drivers. Most intentions are positive. No one seeks to fail, but some intentions must be conditioned as desirable or undesirable to avoid. For example, stealing, robbing, and cheating are not positive and undesirable intents.

In criminal cases justice seeks to find motive based on intent. This qualifies as pre-meditated in the first or second degree for punishment. Some planning is implied and associated to purpose.

Purpose and intent are like personality patterns and traits and not something you easily question or change in an individual. Intent is your early conditioned desire to improve and be curious. Intent and personality traits are mostly fixed by the age of three to five. A personality trait is an unconscious general disposition of personal conditioned behavior.

You learn to ask questions to get answers to satisfy your curiosity. A perceived negative or lack of response conditions not to ask questions. If early in life your intent is conditioned negatively by others, it can take years to overcome and have a positive purpose to approach new skills. Personal success reinforces correct behaviors and build confidence performing specific tasks.

Steps to Improve Your Triad Skills

The first step is to identify your intrinsic motives based upon your personal short-term and long-term needs. Personal need satisfaction is intrinsic to enhance your reward system and reinforce positive work ethic behaviors.

The second step is to be consciously aware of any performance improvement from your immediate past performance or average to feel rewarded. You feel more reward when taught correct performance cues to recognize (cue recognition skills). Early recognition of stimulus cues and correctly responding to be successful develops a conditioned response represented as $S - R > S - CR$ or using the same stimulus: $S - R > CR$.

Imagine having antennae or a satellite dish on your head to take in more information instead of going through routine motions to recognize, receive, organize, store, and retrieve meaningful and relevant data.

The third step is analyzing all your past activity experiences. Draw a line down the middle of a sheet of paper. Record as many positive experiences on the right, and negative experiences as you recall on the left side.

You are conditioned to rationalize your world through a camera lens the way you want to see it. If your experiences are more positive than negative, you are probably rewarded enough to want to repeat similar behaviors.

The pain of an electric shock or any negative behavior reinforces opposite avoidance behaviors. Behavior modification is to reward and reinforce positive behaviors and extinct negative behaviors by not calling attention to them.

The question is, can you learn to perform this process for yourself by self-evaluating the quality of your continuous performance with a feedback model? At some point in your life you must learn to become your own teacher and leader. At some point you must become the patriarch or matriarch of your family to make good decisions when the advice of your elders no longer applies.

NBA star LeBron James recently commented before his first championship career game in 2007 he had to mature early. At age 10 he had to be the man in a single parent mom household. Life changes your needs to create your purpose whether you want to or not.

You may be put into a servant leadership role you do not choose. Plan to be ready. Usually you take these maturity changes in stride and do not focus on them as purpose driven.

Success Comparison

Some top performers use two of The Triad strategies and skills daily without knowing how or why they work, but not all three. They perform them unconsciously through trial and error because they motivate performance improvements.

When I began to study psychology over forty years ago, I became fascinated with how successful leaders and performers stayed motivated and continued to improve. The first athletic icon that came to my mind was watching the development of Michael Jordan.

When I speak to groups, I ask a show of hands who think Michael knew he would be THE Michael Jordan when he was in high school? Not one hand will go up. Then I ask about Abraham Lincoln, Henry Ford, Thomas Edison, Eleanor Roosevelt, Babe Ruth, and Martin Luther King, and still no hands go up.

I mention that Ray Kroc founded the McDonalds restaurant chain when he was 54, and popularized "fast food" into culture. I suggest you can still achieve more in your lifetime no matter what age or level of success you start from with The Triad skills training.

High achievers are not focused on their date next weekend. They increase their awareness to focus on acquiring specific knowledge to live their passion! They acquire a purpose for what they want to do with their lives. Aimless performers are only followers unable to lead themselves and improve personal performance.

Use The Triad to consistently perform above average, find your purpose, and over time become a top performer. A top performer is anyone who is generally average, but consistently performs above average on a specific job, task, skill, or relationship. You can be the best branch bank teller, or custodian at your school when you are consistently motivated to do quality performance.

THE SECOND SECRET SKILL

ENHANCE SELF-EVALUATION

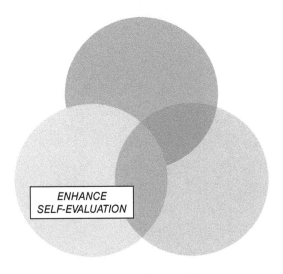

There are three powerful lessons to learn how to self-evaluate your performance.

13

PART TWO OF THE TRIAD
TO ENHANCE SELF-EVALUATION

There are three ways to learn how to self-evaluation your performance. Most people only do the post-performance evaluation after the fact and wish they had prepared better for the interview or competition. Top performers learn to use all three strategies to improve performance outcomes.

Pre-Performance Evaluation. You gather prior performance knowledge to project realistic goals you know you can achieve. You mentally rehearse the methods and cues you have practiced for success. You know your performance need and value to satisfy. You set a low positive goal only slightly better than an immediate past performance to increase your probability for success.

During Performance Evaluation. You process feedback during a performance and make necessary adjustments to increase your probability for success on the next trial.

Post-Performance Evaluation. How your performance feelings agree with your expected goal and result, and comparison of effort to value an improvement. Or, make-a-decision to increase work ethic to ensure improvement on future performance.

How to Enhance Self-evaluation

Self-evaluation is a personal feedback model presented as pre, during, and post evaluation skills. Pre evaluation details how to plan and prepare to get ready to perform at your best. During evaluation reviews strategies to modify and improve your present performance. Correct methods and cues are re imagined in a visual and verbal performance sequence using your abilities. Post evaluation describes using your immediate past performance or average as a benchmark to set and improve new goals.

Pre-performance Objective

Your main objective is to pre-program your brain to execute a specific planned performance sequence. You review stored knowledge of methods and cues you have practiced and trained to perform. You set a realistic low positive goal slightly better than your own immediate past performance or average so you must achieve without an excuse.

You increase awareness of your purpose, needs, and values to enhance your motive to achieve. You may restate and repeat a goal in your brain to enhance the focus. Occasionally you may state a worthy goal to others to create the need for social acceptance. You may compare your goals to performances of top performers and others in your group.

The purpose of self-evaluation is to gauge the level of your output compared to past performances and create a positive pre connection between quality of effort and quality of reward. It is not what you guess about your next performance. It is your awareness to focus on what you have learned to know and value about your performances.

In leadership you can consciously choose a negative or positive view of any task or person. Fearing uncertainty is a recipe for poor performance. As leaders ask questions to make your performers partners in the learning process.

Present information so every performer must decide what is meaningful and relevant knowledge to value. Valued information consciously stored is readily retrieved and applied to improve performance in less time.

The problem with every affluent culture is making unenforceable laws and regulations that retard personal responsibility and accountability. Leadership follows this same behavior. Masses must be directed so they will not hurt themselves. One performer fails to follow the rules, gets hurt, and a new law is created so everyone must suffer a loss of freedom to make personal decisions to enjoy an activity.

There are risks in daily living and frivolous laws are not obeyed. If performers are warned, make mistakes, get hurt, they suffer the consequences. If painful enough, those behaviors are avoided. You stub your toe going barefoot and realize the need and value of wearing shoes. Government shall not create programs that allow performers to abdicate their personal behavioral accountability.

As a behavioral rule, I will state this again. Performers do not value anything they get for free. Consider free college tuition and free healthcare. If granted, expect students to party instead of study, and people neglecting their personal health. There are only so many transplant kidneys, livers, and hearts, or new knees to go around. Hard-working performers will reject paying more taxes to pay for other performers indiscretions.

There are strong leadership values teaching self-evaluation skills. The acquired skill of every top performer is deciding what new information is meaningful and relevant to RROSR. Do-overs and mastery learning instructional practices creates continuous self-improvement by self-evaluation. This is one more powerful lesson in transformational leadership to improve performance in less time.

Basic Strategies to Enhance Self-Evaluation

Setting Goals

The mere act of setting a goal creates a purpose and value system to reward and associate reinforcement behaviors. Writing down goals provides stronger images to store and retrieve in your brain.

Top performers may have primary goals. But they focus on the immediate present performance goals. For example, an Olympic Medal is the primary goal. But objectifying specific component skills of the overall performance is the focus to improve in practices and lead-up competitions.

Top performing leaders are aware of the component skills for good performance. For each component skill they encourage setting low positive goals only slightly better than each performer's personal immediate past performance or average. This increases probability for success and rewards continuous improvement behaviors. Each performer controls the process and cannot control what another performer is thinking or focused on achieving. They can control understanding personal needs, values, and goals and hold themselves accountable for improving.

Recording Improvement

Journaling, workout logs, diaries, and performance portfolios are valuable self-evaluation tools. Create visual performance improvement graphs. Your brain knows if you are improving to remind you of your quality accomplishments. This builds confidence and reinforces the connection between quality of effort and quality of reward.

All good performance requires repetition so consciously record the methods and cues to get better results. There are learning curves to value your purpose and effort compared to a result. Do your results equal your effort? Do you feel rewarded and motivated to repeat those behaviors?

I recorded every swim workout I did in college and Masters' Swimming. There are standard repeat sets each week or every other week to compare times for improvement. The act of recording those repeat times provided a goal in my short-term memory to improve in practice.

Every job, task, skill, or relationship has component parts to separate and objectify. Take time to think of what they are and write them down in the order of importance. Then, ask yourself, "Are you improving? If not, why not?"

Work Ethic Behaviors

Work is pleasurable when you feel rewarded for improving. Otherwise, work can be a pain and avoided. The major difference between average and top performers is the motivation to push past occasional failures. Top performers view lesser performances as a signal to change their work ethic.

Simply working harder is not always they answer until you learn to work smarter. This means focusing on the methods and cues proven to get better results. Top leaders in coaches, teachers, managers, and parents know and impart those correct methods and cues to shorten your learning curve. Provided you increase your awareness to pay attention and value the new information to modify your behavior.

The faster and more you learn to self-evaluate your performances provides greater rewards and intrinsic motivation to repeat and keep improving. Making lists of tasks to complete provides a goal-reward-reinforcement connection to feel good about getting tasks accomplished to cross off your list. This is purposeful intent in action.

Positive Self-talk

You must be realistic to use positive self-talk. Your expectations must be in line with reality. For this to work you need a lot of performance knowledge to draw upon. Then compare your performances and abilities and contrast against others with similar abilities competing in the same arena. You cannot control other performers so do not worry about them. Instead focus on doing what you know to do best. Last, TRUST.

There are several well-known strategies top performers use. Most are reminders of past performances and successes. You can do this! Have a personal conversation in your mind. Review all the component parts to focus on in sequence to build your confidence. Program your brain to execute the performance the way you visualize it.

Visualization

Top performers make mental movies imaging perfect performance sequences. To make this personal movie requires a lot of prior experience with the performance. Get your brain focused to automate awareness of cues to trigger correct responses.

Your short-term memory holds the movie, so you want to visualize your performance closer to your actual performance. In golf, it may be your next shot in a matter of minutes. In swimming, I like to sit quietly alone about 20-30 minutes prior to my events. The last thing I want is a meaningful conversation or distraction. Stay focused!

Pre-Performance Routines

I use several examples from sport because more performers seem to identify with the effect. Every job, task, skill, or relationship has a pre-performance routine. You want to transfer the same identical elements you have assimilated in practice to the actual performance. Watch pro golfers or basketball players. Each one has their own pre-performance routine. This settles down your nerves and maintains a positive focus.

For a job, the routine is like preparing for work. For tasks, you may use the same routine to wash dishes or your hands. For skills, you make a fast review of the cues in the same order of importance. For relationships, you start with a routine greeting and smile.

14

PRE-PERFORMANCE EVALUATION TECHNIQUES

A top performer is willing to risk failure to test their limits and capacity to improve. Constantly measure your purpose against your abilities and skills. Use a variety of information to predict the value of a future performance to increase your intrinsic motivation. Then, super-impose an immediate past performance or average as your baseline standard to improve.

Self-evaluation validates your performance against a personally selected standard. Pre-performance evaluation is a review of a conscious plan to improve upon an immediate past performance or average. It is not wise to compare or set goals based on the performances of others.

You can be aware of your competition, but the greatest motivation is to focus on improving your past performance. If you improve but still lose the job or contest, there is no shame or need to beat yourself up.

Top performers consistently use their own immediate past performance as the basic standard to evaluate the worth of every new performance. This personal standard constantly changes as you improve your performance. They record and log performances in practices and competitions, so they are consciously aware to set realistic goals.

The key strategy is to break down your performance into component parts you can create and objectify using a scale of 1 poor to 3 average and 5 excellent. For timed events you simply record the time to improve on your next trial. If a performance scoring system is not feasible, then video tape your performance to view later and process for performance feedback.

You can control your focus on specific methods and cues in practices to improve performance. This is hard enough to do for yourself. Why waste your time figuring out and worrying what your competition is doing? It takes years of dedicated practice to become a top performer. Forget about being an overnight success or someone you are not.

Adjust your personality to get real with matching your abilities, past performance experiences, and realistic goals or expected outcomes. You can change your needs and purpose once you identify their meaningful and relevant performance value. These primary factors create your intrinsic motivation system learned with The Triad.

In the first skill of The Triad, Increase Awareness, you learned to identify your needs from desires or wants, and matched your abilities to performance outcomes. Being smart is knowing what you are good at performing and feel some personal reward to motivate your need to continue to improve.

In the second skill of The Triad, Enhance Self Evaluation, you learn to reverse the flow of knowledge from extrinsic or outside sources like parents, teachers, coaches, and managers. The paradigm shift is to self-evaluate and be your own judge. If you were alone, would you evaluate and self-correct your performance skills?

You have learned needs and values and goal setting to define your purpose and create your personal intrinsic motivation system. Now you must increase awareness to set up and improve a personal self-evaluation system. The purpose is to properly affect positive realistic plans to succeed on given jobs, tasks, skills, and relationships.

This strategic purposeful planning builds realism and intrinsic motivation by increasing your probability for success. Success does breed success because you reinforce a reward system to keep working to improve and feel pleasure.

Pre-performance evaluation is programming your brain to auto respond without thinking. Without a prior planned program processing more unfamiliar information inefficiently confuses the brain and delays timing for accurate responses. This is another powerful lesson in transformational leadership.

Strategies to Improve Pre-performance Evaluation

Visualization Strategy Prior to Performing

This is my personal preferred strategy to use immediately before competing or an event. With mental practice you can visualize specific techniques and mechanics for any physical skill or points you would like to make in an interview or a conversation. I assume this also applies to jobs, tasks, and relationships. You program and mentally rehearse specific cues to trigger correct responses in sequence to automate performance routines without delayed reaction.

This strategy works well only if you have enough prior success experience to draw upon. It does not do you any good to focus on the wrong cues to avoid and get poor responses. The pre-performance self-evaluation must be accurate with proven results. Unfortunately for some performers making mental images and movies are difficult.

The "third eye" strategy is to see yourself from the view of a movie camera behind you. If you can, video tape your performances to self-evaluate.

You can do whatever you like to prepare and get motivated. Some like to listen to upbeat music using ear buds. Others jump up and slap their bare skin. You may want to repeat your start or pace times repeatedly. You want to mobilize all your energy for that one moment in time. Program all the correct positive things you can imagine. Then, after a short break, let go and trust your brain to execute your plan.

This photo was taken prior to an event at the 2012 Master's Long Course Nationals in Omaha, NE. Some swimmers thought I was an old man taking a nap. Instead, I was visualizing my perfect race. I was programming my brain to execute my race based on all the positive cues for proper mechanics, and race pace from start to finish. This is pre-planning for success and getting in "the zone."

Mental Practice is a Variation of Visualization

To effectively use visualization techniques takes practice. Use positive experiences from practices and performances to visualize the same sequences. Find a quiet place free from distractions so you can focus a good image. Add as many of your other senses to make it more real.

Performers who have used mental practice at least one-third as much time spent during actual physical practice improve much faster. I used to practice my timing and pace splits. With experience I can predict my split times within one-tenth. For timed events, start your internal clock at the same time as a stopwatch to see how accurate you are to the split times.

Recently I fell asleep on the couch after lunch watching the news. In a dream a large ball—maybe a basketball from my grandson—was headed for my face. Of course, I flinched throwing both hands up to block the ball. Has this ever happened to you? I know visualization and mental practice help to improve physical and mental skills by the muscle response I got.

I cannot recall where I read an article about a pro baseball or golfer who was a prisoner for several years during the war in Viet Nam. He mentally practiced his swing almost daily to occupy his time. He visualized the pitch or maybe it was where he wanted to land his golf shot. After his release he either hit over .400 or played scratch golf. Mental practice works. Top performers use it.

Perfecting Sub Routines with Mental Practice

Top performers make wonderful subjects to study how they efficiently learn and improve their skills. They succeed in short periods of time. They naturally apply skills even they are not able to describe. But with close observation can learn from them to teach other performers.

By questioning a top performer for any skill, learn what cues and associated responses they perform. These important cues should be emphasized in practices simulating actual performance.

Top performers, prior to performing, create positive images of successful performances. Visualization is the technique of making a mental movie of your best performance. Then trust your brain to execute the programmed movie.

The problem is getting top performers to describe what they unconsciously do. Most have highly developed conditioned responses to cues they no longer think about to perform.

I was teaching golf skills to a class of physical education majors and elective students at Furman University. Two of my students were Betsy King and Beth Daniel. Both were members of our National Championship golf team and elected to the Women's Professional Golf Hall of Fame.

Betsy was a magician with a golf iron. She could hit the ball around a bush or tree on an uphill or downhill lie and tell you how to do it. I asked Beth to teach putting. She had perfect form but could not describe what she was doing or why.

To mentally practice all the parts to my swim races in college I developed sub routines. Observing Michael Phelps win his record setting eight 2008 Beijing Olympic Gold Medals, he mentally perfected all eight races as sub routines. He cleared his mind to block out the pressure and focus on executing his program for each specific race.

This practice skill can be learned and applied to improve any job, task, skill, or relationship. Preparing to take an exam, close a sale, prep for a job interview, or develop relationships with a spouse or employees.

Task Familiarity

This was the central focus of my doctoral dissertation personality research. When you approach new unfamiliar tasks or skills with less experience your typical personality patterns are less confident, no trust, and insecure. As you become more familiar with any task or skill you gain confidence, trust, and feel secure in your performance. Sometimes this process takes weeks and months to occur.

Be patient with new employees or performers. Provide a brief job description and remind them of the outcomes you need to achieve. Then let your performers sort out the process details to get the results. Patience is a virtue.

Displace – Replace

Be more aware of nervous energy. When negative thoughts creep into your brain prior to performing, simply put up an imaginary STOP sign or see an open hand raised to signal a dog to stop. You want to extinct all negative thoughts, so you do not reinforce repeating them.

Recall how your brain is a micro-processor. It does not know right from wrong. In sport psychology this example is used to demonstrate how easily you can displace a negative and replace it with a positive. I can yell at you NOT to think about oranges (a negative) but your brain still makes an image of several oranges.

To displace and replace a negative image of oranges, replace it with a positive image of bananas. Your brain immediately fades out the negative oranges image and replaces them with the positive image of bananas.

Imagine playing a 380-yard par 4 golf hole. A pond left of the fairway is about where you want to land your tee shot. You tell your brain NOT to hit the ball in the water. But your brain says, "Oh, I see you want me to hit the ball into the water." A better positive approach is to visualize where to land the ball and only that image. Program that instead.

Never ever just go through the pre-performance routine motions. Increase your awareness to program your purpose or why to get clarity. This puts your brain on alert to focus on the positive performance cues.

Identify Task Difficulty for Needs and Values

It is okay to be challenged but not with low possibility for success. Be your own best friend and realistic with your activity choices. Know your purpose or why you are performing the job, task, skill, or relationship. Write it down. What do you need and value to achieve? Is your intent to succeed, just get by to participate, or lose to be accepted or liked? Know your abilities well enough to project some idea of the per cent of effort it will take to match your purpose, needs, and values. What are the aspects about this activity that motivate you to try and improve?

Surveys your needs and abilities in the Appendix. If you do not identify any needs to satisfy, you are wasting your time on the activity. Do your abilities match up with other performers in the activity? If you are built like a football tackle, you are not designed to swim like a dolphin. Be realistic to match your needs and abilities to each selected job, task, skill, or relationship. This improves your probability for success and continued improvement. There are performers who believe you learn more from failures or mistakes to correct and get better. I believe it is better to learn a system of progressive success using The Triad and RROSR. This shortens the learning curve and reinforces correct behaviors to continuously improve and become a top performer.

The Activity Value Index is an important visual chart presented in Chapter 3 Values you may want to go back and review. There are optimum values achieved from activities. Essentially the greater value of an activity increases intrinsic motivation to succeed. Failures lead to avoidance behaviors. Successes lead to a motive to repeat those behaviors.

Personal Personality Evaluation

Take time to reflect on your past performance behaviors to discover who you are. Are you honest with yourself and others to hold yourself accountable for your performance improvement? This is your integrity.

Are you in a normal range or off the wall in your behavior? Do you think things through before you act, like this exercise is suggesting you do before you perform?

Are you inner or outer directed? Recall no top performer ever waits for the approval of another person.

Your ability to perform as you expected to perform suggests realism an important personality trait of top performers. Will power, mental toughness, persistence, and committed are hallmarks of top performers.

However, if you have phobias and addictions, you have lost self-control of your performance. Assess where you are going in life, and plan for the necessary transformative permanent changes to succeed starting now and commit to doing them. Write down specific measurable steps as goals with realistic time frames for their achievement. A lot is accomplished in a year when you are aware of your goals and purpose. But you cannot finish what you do not start. Take action NOW!!

Self-discipline

Discipline and motivation are not synonymous. They are co-dependent upon reward and reinforcement. When you apply self-discipline, you understand your needs and why you want to perform. You know what it takes to produce a quality performance. You adhere to a strict personal set of criteria to predict your success. You value the quality of your effort and reward.

When others apply discipline to you it is extrinsic and less meaningful to control your behavior. The effect provides negative reinforcement in avoidance behaviors but does little to refocus on your positive behaviors for good outcomes. In the traditional educational system, what matters most is the evaluation performers receive from others.

The 3 Secret Skills of Top Performers seeks to transform leaders of traditional educational systems. The paradigm shift is to educate performers as teachers, students, athletes, employees, and managers to transform to a self-evaluation and personal accountability system of intrinsic motivation. This provides unlimited capacity for performance improvement and growth.

The greatest single fault of American public education is that it is a very controlling and judgmental system. The curriculum is geared to one-size fits all. There are attempts for diverse offerings in gifted and advanced placement, but mainstream teachers are conditioned to leave no child behind. The result is to teach to the lowest denominator in the classroom instead of the middle. The grading system is oriented to create order and discipline. Instead, critical self-evaluation thinking skills must emphasize and foster self-discipline and personal accountability.

It is the performer's responsibility for learning. Leaders need to transform performers to recognize personal needs to become educated. Knowledge is king in any culture or society. In 2020 the highly contagious and deadly Covid-19 virus became a worldwide pandemic. Governments mandated shelter-in-place to avoid spreading the virus. Economies shut down. There were disastrous consequences. A learning curve ensued. Hospitals at first were overwhelmed. States were unprepared. People were not given the freedom of choice to mitigate their risk and take personal accountability for their behaviors.

The worldwide problem with all affluent cultures is creating more laws and regulations applied to all for the poor behaviors of a few. As a behavioral rule I remind you, "The more you do for people, the less they will learn to do for themselves."

Drivers daily assume risk of bodily harm on roads but follow rules of the road to maintain order. It is a choice how and where to mitigate risk of injury. This goes back to educational systems of evaluation and not transforming with a paradigm shift to self-evaluation and personal accountability for behaviors. Learning to learn is a behavior. The intrinsic motivation to learn is based on satisfaction of identified needs and values.

Every top performer has had to overcome this kind of reinforcement system. Our culture looks distastefully at others who would be different by their personal success. If you talk of your success, you are arrogant and conceited. Lesser performers often add swear words for emphasis after arrogant and conceited. I do not think you have to fear success, and there is no law you cannot have a personal conversation to be aware of your performance and improvement.

However, winning carries the responsibility of being a role model to other performers and creates the need and sometimes personal pressure to keep improving your skills. Michael Jordan commented several times in the ESPN ten-part series "The Last Dance" about the sixth and last NBA Championship season, his obligation to perform at a high level to give game ticket holders a show. If you are a winner and mentally tough, all you want to do is win.

If you suggest your opinion to management leaders, you can be labeled a troublemaker and do not get to play or get traded and sometimes fired for challenging your leaders. Top performers are emotional. They get frustrated with leaders who don't display their same intensity to win.

Other cultures have experienced this same problem. A Japanese proverb states it best, "Tallest nail gets pounded down first." Christians learned people "kill the messenger" from what happened to Jesus. Top performers want change to create success. Average and below average performers find change creates unpleasant stress in their personality and upsets their comfort zone.

The difference lies in experienced leaders with proven results who direct the show. Top performers want to be more in control of their lives and accountable to themselves more than to others. They desire to improve their personal rather than group performance standard if they think there are a bunch of deadbeats not doing their job in the group, but who want the same credit.

Achieving Confidence in Pre-Performance Planning

No one argues you need to feel confident prior to performing. To paraphrase the adage, "if you think you are beaten … you probably will lose …." Visualize your perfect performance and not program a failure.

Create a mental movie to repeatedly play before competition, making deals, to rehearse the job, task, skill, or relationship. Focus on the important talking points, questions, cues, pace, strategies, and skills you have practiced. See the outcome in your mind to program what pattern or sequence to do. Then execute your plan without having to think during the performance.

Confidence is achieved by positive experiences you feel are successful. Positive performance feedback improves the retention value for knowledge and applied skills. As a behavioral rule it is natural to remember more positive than negative experiences.

Take the pressure off. Improve your odds by selecting a goal strategy one point better than your own immediate past performance or average. Mentally practice actual performance simulations to increase positive feedback.

You can transfer more task familiar knowledge to your actual performance with a higher probability of success. Confidence is having the pre-performance feeling the actual performance will be successful. This perception is based on the immediate past performance feedback.

All performers learn about the rate and progress of their learning from processing their own performance feedback. Successful salespersons value their product's features and benefits to meet the needs of their customers. Specialists in mergers and acquisitions value their market analysis before making the presentation. Understanding the valuing process is an essential component of pre-performance evaluation to achieve confidence.

Serial Learning and Other Strategies to Perfect Sub Routines

You can stop action, and slow motion forward or reverse for critical analysis to correct specific S-R connections. This lets you focus on and program details you cannot normally achieve during the actual performance. The process is like writing code for a computer program so that steps are executed in correct sequence.

Mental practice is a proven adjunct to physical practice when you have had prior experience with the task or activity. The more experience you have stored from practice and high-level competition like Michael Phelps has had provides a distinct advantage to perfect your sub routines.

Set up your mental movie and practice rehearsing your physical motions in the correct sequence and timing with your eyes closed. Eliminate outside distractions to focus your lens. Go to a quiet place.

This works well for specific routines where the response for the previous stimulus (S) becomes the new stimulus for the next response (R) in the series. The diagram gives you a visual idea of the process.

Open Serial Loop

$$S_1 \rightarrow R_{S2} \rightarrow R_{S3} \rightarrow R_{S4} \rightarrow R_{S5}$$

Closed Serial Loop

Analyze your activity for a closed or continuous serial loop like running and swimming or an open loop with a specific starting and stopping point like bowling, archery, tennis, golf, basketball shooting, or typing.

Two-Digit Error Information Processing

My two-digit error hypothesis is that on average two bits of information will be processed before you can physically respond to the perception of the error. With older typewriters you usually noticed a typing error after two more keystrokes. Today computers and programs autocorrect typing errors.

This is significant because when you modify a perceptual cue on the input side of the "black box" you must look at two S-R connections in the sequence or two cues before the actual performance error is displayed.

Interruptions or delays in processing feedback while speaking causes stuttering. However, when there is continuous flow in singing the feedback is not interrupted. Mel Tillis stutters when speaking but can sing as an entertainer.

To correct the delayed response, oxygen looking masks are applied over the mouth with plastic tubes carrying the voice directly to the ears to provide immediate feedback. What is more mind-boggling is why elementary students who learn to play music develop better math skills. Is it the continuous processing of sound or the visual recognition of cues?

To be a top performer creating personal mental movies, you can perfect your sub routines by correcting specific stimulus-response connections prior to and during the actual performance. As the leader or coach of a physical skill you must subjectively project back two bits of processed information in the pattern sequence prior to the error.

Then use a new cue to re condition a change in perception to recognize (the first R in RROSR) for a specific S-R connection and repair that link in the performance chain. Your art of coaching will try one cue after another with a performer until you unlock the stored code to repair the link and improve the output performance.

As the leader, manager, teacher, or coach, all you can do is keep modifying the cues in the input phase until you get the correct output from each performer.

You can focus on these kinds of corrections to think about on a conscious level, and then practice to program them to happen during the performance evaluation of your personal feedback.

Applying RROSR to Mental Practice

Focus on the specific S-R connections of cues and response feelings to mentally practice the association for faster cue recognition and response. It is doubtful the actual speed of nerve transmission is much faster, but there is evidence of electrical activity in specific muscle groups during mental practice.

The two strategies often used are *keyhole* to visualize performance details looking through an imaginary keyhole of a door to narrow your focus and eliminate distractions. The other strategy is *third eye* to view your performance from a camera lens instead of your eyes. A third eye sees every cue and response detail.

Some top performers refer to this as looking through a different lens where you can focus a close up or far away view to observe your body parts in space, and project how you might feel at each stage of your performance.

Mobilization of Energy to Improve Performance

The expected outcome of energy mobilization is *peak performance* and getting into the *zone*. However, equally important are increasing *focused concentration* and *mental tension control*. Nervous energy, if not directed properly, can sap your energy and ability to concentrate. It will deplete your muscle glycogen or fuel needed to perform.

Some techniques shown in italics are used to control nervous tension. *Diaphragmatic breathing* you inhale more by lowering your diaphragm than by raising your chest wall. *Relaxation training* initially authored by Jacobsen (1938) is also popular to control tension.

You lie down and initially contract a muscle group, and then consciously feel the tension being released from the muscles. Top performers may prefer to listen to *energizing music* like the theme from the movie *Rocky,* or other favorite to distract their nervous thoughts temporarily away from the competition.

Energizing music becomes associated and conditioned with your response. Like *mental practice*, it is used to program a perfected sub routine ready to execute as another file in your computer. You simply add music to your movie.

Positive self-talk is implied. Focus your highest concentration on positive performance for the entire sequence of the sub routine. *Trick your brain* by telling your brain what to expect and perform. Then trust you execute your realistically programmed routine.

To effectively mobilize your energy for peak performance, your motive to achieve success must be greater than your motive to avoid failure (*MaS>MaF*). You do not want to focus on and visualize past errors, what not to do or avoid, or watch other competitors immediately prior to your performance.

Watching others creates a visual bit map of their performance in your short-term memory. Several United States Women's Olympic gymnasts made this critical mistake in the 2008 Beijing Games. Then they made unusual performance errors because their programmed sub routines were disrupted.

Visual sensations are dominant and why your demonstrations must be exact. The old phrase 'monkey see, monkey do' when your performers copy your good or bad demonstration or speech. You do not want to program any visual performance other than the positive one you created in your pre-performance routine.

Increasing Your Pre-performance Thinking with Visualization

Besides mental practice and visualization to improve performance, try these other strategies. Focus on your positive work ethic behaviors to raise awareness of work accomplished. This opens the door to feel you deserve rewards for a good performance. If you have not done the work, you will doubt your performance and have less confidence.

Keep performance logs of practices to gain feedback awareness and rate your smaller improvements to parts of the whole routine. Be aware to reward yourself and stay motivated. Use mental practice to imagine successful performances with the game or contest on the line and all kinds of distractions to *mentally rehearse* a positive outcome.

Top performers practice pre-performance routines to concentrate on the skilled performance and block out distractions. This strategy works best when you have more familiarity with the task.

Another strategy to use is *be your own best friend*. Top performers tend to be overly critical when higher expectations are not met. At times, this frustration distracts from seeing positive improvements and feeling rewarded. As the leader or coach discuss how to set goals and keep expectations in line with reality.

I recently took my 12-year-old grandson to play his first ever round of golf on a challenging par 3 course. I taught him basic skills a couple of times on a driving range and included chipping and putting. On several occasions I observed his disgust with missing a close putt for a birdie.

He clearly was mad he did not get rewarded. He created a negative to reinforce. I corrected him to think positive and reinforce what he did right to get his put to the hole. Always look for ways to reinforce the positive and extinct the negative. Words and feelings matter. This is one more powerful lesson in transformational leadership.

Many performers are conditioned by others to be overly critical of their performance. A perfect example are parents and coaches who want to vicariously see in others and feel the success they never had. Comments are made without regard for the performer's feelings.

As a leader, if you extol the virtues of hard work, then let your performers reap all the rewards. The fastest way to kill morale and intrinsic motivation is for the leader, manager, coach, or parent to accept all or part of the reward they do not need.

It's as if to say, "Yes, I know I made a mistake. I am upset, and I don't need you to tell me." The result conditions negative behaviors instead of conditioning the positive improvements to several parts to increase intrinsic motivation.

Your awareness of pre-performance evaluation strategies conditions your performance needs and values. You value your work and need to fulfill your performance successfully to feel rewarded. This increases your drive motivation in pre-performance evaluation.

When performing hands on practice or conscious mental rehearsal and positive self-talk these strategies increase your awareness to value your performance is meaningful and relevant. Unsuccessful performers seldom pre plan how they choose to perform or feel because they have not learned The Triad and RROSR.

As the leader help your performers understand their personal needs and common purpose. Performers who do not have a strong purpose automate their routine tasks going through the motions aimlessly with lower values. This results in inconsistent average performances.

Conversely, consistent successful top performers create a strong purpose, and increase awareness to a higher conscious state of needs to satisfy and value the work they perform. Prior to notable performances this increases the need or motivation to feel rewarded.

The top performer mobilizes all their talents, abilities, and energies for a selected moment in time. This pre-planned process starts with a realistic positive pre-performance evaluation. You set up an internal clock to prepare a set time to perform like an-alarm-to-wake-up-call by having all your systems ready to execute your plan. This process is also called *peaking*, when your best performances come at the end of your season.

Choices to Make in Pre-performance Evaluation

You have many choices to make in pre-performance evaluation. You can look at your life as half full or half empty. You learn and achieve what you focus your efforts on to improve whether it is mental, physical, emotional, or social skills.

The child's program Sesame Street often plays this catchy tune, "Be what you want to be, learn what you want to learn." Preplan, commit to your plan, and focus on continuous small improvement of your skills over time to be successful and feel rewarded for your efforts.

Why wait for someone to tell you what to do when you can do this for yourself? Value your work to practice improving your abilities and skills to feel rewarded enough to reinforce future efforts.

Get an idea of your rate and progress for learning to predict a future performance. Use your performance logs from your practices and performances. Record specific goals, cues, triggers, and any kind of psychological data you like to use to aid your learning and motivate your top performance.

Use a predictive equation to select the important cues and strategies and focus more attention to value the higher beta weighted variables. Know how to set personal goals based on a perceptual anchoring point known to you but unlikely known by others.

Perceive value from need based behaviors assigned to your activities and knowledge gained from your personal performance feedback and leadership. Know how extrinsic values set by others are their goals and less powerful than goals you set.

Create significant positive thought processes in your brain with pre-performance thinking to apply to your performance and increase your probability of a positive outcome. These are all personal leadership choices you need to make.

Set Up Pre-Performance Routines

Pre-performance routines clear your mind of conflicting sensations, distractions, and negative error messages to correct at the last minute. You apply the same routine before every performance despite changes in the environment or specific task.

For example, pro golfers have a pre-shot routine for each club. They set up for the tee off using the driver differently than for making a putt. But the routine is always the same. You practice them as you would any other skill. But first, set them up with a plan to know ahead of time what will work best.

With experience and task familiarity you anticipate what to expect. If you lack experience performing in a new environment, then ask those with experience to describe what to expect. Go to a quiet place, close your eyes, and run your mental movie as you want to see yourself perform your skills.

In chaos, block out the noise sitting in your chair. Go to your favorite quiet place in your mind you have already programmed and mentally practiced. Create the image. Maybe a favorite beach scene like a sunset, a reflecting pool, or simply your private bedroom. Add your favorite music.

This puts your program in the ready queue and eliminates conflicting sensations for the brain to execute the performance. This is not the time to wonder if you ate the right foods, rested enough, worked hard enough, etc. Perform your checklist and make this a routine to plan pre-performance evaluation.

Cramming the night before a performance test or big event is never a good idea. It takes a minimum of five days to accommodate and assimilate information or program changes to a sub routine. And it takes six to eight weeks for muscle adaptation changes. You do not get in shape physically or mentally overnight.

To perfect mental skills and warm up routines, prior to performing, takes time. When Michael Jordan returned to pro basketball after a two-year layoff to play baseball. His body was in shape, but it took several months to get back the mental skills.

When your programmed sub routine is perfected with mental practice, reviewed immediately prior to performing and placed in the ready cue, set up the final trigger to start the program. In swimming and running, the blast of the horn at the starting blocks is what you concentrate on.

For golf or target shooting, typical open serial skills, rushing your beginning does not create good performance. Getting into a comfortable stance, aiming, and exhaling slowly relaxes the muscular tension for a smooth contraction to aid your performance. Watch top performers and learn why they concentrate on the routine sequence to perfect their performance.

Summary

Whether you are planning to perform in a sport, close a business deal, or prep for a school test, your pre-performance evaluation process motivates performance improvement. True success is being consistent and successful over time.

Planning is the key to success in any endeavor. Success also takes hard work to create value for your achievements. RROSR promotes faster retrieval of stored information to apply in a pre-planned sequence. When you make this a part of your performance routine, you significantly increase your odds for a good performance and feel rewarded.

15

DURING PERFORMANCE EVALUATION

A wise man envisions opportunity, and an intelligent man capitalizes on it. During performance emphasize your strengths and capitalize on your opponent's weaknesses.

Timing is everything. Top performers have the awareness to sense when to mobilize their energy and increase their performance output when it counts the most. Emotion or arousal is critical to apply energy to peak perform.

Performance and emotion have been linked. The classic study presented earlier is the 1908 Yerkes-Dodson Law. The relationship looks like an inverted U-shaped curve. Performance improves as anxiety or emotion is increased up to an optimum level when exceeded performance is decreased.

Top performers have years of experience with a variety of stressors, and conditioned responses from jobs, tasks, skills, and relationships to control their anxiety. They raise or lower their anxiety to meet an optimum level of performance with a concept I introduced as *at will on demand*.

Another new concept I introduced is *task familiarity*. During competition or on the job, you do not have the advantage of practice to condition a familiar response to a stressor, and your anxiety increases more for unfamiliar tasks.

In sport psychology, a performer who has too much anxiety is "over-amped." There is too much juice running through their nervous system. Nervous performers who are less than confident will have cold sweaty hands in a warm room. Perhaps nothing kills an interview or welcome faster than to present yourself with a cold hand. Leaders use this feedback to gauge how performers react to learn new unfamiliar information to affect performance. The strategy to use is to familiarize performers what to expect to reduce anxiety and build confidence focusing on what they do best.

The ability to modify a performance during a performance is based on prior conditioned stimulus-response connections. Task familiarity plays a key role to draw upon those past experiences. To keep your head in the game, refocus on the methods and cues practiced. Be sure to break complex skills down into component parts. Focus attention to the key variables proven to get results. This is a fast review of pre-performance routines. Adjust the goal and visualize performance outcomes correctly using RROSR.

Whether performing your part in a game or making a presentation to close a deal, each can be broken down into sub routines or parts. Once you acquire experience with all the parts, chain them together in sequence for a top overall performance. The process rebuilds your confidence.

I use relatable sports analogies. Whether you play golf or have seen it played on TV each shot has a pre-shot routine. If you hit a bad shot, you must let it go to refocus on your next shot. Writers can let their work sit for a day and review later. But in sales and marketing in front of a customer you must modify your presentation as you uncover objections.

In the middle of a timed test, you cannot waste time stymied by a question or two. There are test-taking strategies to learn and how to study for the kinds of questions you may be asked. Prep to answer typical interview questions. You adjust your answers using during performance evaluation strategies. For example, to buy time to answer to a difficult question always answer a question with a question.

When you feel your performance is going all right you relax and can think. You can process information. But if you are nervous and feel under qualified for the position or your ability to perform, your brain will not think clearly. You need to learn during performance evaluation skills to apply to any job, task, skill, or relationship. Be prepared and familiar how and what to respond.

With more experience top performers learn S-R connections to best perform under a variety of emotional stressors. These are predictable fundamental variables identified by your subjective pre-planned during performance evaluation. This is the multiple regression equation presenter earlier.

Top performers continually work on the higher predictive variables of skilled performance to improve. When you subvert mundane tasks to a subconscious level, you cannot control the unexpected during performances. You quickly lose your confidence.

If you make a few errors during performance your choices are limited. The best choice is always to refocus on what you know you can do. Remember the displace-replace strategy? Wipe out negative thoughts by visualizing taking positive action steps proven to get results.

Apply the MaS>MaF concept. The odds are not good to modify any performance if you focus on your motives to avoid failure. You must re focus on the specific pre- planned familiar fundamental cues you perform best to rebuild your confidence.

A classic example was in the 1961 movie *The Hustler* starring Jackie Gleason who played a pool shark named Minnesota Fats. In a match he was getting soundly beaten at his own game. He took a time out and went into the bathroom to wash his hands, look himself in the mirror, and came back to win the overall match. Winners and champions have this little voice inside their head that will not let them accept defeat.

I clearly remember competing in a Masters' Swimming National Championships several years ago in Santa Clara, California. For years I have won this

50-yard breaststroke event in my age group. I even told a good competitor friend how to beat me by describing all the key component parts of the sprint race the summer before.

The horn blew and we dived in. In a short sprint there is really no time to use during performance evaluation if you have not pre-planned contingencies. We both surfaced and I could see his shoulder meaning he learned how to start. Now you are not supposed to think. The race has been pre-programmed.

I was losing and my brain was thinking I could catch him on the turn. We made the turn and he was still a good two feet ahead. I thought, damn, he has learned how to turn. This is only two short lengths in a 25-yard pool. Half-way back I was not catching him no matter how I tried. My thought was, "well, he's finally going to beat me after trying for ten years." Then that little voice said, "you are the champion, you have to at least make it look close."

My usual finish was to focus on the touch pad and not breathe the last three strokes. I kept my body position and on the last pull sculled my hands faster and stretched forward. With my goggles I saw the two middle fingers on my right hand touch the pad.

As I looked over, he appeared to be resting on the wall, so I thought he had won. From the sidelines my friends thought so, too. Then I looked up at the official scoreboard and there was a "1" next to my name. Surprised I won by only .087 seconds or about 4 inches. Every skill has its components to condition. Glad I had conditioned how to finish.

There are ways to refocus. Condition the responsive contingent steps to make when things are not going your way. This is how to use during performance evaluation. There are dependent variables like performance time you need to control. Less time requires better pre-planned strategies to react.

If your performance does not have time outs, or you cannot break during an interview, you must define your next move. Keep it simple so your brain has time to process the information as input. If you are overly emotional or super aroused even mad, you need to put yourself back in charge of your brain to direct your mind and body to work together.

Rely on Feedback During Performance Evaluation

You know quality when you see it even if you cannot describe it. You also know: 1) how you perform under similar circumstances, 2) to project how you perform under less pressure, 3) have a realistic goal you know you can perform, and 4) current performance input-output.

Racing through your mind are many ideas. They distract your ability to focus on performing one or two essential fundamentals. When times get tough, others who extrinsically motivate you to meet their needs could care less about your hurt feelings.

They expect you to satisfy their needs. But to be intrinsically motivated the exact opposite is what you need to focus on performing. Your immediate need is to perform **ONLY** what you can do best during the performance. This is important for leaders to transform this process shift to each performer.

As the leader, coach, or manager of a team, quickly remind each performer of their capable role and fundamental expectations. Refocus your top performers to lead the others.

In my first year as a young head high school swim coach, our team was losing several close races. I could see our confidence was poor. During the diving break I invited four of my tough-minded top performers into the locker room. All I had to do was ask them if they felt okay with how the meet was going.

I knew they would change their attitude because I reminded them of the work they had put in during the week and deserved to swim faster. It was a green light to perform. They swam well and excited the others to improve so we could do better on relays and we won the meet.

As the leader you must identify your top performers and use that during performance evaluation so they can lead your team by their example. You create a culture of improving under a variety of circumstances. Continually ask your top performers for suggestions. And never ever take credit for what they suggest or perform.

Huddle up your top performers fast and trigger the response you have practiced and conditioned them to perform. Bring their anxiety level back down by changing the expectation to a specific smaller element of the whole performance each performer can perform well as a part of the team.

You cannot control what teammates or competitors are thinking. You can control your focus to concentrate on what stimulus-response connections you can perform best under the circumstances. As a teacher-leader or coach, all you can do is present and modify the input cues and look at the performance output result. Every performer processes information differently because of their varied experience. During performance, a change in the input cues may be needed to get the correct personal output. One input cue may work for one and not another performer.

As the leader with experience you must continually try different input cues to find what works best for every performer to get the correct output. It may be a visual, verbal, or kinesthetic feeling cue.

When I was in my thirties, I wanted to learn how to snow ski. The instructor had about 12 of us on a bunny hill. He did a good job demonstrating and explaining all the basic skills. How to tuck in your poles, snowplow to stop, put a lean to lay down a ski edge to turn, etc. After 45 minutes I lost my patience. I had to try it and feel the edge of my skis. I was more of a kinesthetic skills learner.

As a leader let your performers process doing jobs or tasks that fit their learning style preference. Teach how to self-evaluate during performances to keep improving without having to manage them. Later, during performance, those best cues become the most reinforced triggers to refocus your performers.

You can set up any kind of trigger. It can be a simple hand signal, whistle, a keyword or phrase. It is like an audible at the line of scrimmage in a football game. The trigger changes the play to refocus on the performance.

It is extremely important to get off to a good start in any kind of performance. This sets a personal standard baseline or perceptual anchoring point for the next goal. Performers are motivated to do more and ensure improvement.

Focus on performing the most familiar patterns and sequences or routines. Your quality of achievement is defined by familiar cues you focus on during your performance. Your familiar task experience happens with specific practice to connect appropriate responses to the selected cues.

Top performers with more experience in specific tasks are paid more to achieve results other less experienced performers cannot. They enhance their performance feedback system to a higher level. Cues for peak performance are consciously automated. This provides more value and meaning to each performance and increases intrinsic motivation to improve performance.

During performance evaluation raises awareness to focus on the best cues to get results. Learning and performing is aided by these data stored as compressed bit maps in various lobes of the brain for easy retrieval. Then prior to and during performance, your pre-frontal cortex creates sub routines for immediate retrieval of the compressed bit maps required to execute the performance at will on demand.

Refocus Turning Negatives into Positives

This is a variation of displace/replace strategy. During your performance you may hear criticism from boos to insults from the audience, teammates, or management. Learn to shut down this noise. Then refocus on the correct cues proven to get positive results. What you intrinsically program yourself to think and respond is far more powerful than the extrinsic motives imposed on you by others. You are the performer, not them.

Reflect on your specific immediate past performance. When you performed specific jobs, tasks, skills, or relationships successfully, you had a defined purpose. Your intent was to see improvement to feel rewarded. Mistakes happen by chance for lack of planning or having a positive purpose and intent. Some refer to this as attitude.

You learn a lot by observing professional athletes who already have advanced physical skills. In short periods of observation, learn the effect of specific positive or negative consequences on their sports performance. How did they refocus their attention to different cues to get better responses, and turn a mistake into a success?

These are those "momentum swings." Observe what happens when a player sinks a few baskets or putts or makes a hit with a player in scoring position. Their whole mood changes. You see a smile or glow that exudes confidence for the next several trials.

Conversely, if you negatively focus, you are more likely to make another mistake right after it. Refocus your energy into a positive visualized outcome. What can you learn from observing these examples? In sport psychology, the strategy is to condition how to "let go" and refocus on select cues to correctly perform the next skill.

You pre-condition the focus on how to recognize a specific cue to perform the correct associated response that you have simulated in practice. This specific practice helps you transfer the identical elements to the competitive situation.

Rather than focus on and condition the error mental image, refocus on the positive image from practice and prior experience of the correct response. If performance is really going badly during your competition or in life, resist the temptation to get it all back on the next play or in one day of your life.

Those temptations involve luck and not skills. Change your focus to know how, what, and why to take necessary steps to improve. Sports applications can be applied to your life. Do marketed dieting plans provide you with skills to permanently change your behavior? Is skill involved in choosing a marriage partner or developing relationships? Can you effectively lead others when you cannot demonstrate the ability to lead yourself?

Reflect on past performances when you knew your positive purpose. Compare these to your performances when you were just going through the motions with a negative attitude like "I hate school" or "I don't like …." You may feel lucky but at best get a 50-50 chance for success, the same as flipping a coin.

With pre-programed refocus strategies, you increase the value learning from the performance experience to 95-99% whether you met your personal goal or not.

During performance evaluation increases your awareness to turn negatives into positives. If not, performances have little value and waste your time. Your time to learn is valuable. You can earn more money, but you cannot earn more time.

Input Phase

As a transforming leader do your stimuli in the form of cues and triggers initiate correct responses? What input is your performer thinking? If the input is incorrect how likely do you think the output will be? Remind your performers to refocus on proven cues during performance to get good results.

Refocus on already learned and practiced correct cues or strategies to change negative to positive performance output. You can "shape" behavior by conditioning repeated practice of correct stimulus input—response output cues. Focus on small specific behaviors to rebuild confidence. Total performance thinking is too broad and general and less effective.

A big mistake during performance is pointing out errors. A mental comparison of the performance error with what was expected has already taken place. Talking about the error reinforces a mental image to repeat the behavior. The best strategy is to refocus only on cues to get the correct output. Extinct the negative and reinforce the positive.

Output Phase

Self-correction skills are based on during performance evaluation of your performance output. You know what the correct performance looks and feels like. You learn these skills prior to performing by conditioning the verbal, visual, or kinesthetic cues for the expected output.

During performance recognize the input cues and compare to your expected performance output. When immediate evaluation output is not as expected, top performers change or modify which input cues to focus on.

Learn to process your performance output as feedback to compare to your immediate past performance or average or against a known standard. Then judge the value of your next performance. If poor, you may not care to improve. But if you know your abilities and believe you can improve, your motivation increases all based on personal value.

Value is determined by satisfaction of personal needs. When you know you can improve a poor performance, your ego and social condition takes a hit. That is a painful feeling to avoid. Now you pay attention to focus on the details and work ethic to ensure improvement on the next trial to avoid embarrassment.

The conditioning process to connect a stimulus cue with a correct response is essential to learning how to learn. You take accountability to teach yourself so you can improve performance in less time. Pay attention to your output behaviors and learn to self-correct the next output by changing the input cue. Your skill to apply subjective values to your feedback and see performance improve and predict future success is how learning occurs.

What you think of your performance must matter more than what a leader thinks of your performance. Use your performance feedback to self-evaluate the worth and value of every performance. You cannot control what others do, but you can learn to control what you do during performances. You are a leader of one using The Triad to keep improving your performance in less time.

Recently I had a brief talk with my 12-year-old grandson to explain how to be more aware of his performance output as feedback. I asked, "Why do your parents have to direct a lot of your behaviors? What is it you are doing or rather NOT doing to give them the need to direct you? If you behave responsibly, parents as leaders do not feel the need to direct you. Try not to give them a reason. You know what to do so self-evaluate your performance output. Are you happy with helping your parents without being asked?"

Error Correction During Performance

Picture a basketball free throw shooter during a game. They miss the first free throw and refocus on the best cues. The adjustment usually results in making the second free throw.

Performers who go through the motions, and do not process their own feedback never learn to improve at the same rate. They have a difficult time becoming a top performer.

The central idea of learning to process performance feedback in the "Black Box" loop is to condition appropriate cues to get faster and better responses in succeeding performances. For any performance error, evaluate the specific S-R connection and mentally visualize a positive response to repair the link with the correct association.

This strategy is a refocus skill top performers apply during performance. Shamefully, many students cannot tell you what their score was on their last math or science test. Feedback from your immediate past performance is needed to set a low positive goal to improve. This same process occurs during performance evaluations and increases your intrinsic motivation. With a low positive goal, your brain has no excuse.

Getting in the "Zone"

Top performers do not perform at a high level or peak performance every practice, game, or event. They know how to apply all their talents, abilities, and energy to get in the "zone" on a performance at will on demand for brief moments in time. Golfers report the cup enlarges. Basketball players see the hoop as larger than a peach basket.

To get in the zone you must have extensive familiar task experience. It usually occurs under duress when the need to perform is high. All your senses enhance your feedback. Higher awareness of cues and correct responses become automatic without thinking. Visualization of pre-programed perfect performances may help get into the "zone."

Top performers get in the zone with awareness and experience with the job, task, or skill. The move subconscious go-through-the-motions performance to a higher conscious awareness. The Black Box feedback model serves that purpose to evaluate during performance. Until you learn how to process feedback, getting in the "zone" may never happen.

Visualizing pre-planned sub routines or smaller parts of the total performance improve your focus. Getting familiar with the job or task also reduces stress so you can concentrate on one small element at a time.

In the 2005 NCAA basketball playoffs, the University of Illinois with a 29-1 record and #1 seed was down 14 points 77-63 to a talented University of Arizona team with only 3:28 remaining in regulation. Illinois coach Bruce Weber admitted in a post-game interview he had quietly given up hope of making the Final Four before he watched his players take over the game.

All throughout the year, I observed his interviews. He did not make the crucial leadership mistake of taking credit for what his players had accomplished. He added a subtle trigger statement few sportswriters and fans may have heard. All year long during their 29-0 unbeaten string, he said the boys would listen and be energized by the crowd.

This subtle trigger was programmed into all the players to trust teammates to perform during performance evaluations. During close performances and blowouts all season, the players increased their awareness (the first Triad).

With practice they learned to recognize cues to pass the ball and score or defend and steal the ball or be in rebound position. Each player was conditioned to enhance self-evaluation with immediate feedback (the second Triad) and was programmed to make a positive response.

What happened next was Williams drove to the top of the key and sank a 3-point shot to reduce the deficit to 12, and the Illini crowd lightly applauded with hope. The Illinois players heard the crowd. They were programmed to be energized by the noise. The players increased their awareness.

The ball began to appear like a beach ball in slow motion to pick off passes. The hoop suddenly became much larger, and the next 3-point shot quickly made it 9. The crowd grew louder, and the boys' awareness grew. Time slows down to make 3 seconds seem like 20 before impact in a car crash. The boys got in the "zone."

Illinois made a 17-3 run to tie the game 80-80 and send into overtime. Then Illinois took over to win the game and ended up winning their next game to make it to the championship. There North Carolina beat Illinois.

Extraneous insignificant stimuli are totally blocked out. It is a brief outburst of mobilized energy. The positive feedback is coming in and compares well with past input already in the highly practiced retrieval system to reward and reinforce the next attempt (the third Triad). Confidence builds with each new successful attempt. The output is positive and congruent with previous results that produced a good outcome.

You can teach performers how to get in their zone using triggers consistent with their level of talent, ability, and experience. These consist of a variety of cues and responses that also include pre-set goal routines to value minor positive achievements. You cannot correct a big error in a single play or one event. Go back to smaller achievements with low positive goals to rebuild your confidence. And evaluate during your performance to trigger your mentally rehearsed response.

Thinking it Through

During competition, there is little time to think through the necessary stimulus cues and physical responses to be successful unless they have been pre-programmed. Scouting an opponent and watching game films gives you the chance to specifically prepare to meet your opponent's strengths. Research the company you plan to interview with. What do they need and value? Visualize how you would fit in to fulfill those needs.

Develop pre-planned strategies to use during performance to combat the other team's positive tendencies. Put your best basketball guard on their best shooting guard to improve your defense. Task familiarity and task specificity play key roles. You do not visualize bowling to perfect your basketball skills.

Getting your mind focused on the specific task ahead centers your thinking during the performance. You cannot be thinking about a past error and expect to have a positive focus for the next play. Learn to let go and refocus on the positives. If you let your emotions get the best of you the Yerkes-Dodson Law will take effect.

You stay in conscious control, or your performance will suffer. Queen Elizabeth said, "Anger may make dull men witty, but it also keeps them poor." By thinking it through you pre plan how to approach the next play, point, swing, or deal.

Dr. Wayne Dyer published The Power of Intention in 2004. The premise is to create positive thoughts for what you intend to happen. The applications are the same as The Triad to improve performance in less time for any job, task, skill, or relationship. If to fulfill the intention is realistic and in line with your abilities, then the subconscious mind takes over.

During a performance you use specific cues to trigger specific responses you have pre planned to perform. You can trigger a cue in the time it takes to take a breath. This is a hallmark of top performing coaches at half-time. As the performer you can choose an attitude to think positive or negative. Which do you think is more likely to succeed?

Beating on lockers and yelling at players to excite their emotions has been replaced by an intelligent stimulus response approach to create a winning strategy with a focus on a common goal. A strategy helps identify your weaknesses and provides a positive means to improve your performance.

This is accomplished by creating a higher order need. In a team environment, leaders must align the needs of your team with the personal needs of your performers. Finger pointing fault sessions lower your morale and performance focus. Focus on specific smaller and more manageable skills you can perform correctly to build your confidence.

Program a practical positive visualization of your performance as you intend for it to happen. Keep your expectations in line with reality. You cannot expect to achieve what you are incapable of physically performing. But neither do you want to introduce negative thinking that you cannot perform higher with proper conditioning.

Set low positive goal expectations like stepping-stones during the performance to create a highly probably reward-reinforcement effect. Your performers will notice and put forth more effort. If you get off to a bad start, your team will not be crushed and give up.

Teams that exceed early expectations are motivated more for the rewards they are conditioned to value and feel. Your performers need to be taught how to self-evaluate their effectiveness during performances and give themselves a short pep talk (positive self-talk) to refocus on the correct S-R connections to be successful.

Focus on a positive performance to think it through to a positive result. Condition a practiced response to immediately react correctly to changes during the performance in all your performers. This avoids surprises.

The value of great leaders is task familiarity. An experienced leader can fully describe tasks to familiarize performers about what to expect and remove uncertainty. Remind your performers they only need to focus on doing their job playing the one position well.

Your opponent puts their pants on one leg at a time just like you do so outsmart them with your pre planned play. Visualize an expected outcome to use during performance. This mobilizes your energies to peak perform at will on demand.

Top performers and leaders perform best when it counts because they know what to say and do during performance. The great leader paints a vivid impression of how an expected outcome can occur to focus all the performers on a common realistic and achievable goal effort.

The key is to align the mission goals with the personal needs of the performers to feel successful. Leaders clearly outline the positive steps to accomplish the mission. The described task becomes familiar to all the performers, and more likely to turn out the way the leader explained it would happen.

When you lead yourself to accomplish a realistic goal, you perform the same steps predicting you can do it. Adjust your plan during performance with preplanned strategies. Set up possible contingencies to adjust your performance so you are not surprised to lose confidence.

Increased Expectancy of Reward

A hallmark of top performers is work ethic and ability to delay the onset of rewards. Inexperienced performers expect immediate gratification. Experienced performers know it takes time to perfect skills to achieve good results and feel rewarded. They accept early failures as feedback to change input cues to improve output performance.

Congruence is important during performance when events are turning out as you predicted. Your expectations are in line with reality. A strong evidence of your personality. Based on early during performance evaluation sampling and doing as expected, your confidence fuels your intrinsic motivation to keep putting forth the effort to ensure success.

Your performance equals or slightly surpasses your realistic and achievable goal. Although unnecessary your self-evaluation is closely aligned with the evaluation provided by others. If you are a top performer and your leader or manager is not in agreement, then you must move on or suffer the conflict. If you trust the leader with more experience and proven results, perhaps they know you have room to improve and get even better. They have confidence in you so listen to what they suggest.

Effective leaders of organizations recognize and encourage talent to perform above average and provide a rewarding means for self-satisfaction on the job. Confidence is anticipating events as you predict during performance.

Top performers often adjust goals during the performance to achieve smaller success elements. With multiple trials as in golf or basketball immediate past performance changes during the performance. Set low positive goals only slightly better to increase frequency of reward.

This builds confidence faster and is easier to predict future performance and condition a needed positive reward. Those who set unrealistic goals, condition failure, and feel miserable, and infects others around you.

During competition you cannot control the other team or teammates. You can control your reaction and feelings to respond and perform in a positive way. Setting goals follows this same premise. How can you predict what another person is thinking when you have trouble getting in touch with your own thoughts?

Top performers practice using specific methods and cues proven to improve performance. Skills are broken down in small parts to be objective and plot results. Those become your immediate past performance. When you exceed your personal goal—no matter how slight—during practices or during performance events, you take away a personal feeling of satisfaction or reward you want to repeat.

You have learned to equate quality of effort with quality of reward. You no longer wait for the approval of others to feel rewarded. Your will power is self-rewarded and reinforced to repeat the work in practice to keep improving.

Conscious Execution

To increase your awareness during a performance work on conscious execution of smaller movements. This means processing your output as feedback to make immediate input adjustments during your performance. This assists your recall of cues and responses to events while practicing and during performances to apply to future performances.

Your mind and body are set up to automate responses. Learn to override this natural occurrence at will on demand. Focus on a specific stimulus cue and response connection you perform well. Then apply that first during your performance to reduce anxiety and build confidence.

Continue to set realistic intermediate goals based on how you last performed. Any subjective skill can be made into an objective raw score to record. Keep a log to compare with your past performances and expected new goal. Break complex skills down into sub skill components to provide each part a subjective-objective rating.

Select no more than five sub skills to describe the whole skilled performance. Create a rubric table that describes a 1-2-3-4 or 5 performance rating for each sub skill. This enhances your personal self-evaluation system and become more familiar with your standard perceptual anchoring point to set new goals.

Auto Suggestion

Increase your awareness in activities by practicing visualization also known as mental practice during the performance. Mentally rehearse the association for specific cues and responses to speed up your performance reaction in sequence. Efficiency improves when you associate specific cues with repeated practice responses.

Auto suggestion is a variation of positive self-talk. Top performers rely on a wealth of past experiences. They make accurate predictions for the pace or type of probable performance. Then they program their mind and body to execute the performance.

Auto suggestion works as if you had put yourself into a hypnotic trance, snapped your fingers to come out, and then respond to the pre-programmed trigger cue. Did you ever get excited about getting ready to leave on a trip? You set your alarm but wake up ready to go 30 seconds before the alarm goes off.

This strategy lets you step back and trust your system to respond. You mentally review pre-programmed responses during the time out or between plays. If the during performance evaluation is not going well, mentally remove yourself from the competition. Reset your stimulus-response approach. Focus on the pre-shot routine or see yourself performing your best skills. In golf visualize and suggest a stroke and ball flight to take dead aim at a target (goal). Then relax with a deep breath to trust your performance. Make a fast evaluation of the cues and responses you have been making. What caused performance errors you can self-correct?

Then mentally rehearse a correct response for the same kind of cue and put in auto suggestion. This is stimulus generalization or non-specific cue recognition. You get faster nerve transmission rates to improve reaction time and performance. Use this auto suggestion strategy to get back into the competition.

If talented, your skills are already in place to perform. Self-induced hypnosis works on the same principle. Go to a quiet place in your mind during the heat of competition, put yourself in a trance and mentally rehearse what you want to perform. Set up the cue recognition trigger and go for it. The entire process creates the need and value for the activity to have a positive effect.

Summary

During performance, The Triad is put to the test. Use the principles found in B.F. Skinner's "Black Box" feedback model to increase your awareness of performance output during the feedback loop. Then compare to past performance, others, or a standard to evaluate whether to change input cues. Top performers create personal performance standards and need to keep improving their immediate past performance to feel rewarded.

With each new success proper cues and responses are conditioned and reinforced. Setting realistic low positive performance goals for smaller performance components are met with greater probability and frequency. More frequent success builds your personal reward system and improves your confidence and self-esteem.

Inconsistent or poor responses are displaced and replaced by refocusing on pre-conditioned cue response connections with positive visualization during reflective time outs. Find time to practice mental rehearsal to visualize correct associations between cues and appropriate responses.

Trigger responses with brief visualizations prior to performing or during time outs. Adjust goals for smaller parts of the overall performance to increase your probability for success and reward system. This reinforces your positive work ethic.

16
POST-PERFORMANCE EVALUATION

Most people only do post-performance evaluations. They remark how they should have said this or that in the interview or trained differently for an event. Coulda-shoulda-woulda does not cut it. But take-away something positive to better prepare for your next performance.

During performance you learned specific strategies to adjust a performance. These strategies evaluate the immediate use of performance output as feedback to adjust the input quality. Your input comes from awareness skills to recognize familiar cues in practice or other competitions. Top performers benefit from more experience held in memory.

In post-performance evaluation, work on improving prediction and projection skills by analyzing what you did right from what you did wrong in your control. What would you change for future performance? Compare your performance output to the input adjustments you made to affect a positive change in actual performance.

Reflect on the intensity of your response and emotional control is equally important to think clearly and stay focused while performing. The Yerkes-Dodson Law showed some pre-event anxiety is important. But too much hurts performance. Too much nervous energy also depletes blood sugars and muscle glycogen prior to performing.

In sport psychology, Dr. Bob Rotella, of the University of Virginia and Golf Digest magazine advisory board, coined the phrase, "getting your butterflies to fly in formation." Rather than pass off your performance, review, and plan to control your nerves. Here are some strategies to help align those butterflies.

Congruence

Was your actual performance closely aligned to your predicted realistic and achievable goals? This requires an understanding of your needs, values, abilities, and skills as they improve over time to maintain a consistent intrinsic motivation. Top performers continually self-evaluate this process.

In simpler terms, are you improving, and if not, why not? Are you being fair with yourself, or setting goals that exceed reality to cause your frustration? Frustrated performers seldom learn to self-reward and reinforce work ethic behaviors.

There is an optimal performance reinforcement value when your performance more closely approximates or slightly exceeds your goal. Go back and review The Activity Value Index in Chapter 3, Values. This demonstrates the personality trait of realism and with frequency of improvement has tremendous reinforcement value.

Personal Accountability

Top performers hold themselves accountable through the process of self-evaluation. Top performers do not usually wait for the approval of others? They know what they need to perform. As a leader, manager, or coach, know how top performers tend to be more critical and tougher on themselves than their coaches and teachers.

They set personal standards to promote and reward consistent improvement in small increments to maintain a high motivation. Those personal standards are based on immediate past performances they continually evaluate. Top performers take accountability for what they can control. They recognize the most important cues to process and apply to their next performance.

Common Goals and Mission

These variables are improved when each participant pays an equal price for success. Companies ferret out the lowest one-third of all their employees. These employees complain because they feel their personal needs and values are not being met. They damage the perception of the mission and goals to reduce group motivation to succeed.

When all pay the same price, they value the same benefits and enjoy working together for a common purpose. And the common purpose is aligned with the personal needs and values of all team members who work collaboratively like a family in a common bond.

Personality Components

Do you have what it takes? Are you willing to change your personality to be successful? Top performers exhibit common personality traits to believe in a work ethic, performance effort, and success. They do not take shortcuts. They remember practices more efficiently. Some keep workout journals and logs to evaluate their progress.

Reflective Thinking

Top performers do not wait to be evaluated. They continually reflect on post- performance evaluations to set personal standards. Traditional post performance evaluations by leaders, managers, and coaches are too general and non-specific. The cause and effect are lost on the group with far less significance. Not my fault. Others are to blame.

However, there is value teaching each performer post performance self-evaluation skills. This instills personal accountability and builds trust and confidence in the process.

Dichotomy Comparisons

A dichotomy exposes evaluation differences between organizations, companies, or groups and performers. Boss or principal evaluation, organizational evaluation, peer evaluation, and personal evaluation. The best practice is to provide the evaluation form so performers can first self-evaluate. Then in a meeting compare to the boss's evaluation to the self-evaluation to find agreement, strengths, and weaknesses for improvement. When done correctly, your personal intrinsic evaluation is more powerful than an extrinsic evaluation provided by your boss or organization.

Post-performance Actual Versus Expected Goal

This form of dichotomy and congruence is linked to personality. To gain realism, a personality trait found in top performers, your actual performance should closely approximate your goal expectation. The greatest intrinsic motivation comes from knowing yourself to accurately predict and perform to a goal outcome. There is an optimal performance reinforcement value you can index to monitor improvement.

Individual and Team Satisfaction of Needs

Winning is another measure of your performance improvement. Whether the team wins or loses, how well did you perform? What areas did you contribute most to the success or failure of the team?

Overview

There is a distinct difference in how others see your performance and what you see in your performance. Top performers value their own evaluation more than the critics. Good leaders teach self-evaluation skills to build personal accountability. They introduce key factors to focus on improving and gaining intrinsic motivation. They also give all the credit to performers who improve.

Top performing leaders and managers cannot be with every performer every moment. They depend on a practiced positive system to continuously improve every performer's performance over time.

Leaders need realistic expectations, too. They must also hold themselves accountable, reflect on immediate and past performance averages, and be congruent. When leaders accurately predict stated outcomes and the group experiences success to feel rewarded, they will have followers.

As a parent of six children I tried to create an expectancy for success if they would follow certain ideals to self-evaluate and hold themselves accountable for their performance. Then I would give all the credit and rewards to them to reinforce my words. Words do have meaning, and when true to expectancy and actual performance creates followers you can lead and who will listen. Read the Pied Piper fable.

Select low positive goals only slightly better than your own immediate past performance or average to increase your probability for success and reward. As you improve, your immediate past performance also improves to challenge you to set another slightly higher but low positive goal.

Over time, this reward-reinforcement strategy increases your intrinsic motivation and work ethic to keep improving and feeling rewarded. It is simple, you value reward and avoid pain. You value commitment, dedication, sacrifice, focus, and concentration on the specific cue-response connections. This leads to Planer Thinking or thinking in higher planes as tasks become increasingly familiar to perform at higher and higher levels.

Leaders Take Note

 Judging another person's performance automatically converts the valuable intrinsic motive into a less valuable extrinsic motive. Your performer is not able to accept all or a major portion of the credit. Imagine a small scale. The more you take credit, you reduce the amount of credit your performer can accept and feel positive reward to reinforce succeeding attempts. This is a powerful lesson in transformational leadership.

When others accept portions of the reward you worked to earn, they diminish the value of your personal intrinsic connection between quality of effort and quality of reward. This reduces your desire to increase your work output on succeeding attempts to ensure your success and feel good. Performers may not know how to define their personal needs, but they still know how their performances make them feel.

In excellent organizations, performers ask peers their opinion without fear of ridicule or retribution. This provides a match between how you see your performance, and what others see you perform. Performers who experience repeated failure are not easily motivated. To do more work and feel success show how to set a low positive goal for a small part of the overall performance. Wanting to do better is a natural drive. If failing, change your perception of success by adjusting your personal goals to be more achievable and realistic.

In Post-Performance Plan for Initial Success in the Next Event

Serious morale problems result when leaders ...:

a) in the name of accountability, blame the performers for a poor start in the post-performance review
b) accept the credit for the suggestions or work of others to modify the approach to the next event

These set up a negative cycle and mistrust. Performers learn to hate their job, leaders, and managers. Their roles are not reinforced to feel rewarded in small positive incremental steps improving immediate past performances.

When expectations exceed reality, it leads to frustration. Performers enjoy working when they can feel a personal reward for seeing improvement. Money is not the issue. Performers leave jobs or teams because there is little or no job satisfaction. They dislike the manager whom they feel cannot do the job as well as they do but are overly critical.

Intrinsic motivation leadership skills help performers define and value their role in the organization and keep people on task. Successful performers are generally happy to reduce job turnover and transfer a positive work ethic to other employees.

Post-performance Evaluation Leadership

For post-performance evaluation to be beneficial, pre-design several key strategies or rubrics to focus your desired thinking or thought process. The goal is to learn how to process performance feedback, make positive adjustments, and efficiently improve your performance consistency. Selectively attend to specific strategies you feel predict your performance improvement.

Top performers who have achieved consistent success look for more. At the top of Maslow's Need Hierarchy is self-actualization. Top performers feel the need to give back to others what they have achieved. They are driven by a higher power, a calling or purpose.

It disturbs me to see leaders, coaches or teachers spending most of their time on their best or well-behaved performers. If you manage or coach a team, whether in sales or athletics, the practice to only work with the best leads to serious morale problems. A few top performers may be happy for one or two events in the short term. But overall contribution of the entire team will not improve very much.

As the leader you must find a simple and personal way to recognize the contributions, struggles, problems, and improvements of every performer in your organization. If not by you, then delegate your staff to permeate personal recognition in the organization. The greatest coaches view their success more by the development and improvement of their average performers.

In college, I was fortunate to be one of those performers for my Indiana University swim coach Doc Counsilman. I was a below average high school swimmer. I enrolled in Indiana because I wanted to be a swim coach and learn from this top performing coach. We already had numerous world record holders and All-Americans coach could have spent all his time. But Doc provided attention to details to all his team. I became a five-time All-American because I learned how to set workout goals and evaluate my improvements.

Self-evaluation is key to intrinsic motivation. The following is an example self-evaluation exercise using a rubric. As the leader you can create a rubric to evaluate any kind of performance.

Post Performance Evaluation Rubric

External Evaluator —————————————————————— Self Evaluator ——————————————————————

Rubric	Score 0	Score 1	Score 2	Score 3	Score 4
Improvement	0 part of whole	1 part of whole	2 parts of whole	3 parts of whole	4 parts of whole
Purpose & Value	had none	knew for this part	knew for these parts	knew for these parts	knew for these parts
Congruence Goal-Result	not even close	+/–6–10%	+/–3–5%	+/–1–2%	right on target
PAP Perceptual-Anchoring Point	had none	used group performance of others	based on stated goal to others	combination verbal & past performance	immediate past performance/ average
Sub routines	viewed whole performance	broke task down into two parts	broke task down into three parts	broke task down into four parts	connected cues and responses each part
Accountability	blames others & finds excuses	has idea to do better next time	identified needs & abilities to develop	created steps to improve	gives credit for success to others
TOTAL SCORE					

0–3 You are wasting your time.

4–10 You are starting to get a clue how Triadskills improve your performance.

11–17 You have the idea and it is a matter of time until you are a top performer.

18–24 You have what it takes to be a top performer.

Value Every Performer

If you are in the business of helping people, then model and teach all your performers methods to improve. This includes the troubled, mentally weak, misguided, and unfortunate performers with low abilities. Performance is based on each individual able to see improvements better than their own immediate past performance. Teach positive views for success to feel personal reward for improving.

As the leader or manager or coach your initial evaluation of talent could be wrong. Dean Smith said he thought Michael Jordan was another good basketball player on his team. He and other great coaches have not predicted the ultimate success or failure of great athletes. Why would you completely accept the improbable evaluations of others when you could learn to self-evaluate your performance?

Learning a post-performance evaluation system determines your improvement progress. Only you can predict how far you want to go by your personal motivation and work ethic.

Schools and organizational systems do not ordinarily use rubrics to teach you how to self-evaluate your performances and hold yourself accountable for improving. School teachers, coaches, parents, and managers condition you to believe they know what is best for you. Then, after you get your evaluation or grade, little is done to suggest how you can immediately improve your next performance.

No matter at what age you begin your education, it is always uncertain how you will end up. What is certain failure is not trying. You only regret the opportunities you passed up in life. The road to be a top performer is a process to enjoy because you set the goal, do all the work, and get all the reward.

The value of rubrics is learning how to self-evaluate your performance before the final external evaluation by others. Carefully crafted rubrics greatly benefit teachers and coaches to teach physical and mental skills. Leaders can use rubric strategies to teach individuals in a team environment how to continuously evaluate and improve all component parts of their performance.

Top performers process their performance feedback and assign a relative value to reinforce the input-output and goal-performance relationship. They increase awareness of the goal objective and actual performance outcome as predicted. You improve conditioned responses through post performance evaluation to build confidence and realism to lead.

You speak with more believable conviction to lead. Your performers believe what you realistically suggest and raise their positive expectations. They follow your leadership when performances turn out as you stated they would.

Your leadership is to familiarize your performers with what to expect prior to performing unfamiliar tasks. Your consistent positive winning behavior benefits your performers and the organization.

To focus on mistakes thinking to avoid them, you condition that stimulus-response connection the same as if it were a positive performance. If leaders berate and criticize performers focusing on all the mistakes, they condition more performance errors. This is one more transformational leadership lesson.

Condition positive performances and extinct the negative ones by not calling attention to them. When you focus on the faults of your performers, they stop being creative and contributing to fly under management radar. You want to reinforce the positive steps taking place in the organization. Making negative comments undermine your leadership focus.

Performance improvement requires leaders to understand the psychology of human behavior. No one likes anyone to find fault with every little part of a more successful overall performance in order to strive for perfection. That strategy does not reinforce positive performance improvement. Your performers are driven to improve and feel rewarded not criticism for trying and taking some risk to increase the reward.

A better strategy is to increase awareness by focusing on specific steps for improving each task within your organization. Another strategy is continually focus on the positives and not talk about the negatives of performance improvement. Boss leaders have an intrinsic need to seek power and set extrinsic goals for their performers. The design meets their needs first, and why their performers are not motivated to extend their work effort.

Lead managers believe the opposite trusting performers to set goals and do their job well when they are not looking. Their performers are empowered with a conscious purpose to improve performance and achieve self-rewarding quality.

To achieve long-term performance improvement all your performers must reflect and evaluate the quality of their work in relation to a standard you set. Performers who see the standard as a realistic expectation increase their work ethic and self-rewarded behaviors. But guaranteed, the top performers will set higher personal standards for their performance to value. What follows is another value index. Chapter 3 used an activity value index to signify intrinsic motives. This index reflects optimum reinforcement value for performance.

Optimal Performance Reinforcement Value Index

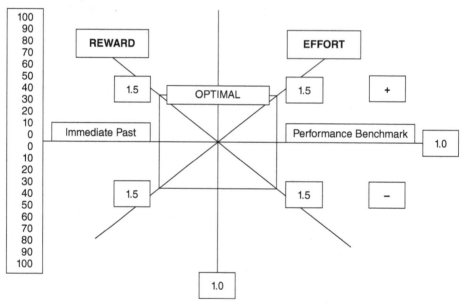

The Optimal Performance Reinforcement Value Index is formed with an upper and lower-half mirror image. The index is applied to actual performance results by dividing the perceived reward R by the perceived effort E. The equation is $V = R/E$ as an index of optimal value. After a performance, you self-evaluate your actual performance results. There is a positive and negative scale to 100%. The base line in the middle is your immediate past performance. Your goal is to improve your baseline intersected by the % reward and effort lines.

If your performance has improved over your immediate past performance, you use the positive upper half scale. If your performance has declined from your immediate past performance, you use the negative lower half scale. You still subjectively estimate your perceived effort and reward scale to compute your index.

Value becomes an empirical index. V is a value index from 0 to 10 found by dividing R, the perceived % reward strength by E, the perceived % effort strength. The optimal reinforcement is a perceived value index of a positive 1.0 to 1.5. You expend 30-50% effort more often to increase the valued frequency of reward.

If the perceived reward is approximated at moderately high 70% and easy to attain 30%, you have a Value index of 70/30 = 2.3. If the perceived effort is easy (20%) and the perceived reward is slight (20%), your Value index 20/20 = 1.0. This is not optimal. You must expend more than 30% effort for the value to condition a reinforcement effect.

If the perceived reward value is a high 80% and the perceived effort is 80%, then your value index would also be 80/80 = 1.0. However, the difference is above the 50% base line. However, you expended a greater effort to get a better reward. You are not likely to repeat this activity often. Therefore, this activity would also have less motivational value to reinforce your future efforts.

An index below the base line still has relative value to improve your motivation, but probably is half the strength of a positive index of the same value. When you increase your training effort, the perceived effort comes easier with more physical practice conditioning and knowledge 50%. The perceived reward may stay the same or slightly increase to 80% to give you a value index of 80/50 = 1.6 slightly above the optimal reinforcement range.

With improved performances the perceived rewards begin to exceed the perceived effort. You gradually become more aware of a higher index value, increase intrinsic motivation, and connect reward with reinforcement. Conversely, if the reward is perceived to be high 90%, and the effort is 100%, the value index would be 90/100 = .9 or less than 1.0.

This lower value index reflects a slightly lower probability for positive reinforcement over time. Consistently lower values do not generally increase your motivation or drive stimulus to achieve. A greater number of high value indices reinforces taking more attempts and practicing the specifics to reinforce intermediate rewards.

Thus, the strategy to increase intrinsic motivation is the conscious awareness of your purpose, and projection of perceived value. Shift to positive optimal levels in the value index. This gains realism and congruence between your expected and actual performance, a consistent trait in top performers.

No top performer ever waits for the approval of another person because they develop a personal value system to judge the worth of their performances. The following table of The Triad Performance Improvement Value System provides examples how value perceptions affect performance.

The Triad strength is interpreted as intrinsic motivation to improve performance. The table describes how value is perceived to enhance motivation using The Triad system.

The Triad Performance Improvement Value System

TASK DIFFICULTY	+	AMOUNT OF EFFORT	+	DEGREE OF OBSERVED CHANGE	=	VALUE OF ACHIEVEMENT
PAP perceptual anchoring point		Ability & talent required		Compare new to past performance or average		Expectation of success
Past experience		Task perceived as easy or hard; familiar or unfamiliar		Computed probability of success		Feelings of self-worth
Knowledge of abilities, skills, needs, strategies		Level of commitment		Increasing the odds to succeed		Positive reward
Knowledge of competition & standards		Knowledge of performance conditions		Need to decrease odds to protect ego		Positive reinforcement
		Emotional make up; will-power, persistence				

Examples

SIMPLE TASK	+	LOW EFFORT	+	LOW DEGREE OF CHANGE	=	LOW VALUE OF ACHIEVEMENT
DIFFICULT TASK	+	HIGH EFFORT	+	HIGH DEGREE OF CHANGE	=	HIGH VALUE OF ACHIEVEMENT

Achievement Value and Goal Orientation Related to Triad Strength

VALUE OF ACHIEVEMENT	+	GOAL ORIENTATION	=	TRIAD STRENGTH

Examples

LOW VALUE OF ACHIEVEMENT	+	WEAK GOAL OR NO GOAL	=	VERY LOW TRIAD STRENGTH
HIGH VALUE OF ACHIEVEMENT	+	HIGH POSITIVE ULTIMATE GOAL	=	VERY HIGH TRIAD STRENGTH

Summary

The purpose of learning to perform a post-performance evaluation is to learn how to process your own feedback without having to wait for the approval of others. You judge the worth or value of your efforts. Performance value is a comparison to your immediate past performance or average as a benchmark.

As feedback awareness of your past performances increases you form a "self" perceptual anchoring point to judge the value of each succeeding performance improvement. You cannot control the performances of others. You can control how you approach your goals. Use the needs and talents you identify to set realistic and achievable goals to motivate your work ethic.

When you consistently improve your immediate past performances, you condition your reward-reinforcement value system. You must "connect" quality of effort with quality of reward. With consistent improvement you learn good performances are not haphazard luck.

Boss leaders who assume their performers are incapable of self-motivation lose their ability to lead. No self-motivated performer wants to improve their performance when they are micromanaged and controlled. Remember as a rule you cannot improve accountability in a micromanagement system.

To improve intrinsic motivation, you must align the mission and goals of the organization with the personal needs, values and goals of the performers doing the work. And then give them all the credit.

Top performing leaders demonstrate caring about their performers, opinions, and families. Leaders who care to ask how they feel about the work they accomplish find an improvement in work performance. Your management must find time to effectively listen and communicate with every performer. One more lesson in transformational leadership.

Ultimately, it is not what you think or evaluate in another person's performance but what they learn to self-evaluate that matters most. It is always what the performer perceives to be success or failure. Any performance improvement is success that can be conditioned and repeated especially when recognized by management.

Society has falsely created the notion that only those who are passing, make good grades, or perform outstanding achievements are successful. With The Triad skills and RROSR, you condition a personal success-reward system as you continuously improve upon your immediate past performance or average.

The longer and more continuous you make this quest you become a top performer over time. Reinforce your own efforts to perceive frequent success and reward to continue and persevere where others quit and move on to another task.

In any organization or system, micromanagement will not instill personal leadership and performance improvement accountability. Lead management raises the level of performer awareness with positive feedback. Every performer is empowered to learn a self-imposed pre, during, and post-performance evaluation system. This is the second part of The Triad.

True evaluation starts with a value system to improve performance inherent in the performer. Self-evaluation elevates a higher conscious state of awareness for the quality of work performed. The conscious awareness of quality value enables your ability to readily store and retrieve information to process faster.

This helps you make better decisions and think of performances through for predictable outcomes. And when you set realistic goals and frequently achieve them, you reinforce a stronger personal reward system. By consciously increasing the value of the work performed you perceive yourself as successful anytime you improve your own immediate past performance. You evaluate-reward-reinforce positive behaviors to define your achievements with results over time.

THE THIRD SECRET SKILL

CONNECT REWARD WITH REINFORCEMENT

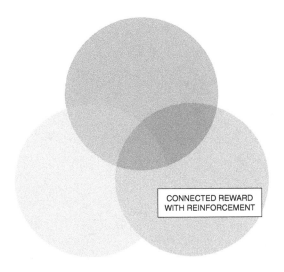

CONNECTED REWARD
WITH REINFORCEMENT

Part Three of The Triad Performance Improvement System is to connect reward with reinforcement. This is perhaps the weakest skill of any top performer. Most top performers I have observed and interviewed take for granted their talents and abilities. They cannot understand why more people cannot perform what they do.

Top performers set up a personal performance value system to feel rewarded and stay motivated. They do not give themselves much credit for outstanding performances. They are conditioned by others less talented to not brag about their performance. Those who cannot perform their skills redress them with labels, "arrogant s-o-b" or "conceited b _____."

There is no law you cannot have a personal conversation with yourself. On your way to and from work review your day. What positives can you take away? How did you improve? Who did you help? Are you happy? Are you proud? When you begin to answer these kinds of personal questions, you connect reward with reinforcement.

17

PART THREE OF THE TRIAD TO CONNECT REWARD WITH REINFORCEMENT

The object of The Triad is to increase your intrinsic motivation to learn how, to think, act, and do for yourself and eventually help others.

Rewards come from satisfaction of a perceptual need or goal. If you do not learn to have confidence in your abilities, no one else will either. Reward and reinforce your success. You do not have to brag, but you can have a personal conversation in your mind to increase your awareness of performance improvements.

In Chapter 4, I identified three new personality traits group, verbal, and self from my doctoral dissertation research.

Your personality uses one or a combination of these types to create a perceptual-anchoring point. The benchmark is different for each personality type. Using that preferred benchmark, you make a predictable goal shift up or down. And when you meet or exceed that personal goal you feel rewarded. You are conditioned or reinforced to apply the same process again the more often you feel rewarded.

Classrooms grade on a curve and teams huddle up to evaluate performance based on a group performance standard. Individuals often state their goals to significant others like spouses, close friends, and sometimes coaches and managers.

The extreme in sports has always been Muhammad Ali's comment, "I am the greatest!" If you make public verbal comments, you better back up your words. Verbal statements of prowess or personal goals are made to increase intrinsic motivation to back up your words. You must perform what you predict or lose social favor.

To open your mouth prior to a competition and guarantee victory more often motivates your opponent. It provides a verbal perceptual anchoring point to live up to your prediction but is not a good idea. Use positive self-talk instead.

Use *positive self-talk* to verbally state your accomplishment privately to your brain. This raises your conscious awareness for the meaningful and relevant value of what you just performed. Others will sense from your body language a quiet confidence and help build their confidence. Give yourself permission to take a pat on the back for a job well done and should be practiced more often. You do not need to wait for the approval of others, especially your critics. You know quality when you see it to compare your performance.

Talking to your spouse or family about your accomplishments may not be a good idea either. They know you in a different light. Your parents and relatives remember you growing up and not as an accomplished performer. So, to them, your words sound like you are bragging. Maybe if you need another opinion have a quiet personal conversation with your mother who probably knows you best.

Remember actions speak louder than words. If you are a verbal personality use caution. Think before you speak.

From my research with Olympic swimmers and goal setting I put them in the self-personality type. They only used their own immediate past performance for the perceptual-anchoring point. In every case where I tried to manipulate them to verbally compete with a teammate's performance, they refused. They all preferred to set low-positive goals slightly better than their last trial on a novel grip strength task.

My analysis concluded they increased their probability of reward. They also improved the frequency of reward to condition future trials and reinforce success feelings. This connects reward with reinforcement.

Failure is a pain to be avoided. No pleasure center in the brain is activated to be reinforced. With frequent non-success you lose reinforcement or motive to repeat those behaviors.

When helping others to improve I do not like to use the term failure. I say there are varying degrees of success instead. You can learn something positive from every attempt. Thomas Edison learned from thousands of trials before inventing the light bulb.

You are probably unaware how conditioning is taking place to make your daily life dull and routine, or exciting and challenging. Repetition and routine create boredom and staleness, and automate responses placed in unconscious sensory reaction mode.

Instead of evaluating, planning and acting to improve your performance your life is centered on following and reacting to maintain the routine and less stress. Change can be stressful. Coach warned us how a change in stroke mechanics feels wrong because it is not the familiar routine.

Performance improvement requires change in how you view your needs, values, and goals. You decide what new information is meaningful and relevant to value. You decide to process and evaluate your performance output as feedback to adjust new input cues.

You must take control of your life and hold yourself accountable for learning and performing new skills. You lose valuable time connecting reward with reinforcement waiting for others to reward your work. What does it take to motivate you to improve upon your God given abilities?

Parents are not role models to blame for your behaviors in the home. I have observed students coming from great homes and professional parents. They still turned to drugs and other maladaptive behaviors because they never learned how to connect reward with reinforcement. What matters is whether you understand your needs to be self-reliant, and value personal effort to achieve quality performance.

The transformational leadership lesson is to equate quality of effort with quality of reward.

What matters is what you think of your purpose in life. What are you here for? Do you really want others to provide for your needs for your entire life? It is sad to see people in affluent countries with loads of opportunities who cannot learn to provide for their own needs.

When your personal needs are provided by others or freely given, you may not value the process to work to satisfy a goal, feel rewarded, and desire to reinforce the feeling. It is a universal human behavior to not value anything given for free.

A real concern in public education and affluent cultures is how people are not learning to identify and provide for their own needs. The answer is in the principle of reward and reinforcement. If all your needs are met by others you lose goal striving behaviors. When personal goals are not created and satisfied you lose all sense of motivation. Necessity is still the mother of invention. This applies to performers of all ages besides students and young adults.

Welfare programs may help the needy, but they do not teach goal striving behaviors to provide for identified personal needs. If you really want to help people, teach them how to help themselves. Build value for minor successes to feel rewarded enough to condition another try to improve upon their immediate past performance.

If a student does not score above 60 or 70 per cent on the first try, the public-school system labels them a failure—a loser who is not trying. This is what gets conditioned and reinforced. School systems can change their grading systems to reward improvement.

A final grade is not earned until all do-overs are finished. No matter where you start, the goal is to increase the probability for success and feel rewarded enough to reinforce the effort. The slower turtle wins the race against the much faster rabbit in the Aesop fable because he kept his eye on achieving the goal.

Part Three examines two points of view to understand the behavioral relationship between reward and reinforcement.

Principles of Reward-Reinforcement. Something so simple can be greatly misunderstood. You can learn to evaluate your performance, set realistic low positive goals, achieve reward, and reinforce those kinds of behaviors to repeat. Top performers consistently follow this process. Conversely, bad behaviors can be enabled when they are rewarded.

Leadership for Success

Every great leader communicates a positive vision that creates "buy-in" from the performers and credit for doing the work. Leaders hold themselves accountable. They align the mission of the organization with the personal needs and values of the people. They build a sense of purpose connecting quality of effort and quality of reward every performer can feel rewarded.

The biggest mistake a leader can make is to take credit for the work or idea of another person. Nothing will kill the morale of your performers faster. Lead management systems empower and trust all performers can connect reward with reinforcement. Boss management systems imply performers are incapable of performance improvement without extrinsic reinforcement. Performers are more motivated to produce quality products and services when they have some say in how they can perform the work to feel rewarded.

Applying The Triad

Here are key points:

*   You cannot appreciably increase intelligence until you increase awareness.
*   No top performer waits for the approval of another person. They have a personal self-evaluation system to feel rewarded.
*   It is natural behavior to repeat activities that connect reward and reinforcement.

When my daughter was inducted into her high school National Honor Society, I asked 18 of the 256 students some simple questions. I asked, "how did you feel your achievements related to goals?" They all reported a preference for using their own immediate past performance and set lower realistic goals to feel frequently rewarded and stay motivated.

Then I asked, "where did you learn that strategy?" Sixteen immediately said at home and two said from a coach. As an educator and behaviorist interested in personal motivation, I thought it was odd that not one successful student in this random sample reported they learned this important strategy from a teacher.

Does this appear to be a powerful lesson in transformational leadership? Not just in educational systems, but in business, government, and other organizational systems.

This may be your conscience or little voice inside that knows the truth. Rely on this voice to build personal accountability. This powerful lesson leaders could use to place accountability on how the performer's feel about their performance. Teach them how to value the worth of every performance.

There are all kinds of dysfunctional relationships. The Triad is a performance improvement system applied to jobs, tasks, skill, and relationships. There are single parent mothers, teachers, coaches, absent fathers, and community leaders who can benefit from The Triad. All behaviors are based on needs and values. When others provide for the basic needs young people do not learn to identify what needs they will have to provide to be self-reliant and independent.

Remember, as a rule providing free goods and services are not valued. More entitlements lead to more entitlement demands. The Triad teaches personal accountability to value oneself and others through a work ethic reward-reinforcement.

Do your homework. Compare and contrast the family environment and discipline asking people over age 50 to what is happening in the world today. There were fewer entitlements. Need satisfaction motivated behaviors. If you wanted a baseball glove your parents could not afford, you mowed lawns, raked leaves, shoveled snow, and worked to get the money to buy.

I often tell the story of a young boy who is given a nice baseball glove for his twelfth birthday. Another boy does odd jobs and earns the money to buy his own glove. Which boy do you think is apt for forget his glove at the park?

Rioters, looters, hoodlums, anarchists, robbers, rapists, murderers, felons, and drug addicts apparently never learned The Triad and its value. Leadership must transform this failed process during rehabilitation. It starts in the home and in the school systems.

One of the first values I learned from my parents was to honor my mother and father and respect my elders. Why? Because elders have the wisdom from living longer. I take time to communicate with all fourteen of my grandchildren the same way I did with my six children who are now their parents. The lessons are the same. Lead yourself and be responsible for your behaviors.

Principles of Reward and Reinforcement

Webster's Dictionary defines the prefix "re" as to go back again or anew. Reward and reinforcement provide recognition for an improved performance. Re-cognition is to think again or reflect on your achievement. Re-enforcement is to strengthen by adding new knowledge to facilitate the connection between a stimulus cue and a response. Re-ward is to give something for something achieved.

Top performers identify their needs and values. They evaluate their performance using a feedback process like B.F. Skinner's Black Box and adjust input cues until they get the correct performance output. They set realistic low positive goals to increase the probability and frequency of success to feel rewarded. This reinforces a work ethic to maintain those kinds of positive feelings of self-reward. That is powerful intrinsic motivation.

Extrinsic rewards like money, grades, or gifts are less powerful motivators. They are not valued. The problem is you must keep increasing the reward, and only a few are recognized. Intrinsic rewards for improving a performance or exceeding a personal goal can be achieved by many.

It is harder to reinforce unrewarded behaviors when only a few are provided extrinsic rewards as a prize. Promotion has long been a tool of companies to motivate employees to work hard for their benefit. But the rank and file performers are rarely promoted and lucky to get a raise or one-week paid vacation after a year of service. Their opinions are not valued or asked for.

Many small reward-reinforcement connections increase intrinsic motivation and desire to renew the performance or activity. As a rule, personally rewarded behaviors are repeated, and unrewarded behaviors are reduced.

Behavior Premise

Micromanagement and leader evaluations reduce personal empowerment and self-evaluation to increase performers' intrinsic motivation. What you learn to value your personal performance is far more powerful than what your evaluator thinks.

Transformative leaders help performers make the connection between quality of effort and quality of reward. The connection of reward satisfying a personal need reinforces the intrinsic motive. But when leaders or managers take credit, the continuing effort the performers perceive in the pleasurable reward is lost.

As the leader, manager, coach, teacher, or parent, when you externally evaluate and lavish praise for an average unearned effort two bad perceptions occur. Your performer does not learn self-evaluation and goal setting/reward behaviors.

You automatically create an extrinsic motive to perform just enough to make you happy. Neither is an ideal method to improve performance. It is not what makes the evaluator happy, but how the performer learns to feel a valued connection between effort and personal reward.

The goal is to learn personal accountability for performance improvement. The Triad teaches a performance improvement system. You can apply to any job, task, skill, or relationship for the rest of your life. The challenge is to keep improving your own immediate past performance and feel rewarded with no set limits. You lead yourself. You hold yourself accountable.

Transformative leaders want performers to do well when they are not looking. There are specific rewards achieving a group goal. Extrinsic motivation diminishes with the personal intrinsic effort of every team member. A strategy to reinforce this behavior would be to *define and assign specific team roles and teach use of performance feedback to compare with immediate past performance*. Then give all the reward to the performers doing the work so they feel accomplished.

To reinforce good performance behaviors, as the leader you want performers to exceed their personal goals. This will not happen as frequently when you have established extrinsic group goals with pre-set limits. Ask your performers to journal how they feel about their accomplishments. This reflection creates value and understanding of underlying needs.

Creating personal value is a far more powerful motivation than extrinsic praise. Every performer learns work ethic behaviors earning fulfillment of their needs and value of rewards. Feelings of success is the intrinsic reward, and necessary component to building personal accountability and connecting reward with reinforcement.

When leaders motivate performers using specific rewards (candy, money, gold stars, check marks, vacations, or excessive praise of any kind) these become extrinsic motivators. The more powerful motivator to change behavior is the performer's internal feelings about the value or satisfaction of their goals.

When tasks are easily accomplished, performers do not value them. See the Value Activity Index in Chapter 3. These tasks are not often reinforced. Leaders must challenge performers to focus on the specific parts of the process using RROSR and the outcome will have a higher probability of achievement.

Focus on the parts reinforces everyone to mobilize their creative personality, skills, and abilities to achieve the result for each part to improve all the steps. There are no short cuts to consistent success. Trainers in sales and marketing who noticed failing results of "approval" systems instituted methods to provide for reflective thinking. This lets performers judge the value of their performance in relation to the group objective.

Excessive social approval and verbal praise diminish reflective thinking to self-evaluate. As a performer and leader of one you need to compare your immediate performance with past performance for improvement. This forms your perceptual anchoring point and new goal.

The comparison can be to what another group has performed, or your verbal statement of the desired goal. But the most powerful is to set a low positive goal one point higher than your own immediate past performance to increase your probability for success. Use the self-personality component of top performers.

With more focused effort you have no excuse. Your motivation to achieve your goal is higher and intrinsic to connect reward with reinforcement. This strategy is a necessary skill component to increase your awareness, confidence and self-esteem that intrinsically create the value of your personal reward.

The quality or value of perceived rewards reinforces and increases your motive to repeat activities on succeeding attempts with more effort to ensure continued successful feelings. The correct process of setting new goals using The Triad enhances your personal reward system and intrinsic drive motive.

Choice Psychology—Burnout, Boredom, and Staleness

Choice Psychology

Dr. William Glasser (1990) popularized choice psychology in his book, The Quality School. Children have a normal drive for independence. Use this drive to teach your performers how to be accountable for their behaviors by not making all their decisions for them. Give them choices like dichotomies to point out the extremes of their behaviors and the consequences for improper choices. Human behavior is predictable.

Performers are not stupid to choose pain and predict failure. Give your performers choices with predictable consequences, and they will make the correct choices. You want your performers to make intelligent decisions to benefit themselves, the company or team, and become independent working without a manager.

This trust builds confidence and loyalty in the people doing the work. Create positive choices that lead to acceptable performance outcomes they can self-evaluate and feel rewarded.

The old phrase, "Do not add insult to injury" applies. Your performers know when they have made a mistake without you emphasizing and reinforcing the error. If your performers care about your organization, they will be stakeholders to make correct personal decisions on behalf of the company. As the leader you must decide on how to display the amount of latitude you will accept as your performers learn and grow with the company to earn more independence in the field. Obviously, you do not let a two-year-old play in traffic, but neither do you treat adult performers like children. You will make decisions for children until you teach them how to self-evaluate their performances to hold themselves accountable for the outcomes. You will teach them a purpose for their performance that is their choice to accept and value.

One strategy is to control your environment rather than let your environment control you. If you choose to become educated, you gain opportunities for rewarding careers. What environmental choices do you think will help you succeed? You can choose where you live and work, the kind of friends you keep, the marriage-partner you select, the courses you need to take, the church to attend, and even the amount of time you devote to exercise and nutrition to be healthy for a higher quality of life.

If you are insecure, you do not risk choosing new unfamiliar experiences to learn and draw upon to fulfill your future perceived needs. This change process creates stress you can handle making smaller incremental steps. With a positive attitude be aware and reward those small changes to keep improving.

Change your thinking right now. Practice self-reward by viewing your success as any kind of slight improvement over your own immediate past performance or average. Forget about that 90-80-70-60 or A-B-C-D idea. You cannot control what other performers do, but you can control what you plan, decide, commit, and work to achieve.

Rejoice in even your smallest achievements to improve. Keep in mind that as you improve, your last performance becomes your new immediate past performance, and your new goal must be one point higher to feel success. With any kind of effort, you are already reinforced to do more of the same things to make it happen again on a higher level.

If you are bored, change your focus from negative to positive. Get clarity why you are performing the activity to increase your enjoyment and reward for any accomplishment. Young performers lack a variety of experience because if they are not immediately satisfied, they quit. They choose mindless activities that decrease sensory awareness.

They are easily bored because they have not learned to apply any of The Triad skills. The focus is on entertainment instead of knowledge acquisition. Valuable time is spent using entertainment tools such as portable music players, mindless TV, instant messaging or texting, repetitive electronic games, socializing, and in extremes self-medicating with drugs and alcohol to prohibit awareness.

Parents and an adult society enable these kinds of behaviors to avoid dealing with their children's problems or to make a profit on their stupidity. Children get conditioned to whine and get what they want. The idea of a work ethic to earn a reward is an inconvenience. That would require supervision and loss of personal adult time.

Entertainment and social emotional learning take precedence over academic learning with an imagination to acquire more knowledge. Whether you are young or old, boredom, burnout, and staleness results from not having learned how to increase your personal sensory and perceptual awareness skills.

Positive Learning is Self-Reinforced

Here are some positive strategies to reinforce motivation to improve performance:

1. Take calculated risks. Set a goal only slightly better than your own immediate past performance to increase your probability for success and reinforce your personal reward.
2. Be more consciously aware of the reasons why you are working at improving in any activity to increase the value. Keep workout logs, journals, diaries, etc., to reflect and record your intrinsic feelings. Reward-reinforcement value increases with effort.
3. Make your motive to achieve success greater than your motive to avoid failure.
4. Evaluate your own progress for improving in smaller incremental steps instead of trying to be an overnight success. You will be less stressed and more in control of the specific cues you need to focus on to perform well and be rewarded.
5. Make every attempt to hold yourself accountable for your learning and performance. Blaming others for your lack of performance will not help you achieve your goals.
6. Learn to be coachable. Accept criticism from those with more experience who try to help you succeed.

Psychology of Intrinsic Motivation

It is counter-productive to extrinsically reward students to learn. They will not value their education. By the time they get to junior high school, the extrinsic reward is never large enough. Each unique performer is what matters most.

Teachers and managers can create the need to learn The Triad if they transform their leadership. Stephen Covey (1989) used the same process in his book, The Seven Habits of Highly Effective People to summarize observations of successful performers.

Every performer brings something positive they are doing correctly. Leaders must look for those positives to reinforce and condition instead of the negative fault finding that reinforces more bad behaviors. When leading create the right environment and needs with The Triad skills training. The rest is up to your performers.

The 19th century German poet, Goethe, said it best, "If you treat an individual as if they were what they ought to be and could be, they will become what they ought to be and could be." You cannot be a boss leader and assume your performers are incapable of intrinsic motivation to improve their performance. If you lead properly, they will perform properly.

Reflect on your successful performances. Were the performances pleasurable and gratifying or painful and a waste of time? What needs did you try to fulfill? Were you aware of your purpose? Was your level of awareness strong enough to process your own performance feedback? Did your success happen by chance or by planned purpose? Did you want to repeat successful performances and avoid activities you perceived you were not as successful performing or as satisfying?

When you become dependent on extrinsic rewards to shape your behavior, you do not learn how to self-evaluate your performance to define and create your personal needs. Learn to operate from within your framework of experience. This forces you to change how you create or adapt to your environment.

The Triad in Action

You repeat what you feel rewarded inside about your performance improvement. You avoid activities that produce negative feelings of failure. Similarly, you avoid others who negatively criticize and berate you against their personal expectation. Any time you see and feel your performance improvement, a kind word, look, or pat on the back from other people conditions this enhanced feeling. But without those extrinsic comments, you can have a powerful personal conversation in your mind to review your day or accomplishments.

Increase your awareness to condition these feelings in yourself. *Be your own best friend.* Top performers do not wait for the approval of others when they know they have done a good job. You know quality when you see it performed by others, and in your own performances. Increase your awareness (first Triad) that it is you who set the goal, did the work, and deserves all the reward.

Cooperative learning does not always condition this feeling. There is some reward in helping others achieve success with your knowledge and skills. Reflective thinking reinforces positive beliefs about what you self-evaluate (second Triad) as quality. Take time to reflect and associate your quality of effort with your quality of reward (third Triad) to build value in what you are learning to learn. Transform your leadership with The 3 Secret Skills.

Creating a dichotomy compares your awareness of early trials with your later successful trials to evaluate improvement. How did you feel when you were not so successful versus how you feel when you know you are successful? Dichotomy comparisons enhance your personal reward system by helping you understand the value of your correct choice to feel rewarded. You can understand the motive and process to condition the rewarding value and mastery for any job, task, skill, or relationship.

Approval System

I repeat this again. Top performers seldom wait for the approval of another performer. This includes leaders. Top performers connect reward to reinforce their own performance evaluations. They keep a positive focus on improving the key component skills of the activity.

Reflect for a moment on your past activities over a two to three-year period. For any activity you understood why you were working hard to improve. Even when you were not as successful as you expected, did you feel that 95% of the time there was something positive you could take away?

Now compare to activities you went through the motions with no purpose or goal to value. Your success was haphazard and inconsistent and maybe only 50-50 at best. If by chance you had a good feeling for a successful performance, you made a positive connection between your effort and reward. This increased your motive to want to repeat those like behaviors to enjoy more of that feeling.

With more repetition and success your passion grows. You begin to self-select more time for activities you feel successful at performing because you condition a relationship between reward and reinforcement. You subconsciously assign high to low values for each activity.

I doubt the great modern art painter Picasso ever contemplated what the critics might think of his creative work. Critics are more often average people who cannot create and do what you have achieved. You need to learn how to evaluate your own work for quality and reinforce the personal value you attach to your effort and results.

Increase your conscious awareness of a specific goal for improving every performance. Self-reward small improvements to each part of the total performance. Otherwise your performances become routine, you lose interest, and quality suffers. Many successful performers fail to recognize this fact and get bored and stop working to improve.

Much of what you successfully perform each day you take for granted because your performances become routinely familiar and common. This does not create a desirable reward-reinforcement. Focus on the strategy to increase your conscious awareness of routine tasks to create value and motivate performance improvement.

Need Based Behaviors and Rewards

Most performers do not think about their short or long-term needs that drive their behavior. Your needs change as you become more familiar with jobs, tasks, skills, and relationships. Knowing your current needs is essential in the pre-performance evaluation stage. How you meet your personal needs is vital to reinforce satisfying behaviors.

In affluent countries like the United States, basic needs for food, clothing, and shelter are usually met by others. Younger generations can focus on higher needs in Maslow's Hierarchy. The problem is they lose awareness to identify those needs to be self-reliant and independent. The result is a growing dependent society with greater expectation of entitlements. And I expect they protest when they do not get what they want for free and must work for it.

Material or immaterial things you do not have to sacrifice and work hard to get are not valued. This is normal human behavior. Most public education is free, and too many students do not value their education to work hard enough to obtain knowledge. Why is an education never valued so highly until you need it?

The more others provide for your needs you lose your motivation to provide for those same needs. You are not reinforced through intrinsic reward to be self-sufficient. Performers with learning difficulties have their need to achieve reduced by others who feel a stronger personal need to provide for their needs. That is not helping.

Leaders can mean well, but you must teach your performers to identify and plan to meet their needs. Ask questions who provides for _____? As a behavioral rule the more you do for others the less they learn to do for themselves.

When I was a school superintendent, some parents complained about their children being unmotivated. I have observed performers and children who play dumb acting like they do not know how to perform certain tasks. Impatient parents and managers end up doing the job for them. This enables bad behaviors with little hope for teaching personal accountability. And then the parent still rewards them with sports and music lessons or allowances. Where is the consequence? The other lament is the 3-count warning system. Of course, any kid knows they get two free passes until the parent will take disciplinary action.

The problem is in the risk-reward system. If there are consequences, then risk is involved. However, a personal quality performance evaluation is a better reward system. Your performer evaluates their performance outcome to justify the amount of reward. Now children and performers associate quality of effort with quality of reward.

When you constantly do the job expected of a family member to perform you negatively reinforce a dependency on you and your system. You may have a need to feel loved and wanted but that is not teaching your family self-reliance.

Transformative leaders must not condition learned helplessness. A cry for help does not mean you perform the work. Teach your performers how to help themselves. *Learned helplessness* is a behavior that conditions others to do the work for you and is not a desirable leadership principle. When you take the fall for your child's mistakes, you do not teach them accountability to learn from their mistakes. If a mistake is painful enough, the behavior is avoided.

Creating Need for Meaningful and Relevant Knowledge

Tell your performers why new information is meaningful and relevant to create useful knowledge they can apply later to improve their performance. The reward from knowing is self-reinforcing and a forthright expectation. Observe anyone who has just improved their performance. Do they look happy and confident?

You cannot be guessing or taking a chance on what your brain must know. The only way to make new information meaningful and relevant is by your thinking.

This is intrinsic. A parent, teacher, coach, manager, or leader can explain the importance of new information (extrinsic), but until you decide (intrinsic) depends on where your brain will store it. Top performers place the most meaningful and relevant information directly on their brain's desktop for immediate retrieval. This single point is what separates top performers from average performers.

You create the need for positive work ethic behaviors to ensure repetitive success. This conditions the connection between reward and reinforcement in repeated trials. As you lead, project the need to improve performance over time. Provide examples of your experiences with other top performers.

Great coaches learned from top coaches they studied and/or performed under in a variety of conditions. Leaders use praise and reproof wisely to gain the respect of their performers. If you give unearned praise, you lose respect. Morale also drops if you do not recognize big or small contributions by all your performers who are trying to improve.

Good leaders are forthright, build trust, and show honest integrity. They communicate a positive vision in an objective and fair way. Their actions speak louder than words.

The best methods to create higher expectations of needs to personally improve performance are:

1. Break complex tasks into more manageable components to objectify success.
2. Place accountability for improving each component on the performer.
3. Teach how to use immediate past performance to evaluate improvement.

Remember the behavioral rule. Any leadership evaluation automatically shifts the perception of the intrinsic value to extrinsic. This makes evaluations by management less valuable than personal evaluations by the performers. When performers learn to self-evaluate by comparing their new performance to their immediate past performance, they intrinsically build positive value for any kind of improvement.

Knowing your purpose for performing creates value and need to improve. The Triad is a performance improvement system designed to make new information more meaningful and relevant. This uses RROSR to readily recognize, receive, organize, store, and retrieve information of value on the brain's desktop.

After your performers have evaluated their performance, the leader—teacher, coach, or manager—can provide their objective evaluation. If the two evaluations agree, you have a congruent evaluation and more powerful motivational reinforcement essential to create the need to improve.

The performer and the leader, teacher, or coach must be on the same page in how they define "performance quality." You want to look for, reward and condition positive behaviors that overlook or extinguish negative behaviors by not calling attention to reinforce them.

This is a major fault for parents who have discipline problems in the home. The more they point out their child's faults they keep reinforcing those bad behaviors.

The same applies to schools that create more rules to violate to improve their discipline.

Whether you desire success in a classroom, boardroom, or any physical or mental skills event, evaluate the results more frequently for each part of the total performance. When your performance feedback shows improvement, you connect reward with reinforcement easier than you could by thinking of the entire performance.

A great symphony orchestrates parts for each musical instrument to blend into the entire performance and is written accordingly in parts to achieve this result. Generally, your brain cannot attend to more than five selected cues at a time, and three would be optimal.

There are specific cues to anticipate and stimulate your conscious awareness. With each new trial, a certain amount of feedback is learned to associate and reinforce reward with the next performance. Great coaches and teachers provide you with the specific visual, verbal, or kinesthetic feedback cues to attend to and improve each trial until a greater consistency of performance occurs.

Innate in all human behavior is the drive to improve. Ideally you want every performer to see and value even small improvements frequently to build their confidence. Frequent reward reinforces intrinsic motivation to keep a work ethic to improve and maintain feeling good abouts performances.

Knowing and observing continuous improvement from your own performance feedback creates a powerful reinforcement schedule. This is highly resistant to forgetting, and conditions personal performance accountability.

Self-control

You cannot control what others think or tell you to perform, or how they will perform. You can control your thinking to focus on the correct methods and cues to improve your performance. Frequent success conditions your motivation to repeat those methods and cues. Hence the term, success breeds success.

Top performers become less concerned with what others think than what they personally have learned to self-evaluate their performance. Once that paradigm shift occurs, they do not wait for the approval of others. You must also make this conscious shift in how you view your performance to take personal accountability for doing the skills that advance your level of performance.

Reflection on Reward

Reflect on your past performances both successful and not so successful. Your intent for both was probably positive. No one gets out of bed and thinks how they can mess up their day. We all start out trying to be positive and desire to succeed. This is a natural drive, and an innate need to improve.

The difference between being successful 95% of the time lies in your purpose. Top performers know why they participate. They understand their personal needs and values motivating improvement to achieve a goal. They project rewards and feelings from success as they view it.

When you simply go through the motions of performing without a purpose or goal to achieve, or being aware of your underlying needs and values, your results are inconsistent and haphazard. You would do just as well to flip a coin to predict your results. You are not likely to connect reward with reinforcement with little desire conditioned to repeat and improve upon those kinds of behaviors.

Organizational Recognition

The central idea of an organization is to see every performer consistently improve incrementally. The most important variable to create is an atmosphere of continuous and consistent self-improvement. When every performer makes timely incremental progressions in more manageable parts of the total performance to feel reward, they will stay motivated to keep improving.

Success is measured by any slight improvement over their own immediate past performance or average. The company or team would see monumental gains in less than one year. Performers who compare their performance in relation to others never perform as well as performers who self-evaluate their immediate feedback against their immediate past performance. This is yet another powerful lesson in transformational leadership.

Large organizations, top heavy in middle management, try to build immediate results using extrinsic goals that place adverse pressure and stress on all performers. The work is no longer enjoyed because no personal satisfaction of reward can be observed. Performers care more about how they feel than worrying how the company, team, or organization feels. This includes the leaders and managers.

A commonly accepted behavioral pattern is people and animals repeat satisfied behaviors and avoid painful unsatisfactory behaviors.

Use your own feedback to compare your performance with your immediate past performance. If you see improvement, then you must feel some reward-satisfaction. When you equate quality of effort with quality of personal reward, you are intrinsically motivated to work harder and smarter to continually improve upon your performance.

There are all sorts of organizational recognition schemes to reward performers. Unfortunately, the predominant rewards are extrinsic with no thought of how performers feel about their performance. There are announcements in the company newsletter, performer of the week or month, closer parking space, a raise or salary increase, increased responsibility for a team role, or some other kind of extrinsic reward.

However, nothing can replace how your performers feel about the quality of their efforts supported by caring leaders who show empathy and personal appreciation. Leadership can provide all the positive accolades and feedback you want, but your performers must learn how to self-evaluate and value the quality of their performance.

When I was a school superintendent in a small rural district, I went to the local dollar store and bought twenty little thank you cards for a few bucks. The next afternoon I wrote a few thank you notes to my support staff and put them in our office mail slots to read the next morning.

Right after eight Laurel knocked on my door in tears. I thought her spouse had an accident. She immediately commented how she had worked as a student-aide for over fifteen years in the district, and no one thought to thank her or notice any good deed she had ever done.

I thought how sad. It only took me five minutes to recognize her good work, but it meant a lifetime of good will for her. Do you think she would stay motivated to do her best? Leaders and managers must know how their performers feel about their performance and take a little time to personally recognize. That personal reward cost little money and time but means more than extrinsic awards.

Periodically ask your performers to evaluate their work in relation to their personal needs, values, and goals. How is it going Fred? Anything I can do to help? Are they on pace or target? A simple conversation works better than a full-blown formal evaluation. You gain a personal connection. Is this transformational leadership?

What must we change to improve? Is training adequate, and have we given you the tools for success? Top performers take pride in their work, and love to communicate this pride to leadership. But too often leadership seems too busy to want to take the time to listen.

As the leader you must build time into your daily routine to regularly communicate with every performer on an informal first name basis. Leadership can provide extrinsic benchmarks, goals, expected outcomes, standards, and a company mission that is the ultimate performance goal. But it is the personal communication by management to care about the feelings of the performers doing the work.

Top performers will still select their own performance standards to improve their immediate past performance and increase their intrinsic motivation. Intrinsically motivated performers more often exceed their personally set standards than those set by management.

The strategy is to get your performers to set realistic standards they can frequently achieve rather than try to impress the manager with unrealistic high goals. That does not reinforce a positive work ethic.

In post-performance evaluation, you learned to connect reward with reinforcement. You do not need a manager to tell you this fact. CEO leaders please ask your managers not to burden their performers with extrinsic goals based on their needs instead of the needs of the performers. The effect of extrinsic management on personal performance improvement is not happening.

Establish Your Personal Reward Standards

Success is not what you tell a performer to feel. It is what your performer learns to self-evaluate from their post-performance to value and feel rewarded. Anyone can tell you some specific new information is valuable. You create the need to value new information meaningful and relevant in your mind. You do this by associating with previously stored knowledge.

The most effective standard top performers use is their own immediate past performance or average. They set goals only slightly better than that standard. When a projected goal is achieved close to that standard you have congruence. This demonstrates your personality trait of realism and level of experience. This is your personal standard. The Triad trains you to control performance improvement in small steps for any job, task, skill, or relationship.

Intelligence is an acquired skill. And how you establish your personal standards early in life with a work ethic plays a critical role for top performers.

The major assumption of this book is for you to associate what top performers do and use that process to improve your performances in less time.

Once you learn The Triad it is like riding a bicycle. You never forget to apply the principles for the rest of your life. They become a part of you to keep improving the Big Four—jobs, tasks, skills, and relationships whenever you decide to apply those skills.

As you become more familiar with each new challenge you increase your opportunity to become a top performer moving to higher performance planes. Your primary strategy is to increase your probability and frequency for success and reinforce those kinds of behaviors. Your awareness of highly predictive cues and self-evaluation conditions your reward with reinforcement to work harder with a purpose to maintain your success feelings. This enables your brain to receive more meaningful and relevant information to apply.

As the leader, avoid the traditional extrinsic evaluation systems and external standards. Instead, provide a personal intrinsic feedback system to correctly evaluate and improve personal performances. This builds personal accountability for performance improvement.

Break down job performance skills into smaller more manageable components your performers can improve and feel some success. They will get the "big idea" and adjust to their role. This builds a self-reward system for each performer to create a higher awareness for all their performance improvements.

To feel success the best value comes from a mental comparison to a personal standard. The traditional standard has been a group performance average. Arbitrary grading results like 90-80-70-60 for an A, B, C, or D and below that would be failing even though you could still be scoring better than half correctly. A new personal standard gives performers some control to see improvements and provide reward feelings. Otherwise, when you show little for your time and effort life is boring.

Eliminate the words failure and loser from your vocabulary and use varying degrees of success. The immediate past performance personal standard goal strategy changes the entire perception of intrinsic motives in your performers. Trying is not failure. You can sometimes learn more from mistakes when you become aware of how to correct future behaviors.

Any score provides a perceptual anchoring point (PAP) to improve. You must start somewhere. It is not where you start, but where you end up that count the most. Your immediate past performance changes as you consistently improve. This is your baseline PAP about which you self-evaluate the worth of your next goal.

The baseline PAP creates your motivation and purpose to achieve. Your goal strategy must always be to set a low positive goal slightly better than your own immediate past performance. This is what you measure the most often in your post performance evaluation to condition the improvement motivation.

As you achieve and reward yourself for small noticeable improvements, so will your immediate past performance change. You keep creating a new low positive goal and stronger purpose to value your work efforts to improve.

You have no excuse for not slightly improving your immediate past performance as your personal standard. You know what it took to make your last performance. Now with awareness of the correct methods and cues in a conscious effort in practice you work to assure your success.

This is the success strategy of top performers. Inconsistent performers set too high unrealistic and highly improbable achievement goals that do not condition their personal reward system. You want to increase your odds for success so your brain functions in a higher capacity.

Use the RROSR strategy to recognize, receive, organize, store, and retrieve information. You have a lot at stake. It is your goal, not your manager's. It is your needs being satisfied. It is your reward for the taking.

If you cannot better what you did the last time out with a little more focused effort, you cannot expect to go from a low to high degree of success with the same effort and focus. You cannot fool yourself. A child knows better. If your performance has less value and no purpose, you reduce your opportunity to achieve personal satisfaction from any improvement.

As leaders, teachers, and managers realize the needs you create for your performers automatically becomes extrinsic and less valuable. Instead show your performers how to identify and create personal needs leading to realistic goals and outcomes. Extrinsic motives set by others lose the benefit of long-term feelings of reward to reinforce your performers to keep improving.

Stay Focused

Top performers stay focused on every cue to see improvement. As a leader if you sense your performers are losing interest it is because they do not see measurable improvements in smaller manageable parts of the total performance to feel rewarded. They will care when they can see the reward value. This is another powerful lesson for transforming leaders.

I had triplet sons and I was a former swim coach so naturally I wanted them to go out for the team. Between them I had three-fourths of a relay. And then they said no. They saw me coach two practices a day plus weights. Their reason was not enough return of the investment of their time. They did go out for other sports. I was proud they could identify their personal needs apart from mine.

I keep advocating breaking down tough tasks into smaller manageable and measurable increments. You increase your reward-reinforcement probability. This enhances your motivation to improve and ensure your succeeding success. Set realistic achievable goals to climb to the first level.

Too often I see performers unaware or unresponsive to their improvement. Take a moment to reflect on where you started to compare to your current level of performance. It may shock you to feel greater reward.

I learned from teaching thousands to swim they are unaware how much they have improved. I give my pupil all the credit. Sometimes in the middle of a lesson I remind them to compare skills when they started to now. This dichotomy points out the before and after as another strategy to make new information meaningful and relevant. It is all about results.

As a leader you can have higher expectations only if you are a good judge of mental and physical talent. You communicate a steady progression achieving results in small steps. As I have pointed out, top performers have common attributes. You gain their attention to set low positive goals for frequent rewards.

A powerful lesson in transforming leaders is getting all the performers to equate quality of effort with quality of reward. Objectify tasks with a smaller more manageable scoring system. Then teach every performer to set low positive goals for each small part of the whole performance only slightly better than their own recorded immediate past performance or average. And be aware of any kind of improvement to feel personally rewarded.

Your leadership demonstrates every performer can improve, and their part of the total production is valuable. You prove their worth and they will value their effort. Failure is not an option, but there will always be varying degrees of success. You choose to feel success when you focus on performance improvement.

Top performers by their respected work ethic behaviors carry over to other members. If improvement requires a team effort, then top performers socially set the tone for practices and the important cues to focus on performing. Members who do not take their focus seriously affect total team performance.

As leaders let your top performers create the need for the team to improve and share in the rewards. Top performers know the needs and values of the members, and their words of advice and encouragement are more powerful.

Observe performers who are aware of their improvement. Big or small you see their heads held up high and proud. Conversely in public school grading systems below 60 is failing. Negative attitudes are harder to change if avoiding failure is the focus. Yet there is some success above zero to encourage improvement.

If you average a 58 and a 74, you are still failing by some standards. Or, you can choose to focus on your 16-point improvement over your immediate past performance to keep your motivation positive. A new goal of 75 has a high probability for improving with a stronger focus and work ethic. This strategy improves intrinsic motivation.

With a winning positive attitude, you retain more knowledge to apply later. All performers can learn when properly motivated from within their own personal need satisfaction system. As the leader help them create realistic and achievable goals to reinforce a positive reward system.

Thomas Edison stayed focused. He found 1119 ways to not build a battery before succeeding. Initial partial success provides a base line to demonstrate improvement and positive reward to condition your effort. To think negative is to learn to perform negatively. To think positive is to perform better than your own immediate past performance, and continually self-reward your own behaviors you have some control over.

You can achieve any realistic standard you perceive as valuable. As the leader or significant other in a relationship your goal is to teach setting low positive goals to improve and value each day. Success is valued more over time than a faster one-time improvement because it takes more time and effort.

Focus and do all the little details that count each day. Goal driven behaviors do not come from infrequent large incremental gains. Those goals offer less opportunity for reward-reinforcement. Although on occasion, your one lucky haphazard shot in a round of golf will reward you enough to want to play another round.

If your job, task, skill, or relationship is not improving, it is because your need is not stronger than other priorities in your life. You must be committed with a purpose to achieve any need or goal you value. Your intensity is reinforced by frequent success to stay on task and focused on each intermediate goal achievement.

You do not become rich or shed forty pounds of fat overnight. You invest small change that becomes dollars or balance your calorie intake with your expenditure through exercise to gain fitness over time. This strategy needs to become habit and to succeed change your thinking and priorities.

Keep it Positive

For every conversation you have with yourself or other performers always start with a positive note and see where the conversation leads you. If you start with a criticism, the performers you lead will naturally become defensive and shut down their brain. They will not accept any points you try to make. The relationship does not improve.

Everything has its price. As the coach or leader remind your team or a performer who has not achieved their potential, they are doing work few people are willing to do. This sets your performers apart and builds intrinsic value for the work each must sacrifice to accomplish every day.

Stress the positive improvements individual or the team is making. And be mindful of the mission. Value improving relationships with every performer. Get to know their needs and values. Help them become aware of those small improvements in practice and watch what happens. Positive attitudes start to emerge. Practices become viewed as enjoyable instead of a pain to be avoided.

My high school swim coach was an existentialist without knowing it. He kept expressing the positive attitude, "you gottawanna." If you did not want to work to improve, no one was going to gift you the race. You had to earn your reward.

You create the value and need to improve and want to reward success. Coach gave us logs to record our times from practices and meets. We became consciously aware of our immediate past performances. We learned a work ethic, a hallmark of top performers.

In study hall I plotted my split times as goals for upcoming races. Instead of reading books and studying, I mentally practiced my races and splits. That intrinsically motivated me more than coach extrinsically demanding performance. He created the need in me to want to improve.

Your personal mission is a powerful intrinsic motivator. Metaphorically, you climb a ladder one rung at a time. You can look at the top step, but it is more positive to focus and securely grasp the next immediate step. If you try to climb too fast or too many unrealistic steps at one time, you may fall to the bottom and must start all over. Haste makes waste.

If you make negative statements, stop yourself and think how to restate the negative into a positive. Increase an awareness for what you say and turn negatives into positives for better performance results.

Conditioned Approval

Performers who are conditioned to wait for the approval of others seldom become top performers. Top performers learn to develop personal feedback systems to self-reward and reinforce a work ethic that leads to continuously improve their performance.

To become a successful performer and develop your personal reward system use the low positive goal setting strategy to set goals only slightly better than your own immediate past performance or average. How many times do I need to emphasize this point?

You can choose to control what skill to learn and practice. Frequently achieving low positive goals conditions your personal reward system. This conditioned reward system gradually raises your personal standards for improving. You are inner directed, and no longer need to be directed what to do. You are on the path to become a top performer if you remain persistent.

Rewarding Loyalty

Sports teams provide insight into how leaders learn to manage performers in business, education, and organizations.

Professional sports teams scramble at the trading deadline to improve their teams. This hurts the morale of players who feel they are needed and counted on throughout the season. Older top performers are traded like horses put out to pasture, but who could guide younger players with wiser team chemistry. Management conditions the opposite of team play. Players are motivated to focus on their personal statistics to increase their value to win bigger contracts or fear they will be traded.

My doctoral study minor was in sport psychology. From 1989–1992 I wrote and published The Sport Psychology Advisor column in the Chicago-Milwaukee area newspapers. I observed sports teams and player interviews. In every case, I noted how championship seasons began in the exit meeting of the previous season. Those meetings came after painful losses. To avoid the pain, every player committed to working out harder than before with a stronger purpose and commitment in the off season.

I see sports teams and management as good and bad examples to apply to business, and educational systems. Owners, general managers, and coaches of successful teams build family relationships with all their performers. They demonstrate loyalty by caring about meeting the personal needs and values of their performers.

Injuries do occur and players know if they cannot perform risk being traded or released. Championships and loyal management are dependent upon unselfish team play. The manager gives all the performance credit to the performers doing the work.

Teams like businesses and school systems seldom become championship caliber with a faulty management system. The Chicago Cubs provide the best example of conflicted management over the past 75 years. It was not until a new proven general manager was hired and built a loyal team of top performing coaches and players to win the 2016 World Series after a 100-year hiatus.

In 2005, the Chicago White Sox traded no one and won the World Series. Players and coaches were loyal. They had team chemistry to trust and work together for a common goal and equally share in the rewards. Loyalty is a measure of trust.

As a company or team, you must align your mission with the personal needs and values of the people doing the work. Quint Studer, author of Hardwiring Excellence, 2003, writes about five pillars of excellence. He quickly points to classify working into three groups based on their personal needs and job satisfaction. Workers in the bottom third have their coats on one minute after the workday ends and complain their personal needs are not being met. They are least likely to become good to high quality performers.

This bottom group will detract company performance by recruiting other workers to join in their philosophy and yield poor performance outcomes. Performers who are not intrinsically motivated need to be identified and ferreted out of the system or change your system thinking to accept lesser performance.

The middle third can identify with and become more like the upper one-third of company performers. They are regarded by management to have personal intrinsic motivation to improve their performance and help reinforce the quality efforts of others.

When I was a school superintendent, we were required to have committees made up of one board member, department chair, and a teacher or staff member depending on the position to participate in the hiring process. After all the hiring interviews, the question I asked them to satisfy was, "What will this person do when we are not looking?"

If you hire intrinsically motivated performers and recognize their efforts, you improve the company by giving them the credit. You gain their loyalty and productivity with less management cost. If you choose to be a transformative leader be certain your managers understand and apply these Triad principles to their performance behaviors as well.

Increase Your Awareness of Incremental Performance Improvement

Formal evaluation systems attempt to define achievement but have similar pitfalls as extrinsic motives. These external systems are based on what someone else believes are the most important predictors of quality performance improvement. As a result, external evaluation systems provide a less reliable feedback system to reinforce positive behaviors in the performers doing the work.

Top companies, organizations, and school systems use the evaluation instrument to let performers rate their performance and then compare with the manager's evaluation to determine congruence. When both agree, the evaluation becomes a powerful feedback tool to reinforce learning and performance improvement.

Leaders in higher management positions must be aware of personality conflicts where a supervisor feels threatened by an astutely creative and intrinsically motivated employee. Harsh evaluations must be reviewed with caution. Evidence must be documented, and if reviewed give employees the right to be heard.

In this case, the evaluation and evaluator must be realistic, and the coaching or request for performance improvement must be achievable to enhance the intrinsic motives of the performer. Law allows employers to fire new employees in the first 90 days without cause.

After 90 days other employment laws take effect. Studies indicate employees leave jobs and positions because they feel underappreciated by their boss for their achievements and contributions. They are not leaving for more money. This places a drain on human resources to recruit and hire, and training programs to maintain levels of production.

Leaders must evaluate promotion practices. Dr. Lawrence Peter in 1969 published The Peter Principle. The Peter Principle occurs when people are promoted up the corporate or organization ladder based on past performance. Then lack the skill set to manage the new position.

In traditional training programs and schools objective scores below 60% of a total possible point total are usually assigned an "F" or failing achievement grade.

This kind of evaluation rarely lends itself to reinforcing new attempts or trials to experience more failure. Take the positive attitude this is not failure but a better start than absolute zero. What matters is whether you can demonstrate performance improvement to your brain.

Awareness of noticeable performance improvement self-reinforces probability for being successful on the next trial. Leaders and trainers need to instruct all performers to keep improvement probability high by setting low positive goals only slightly higher by one point than the immediate past performance.

Increase awareness to process or evaluate performance with smaller incremental and manageable steps. This creates a positive value system of self-reward to reinforce all performance behaviors. It does not matter where you start. It only matters where you end up that counts.

Failure is when you do nothing to help yourself learn and blame others for your poor performance. No one expects a beginner to know all the answers and perform like a professional. Your ability to learn comes from processing your personal feedback as opposed to letting others constantly tell you what is wrong with your performance. Managerial leaders who continually criticize performers who lack a good job description or performance evaluation system never aspire to improve and build self-confidence. They ultimately quit to avoid the pain.

Success Strategy

One team success strategy is to maximize your strengths, minimize your weaknesses, and get off to a good start. This is the objective game plan in winning athletics. You have weaknesses and strengths. You capitalize on the weaknesses of your opponent with your strengths while minimizing your weaknesses.

One weakness to easily correct is understanding your short and long term needs to project a plan of intermediate goals to reach an ultimate goal. In a culture of immediate gratification, fewer performers learn a successful strategy for planning to meet their long-term needs. This is universally happening in all affluent countries.

Older generations and top performers learn early in life the value of a work ethic to provide for personal rewards. Younger generations have been provided free material gains without benefit of a work ethic. There is an expectation society owes them. And they demand more and more free everything.

Whole societies have become literal oriented only for short term need satisfaction. And for some younger generations, if they do not experience immediate success they quit and try something else never learning useful skills to apply. The Triad teaches you how to acquire leadership skills to identify your needs and values to personally stay motivated and meet projected long-term needs.

Another success strategy is "do-overs." In life you get multiple chances to perform. Perhaps less than 5% of your life is spent in a one-time got-to-get-it-right or lose situation. Your one-time decision to merge your car into traffic must be correct to avoid a critical accident. You may not get a second chance if you are wrong.

You must be certain of your decision. You cannot learn to drive by going through the motions on "auto-pilot." Serious consequences including death can result. But for 95% of your life you get another chance to improve. You can afford to continuously plan for your success, take risks, be satisfied with personal rewards, and alter your plan until you achieve your desired level of success for your ability.

Increase Your Reward System with Winning

Failure or winning can become a conditioned cycle and habit. Both take similar energy, so choose skills and strategies for winning. Your needs, values, goals provide a mission and purpose. These are concepts you can control. Passion grows from frequent success reinforcing your feelings of pleasure to keep repeating.

Individuals or teams that consistently fail or perform below expectations have lost their purpose. They are not focused on a realistic identification of needs to fulfill. They may be a collection of quality performers with different belief systems and expectations who lack a common mission or expectation to unify their collective efforts.

You must walk before you can run. Success must be reinforced with small incremental steps by setting low positive goals you can frequently achieve. To break a losing cycle, you must take two steps back to learn where your stimulus-response (S-R) breakdown occurred before you can take three steps forward.

Go back to doing what made you successful to re-build your confidence. Top performers are willing to undertake this process to redefine their needs and values and be more realistic. Failure achieves little; success achieves everything.

Do not make attempts to punish or embarrass yourself to feel bad. Make attempts to fulfill a need and create a positive feeling about your performance. Frequent failure conditions avoidance behaviors. Your brain shuts down like turning your monitor off.

New attempts are harder to perform without a positive focus. No performer wants to feel worse about a projected negative probability to perform. The strategy to avoid failure will never help you to succeed. You must create the need to keep your motive to achieve success greater than your motive to avoid failure.

Avoidance behaviors create a negative focus and reinforces your failures. Student handbooks focus more on what not to do and the consequences than what to do. To perform better, feel good, and repeat behaviors, identify your needs, and create realistic low positive goals.

Self-evaluation Mastery

Children get their educational foundation in the elementary grades using best practice research. Rubrics to self-evaluate performance are being used more often. Mastery learning allows do over assignments to continually improve performance. Do over is a choice or put forth more effort to achieve higher quality on the first try. The long-term effect creates the need to value learning.

Adults get do-overs to get "it" right. Rubrics let you self-evaluate performance before you submit. Learning to self-evaluate rewards thinking behaviors to process achievement and be accountable. You gain mastery of leadership skills needed to improve performance in less time.

A paradigm shift to equate quality of effort with quality of reward is a powerful leadership lesson in intrinsic motivation. Once learned the three secret skills of The Triad are never forgotten. You have powerful learning skills to improve performance in less time for any job, task, skill, or relationships you choose.

The Adult Later Learner

Most adult teachers, trainers, managers, and performers do not understand how to teach intrinsic motivation. As the leader be aware of bias you think underestimates your performers. Teach basic skills in patterns and sequences to get familiar with tasks prior to performance. This is how the brain learns. Performance patterns will emerge.

This process improves personality patterns of confidence, self-esteem, security, and self-assurance. Early success reinforces learning. Top performers learn by trial and error. The benefit of good trainers and coaches is with their prior knowledge they shorten the learning curve. They teach specific strategies proven to predict faster longer lasting results. The Triad is based on the fundamentals of behaviorism and innate drives to improve the quality of your life.

Micromanaged Relationships

You cannot lead and approach performers with the idea you can prevent every mistake in the road. Or, expect performers to do tasks exactly as you would. Micromanagement removes the intrinsic motivation to improve to please and reward themselves—not management.

When I was a school administrator, we identified who micromanaged their children as helicopter parents. They would hover over their children to make decisions and even do their homework to get better grades to assure college entrance. Too often these students were seen walking the hometown streets mid-semester because they flunked out of school. Mom was not there to wake them up to go to class and do their laundry.

Years ago, I developed my personal philosophy of education. I wanted to teach people to learn how to think, act, and do for themselves and eventually others. I applied this same philosophy and the principles of The Triad raising my six children. They learned self-reliance and accountability for their behaviors. I am proud to say they all have successful careers and families.

As a leader you build a level of trust for your performers or your children to make good decisions. I only warned to not lose my trust. I never waited up on weekend nights to smell beer on their breath. I simply told them I am an old coach. I have ways of finding out your bad behaviors. If you lose my my trust, you will never see my car keys ever again. This was a powerful lesson my dad taught me. He reasoned I could shoot a rifle down the middle of a busy street and may harm one person. But in a car could kill five or six people at a time as he visually counted on his fingers to clarify the lesson.

My boys told me later I had given the drinking and driving lesson 101 perhaps a hundred times. Today its texting and driving. You can create realistic expectations leading to quality to build value in the learning process when you forewarn performers. Put the ball in their court. Teach an expectation to self-evaluate, improve performance, and hold yourself accountable.

You understand success setting proper goals, satisfying personal needs, and valuing a work ethic. Top performers know the underlying motives to satisfy their needs with a strong work ethic.

Positive Self-talk Increases Reward Value

Positive self-talk is another performance strategy. In sport psychology we call this "be your own best friend." Top performers make mistakes because they frequently try new and creative solutions to problems they encounter. They accept small failures as opportunities to learn. They take calculated risks and learn from their errors.

Prior to performing you want to get "psyched up." Sit anywhere but mentally go into your quiet place. Visualize your favorite place to contemplate. Tune out distractions and review past performance success. Talk to yourself to focus on specific elements you can perform. Increase awareness of small successes to stay focused on the positives. Then, let go and trust in your ability to perform.

Mobilization of Effort to Increase Reward Value

With each new attempt, you create a personal need to perform to the best of your ability. Top performers know when to mobilize all their energy and skills at will on demand. You cannot control how another person, competitor, or teammate will perform or complete tasks on the job. You can control what you purposefully decide to perform.

You can elect to work harder to identify and overcome your personal weaknesses by creating the need to perform a little better each week. This implies use of RROSR. You know how to recognize, receive, organize, store, and retrieve meaningful and relevant information you value in your learning process. You increase awareness of your immediate and past performance feedback to compare to a familiar standard.

The only difference between a top performer and an average performer is their ability to recognize when to raise their level of performance for a given moment in time. The top salesman knows when to shut up after making the close.

I watched the TV series, "The Last Dance" about the sixth and final NBA championship season of the Chicago Bulls and Michael Jordan. With a background in sport psychology, I followed Michael Jordan's career. Sheer will power is how I would identify perhaps the greatest basketball athlete in history.

Sportswriters tell us about his outstanding performances. I wanted to learn what inspired him. What created his intense intrinsic motivation to keep improving after he had proven his outstanding success?

The top athlete is single-minded to focus all their energy in pre-programmed sequences. They are the epitome of RROSR. The NBA pro rarely misses the second free throw with more concentration and use of the immediate feedback. Success is a learned and highly familiar sequence of psychological events to feel reward value. It cannot be achieved over night. You must connect the value of the work put in to feel a greater reward.

When you see great athletes break down and cry after winning a huge event, you must know they have worked exceptionally hard to achieve their goal. A great example was when Michael Jordan left the NBA after winning three championships to learn to play baseball starting in the minor leagues. After returning to the NBA it took him one and a half years to reacquire the high skilled mental focus to apply his physical skills at will on demand when the game was on the line.

18

LEADERSHIP LESSONS TO IMPROVE PERFORMANCE IN LESS TIME

In all cultures, millions of dollars are spent micromanaging the efforts of others. Rather than develop training programs to intrinsically motivate individual performance improvement for the long-term gain, it has been easier to use extrinsic means to motivate personnel for short term gains.

Performance improvement in less time is driven by needs, values, and goals. The company or organized system has a mission. The leaders create the vision. But the performers doing the work must have their personal needs, values, and goals satisfied to improve the overall performance.

False Assumptions of Management Leaders

One false assumption is that group needs are stronger than the needs of the performers doing the work. As a leader, you need to align your organization or company needs with the personal needs of the people doing the work. This is not an easy task to accomplish, but the dividends are huge.

Too many laws, rules and regulations are imposed on the masses because of the mistakes of a few stupid people. The assumption is all people cannot behave responsibly so everyone gets penalized. This is a subtle loss of freedom to control your quality of life and decide what risks to mitigate.

The powerful lessons in The Triad skills and strategies observed in top performers transform leaders to systematically improve performance. Increasing morale, confidence, and personal accountability rewards changes to the work performance framework. There is trust in others to do their job, performers are more self-reliant, empowered, and not as dependent upon the system. Performers are intrinsically motivated to consistently do their job and take pride in the work and contributions. This satisfies the needs of the performers and the company or organization.

Applied Leadership

It makes no sense to talk or think about a need you are not familiar with. Personal needs and goals are stronger motives than those set by others to satisfy their need for improvement.

Leaders who understand how to get every performer personally involved in the outcome consistently demonstrate performance improvement. Conversely, leaders who take credit for the efforts of others kill the motivation to improve performance.

The best application of leadership is to yourself. Focus on personal performance improvement. You cannot be critical of others if you cannot demonstrate your ability to do the same job, make good decisions, and manage your own life.

Leadership Training

Transformational leadership training is a skill to improve performance with intrinsic motivation. Our changing society and world have become increasingly dependent on external motives. The immediate reward and gratification of a few getting a promotion, bonus, paid vacation, or close parking space is limiting.

For a long time, the attitude for effective leadership was not to care about or be involved in the personal lives of workers. To be fair, managers need to separate their emotional feelings to maintain order and discipline in the organization.

Counter to this idea has been the emergence of successful companies who treat their workers like family. These companies and organizational systems have grown profitable by focusing on the individual needs of their workers to feel successful and personally rewarded to value their opinions. These needs range from a family friendly atmosphere providing day care for working mothers on the premises, relaxed dress codes, fitness centers, excellent in-house cafeterias, and trust to work from home.

It is essential leadership to help performers identify their personal needs and create a purpose to value performance improvement. Job descriptions need to be concise. Every performer is identified with a role in the growth and development of the group or organization. Performers become burned out, stale and underappreciated when they feel they are not accomplishing any goal or making progress to demonstrate personal performance improvement.

This kind of personal leadership to treat workers like family are companies like Southwest Airlines, Smuckers, and Wal-Mart. I am certain some readers will disagree. They routinely identify personal performance improvement. Profit sharing and worker owned companies create stakeholders in performance improvement. Their success formula is what P.T. Barnum used on each occasion to make, lose, and remake millions of dollars. Remember Barnum's three-point formula to motivate every individual was simply to:

#1 Dream the biggest dream,
#2 Market the living "hell" out of it, and
#3 Treat your workers like family.

Top Performers Are Everywhere

You may think a top performer is the iconic athlete or box office actor. In my view a top performer is anyone who excels above and beyond what is expected. This can be the volunteer in an organization, the best branch bank teller, auto mechanic, or elementary school custodian. You get the idea. It is a caring attitude to want to help others improve their skills. The feeling to satisfy the needs of others also makes them feel rewarded.

Natural Rules of Human Behavior

The natural drive to improve may be innate. It can also be reinforced connecting reward with success. There are several natural rules of behavior human animals can copy from wild animals. As a rule, the more you do for people, the less they learn to do for themselves. This is self-reliance.

Signs in wildlife parks; DO NOT FEED THE ANIMALS. You may forget you are a human animal. Necessity is the mother of invention. You do not increase motivation to be self-reliant housing, feeding, and clothing adult children. Tough love is fair warning of an expectation well in advance of the event.

Your children as performers may never learn to think by providing them with direct answers or decisions for them. You want to create the need to know and be curious to discover the answers to their questions. This attitude begins early in childhood.

In the animal world when it is time, birds are kicked out of the nest. Mother bears teach how to forage for food and not allow cubs back in the den. My dad told me he would never co-sign any loan. I warned all my children their freshman year they could not live with me after graduating from high school. They knew I was serious when I said they could not live in a tent in the backyard. They had to go off to college or a trade school or get a job and an apartment. They were 18 to buy their own car and insurance.

As for relationships our advice was to date a variety of personalities to match character qualities, needs, and values. Then go steady, meaning you are not dating others to build trust in the relationship. The sequence in order was to get engaged, married, and then have children. Can you see how The Triad improves performance in relationships and jobs, tasks, and skills?

Leaders are CEOs, managers, supervisors, directors, coaches, teachers, and parents—all models of behavior. You cannot get by with "do as I say and not as I do." To gain respect provide your performers with the tools to learn how to learn, to think, act, and do for themselves and eventually others as good citizens.

You should not hold your child's hand forever and be a "helicopter" parent hovering over your child. Your job is to teach your children and those you lead to be self-reliant so that they can identify and meet their own needs. There will be painful performances and disappointments until your performers increase their probability for success by setting low positive goals. Then the pain for lack of improvement is short lived.

Welfare systems do not work when free handouts are taken for granted and not valued. They do not motivate internal drive systems to provide for personal needs. Free handouts are unearned extrinsic motives. Instead, offer retraining programs.

As a rule, in human behavior those who accept unearned free things like money, and gifts for basic needs like education, food, clothing, and shelter will not respect the giver. The policy should be to provide tractors and plows and irrigation equipment and technology to help countries feed their people by putting them to work to keep their self-respect and dignity. A man earns his self-respect by working for his rewards from his own efforts.

After the Great Depression, our government created the WPA or Works Project Administration, and the CCC or Civilian Conservation Corps. These programs put able bodied men to work to earn a wage and do good work for the country. There are many lodges at state and national parks that were built by the CCC. Unlike welfare today, if you qualify, you do not have to work to earn your pride and dignity.

Welfare programs need to be modified to ween people off the dependency with offers to retrain skills. But the motivation to leave a welfare state is lost when those who are dependent on the financial reimbursement lose it all with any lower pay-ing job. A graduating scale could supplement wages on a new job and reduce the overall financial burden of the current system.

And why not? The government pays farmers to supplement NOT growing crops. Land is put in CRP or crop reserve program for a minimum of ten years. This controls the price of corn and soybeans to avoid over abundance to drop the bushel price.

Focus on Individual Versus Group Performance

There is a phrase, "You are only as strong as the weakest link in the chain." A leader's mistake is not teaching the weak team members The Triad—a personal motivation approach to improve their performance in less time. Top performers may set the example but does not motivate others to equal their performance.

The Toughest Goal to Improve a Company or Organization

Top performing leaders align the mission and their vision of the company or orga-nization with the personal needs, values, and goals of the people doing the work. View your performers as customers. The needs and values benefit improved per-formance in less time to gain loyal performers and happy customers.

If you do not want to believe that then imagine an unhappy worker talking to your customers.

Consumers buy products and services to work efficiently with better results. Salespersons like to market products or services they prefer to use themselves. Performers want to learn methods and cues to see better personal results for their time and energy.

Effective leaders identify the personal needs to benefit the customer and eval-uate the same personal needs to benefit every performer. This process aligns the needs of the customers, performers, and the organization as win-win-win. This is another powerful lesson in transformational leadership.

Leaders establish quality performance standards based on customer needs and values to motivate a buying decision. Then trust their performers to buy in doing the necessary quality work, and still meet their personal needs. Taking pride and being recognized by the boss to produce a quality product or service sometimes means more than the extrinsic paycheck. This happens when you align the needs of the performers for an enjoyable low stress environment with the performance needs of the organization.

If you want intrinsically motivated performers who improve their performance and have realistic and stable needs, then do not micromanage them. When you control a top performer's thinking you lose their creativity and intrinsic motivation to improve. Perception is in the eye of the beholder. It is not what you think about a performer's performance, but what they learn to think or value about their work motivated by their drive to satisfy personal needs.

Top performers are naturally motivated to improve. They become consciously aware of their improvements. Stress comes from being told all their lives to set high goals to be a high achiever. Those goals are not frequently attained to condition the work ethic to get them. In reality, top performers focus on smaller intermediate goals to frequently attain and stay motivated.

A hallmark of top performers is their work ethic. They have a positive attitude and when they set low positive goals only slightly better than their own immediate past performance they feel more in control. They value performance improvement and connect reward to reinforce feeling successful more often. They increase their probability and frequency of success.

Effective leaders create a positive work environment so more people can see the immediate results of their efforts and achievements to enjoy doing the work. The work success satisfies personal needs. Performers are valued workers in the system. When leaders care about their performers, the performers care to share ideas for how to be efficient or lighten up the place without fear of retribution.

Factories and offices do not have to be boring. In a work environment, performers prefer to have some say in how to meet their personal needs. They take ownership and accountability to do the work, produce quality, and feel rewarded to reinforce more of the same quality work ethic behavior.

As the leader continually model a work ethic and sincere caring to enhance the personal needs of your workers if you expect them to learn new skills to improve their performance. Simply, if you want the performers to care about the organization, the leaders must care about the performers who do the work and their role in the organization.

Imagine your managers leading by example leaving work early each week for a golf game. Or to go Christmas shopping, or leave early on a Friday for a weekend. Do your performers have those same needs to respect their leader? As a parent, do you attend lessons and competitions you have signed your children up for?

If you do not create the need to learn and improve performance quality through awareness of self-evaluation and reward-reinforcement, you cannot expect to achieve consistent quality results from the performers doing the work. Disruptive climates occur because performers feel their needs are not being met, or they cannot envision the quality product or service they help to achieve. Or, if they feel the boss could care less?

Morale drops when performers do not connect reward in meeting their personal needs often enough to reinforce their motivation to repeat the work to benefit the company and themselves. Instead, they achieve the "why bother syndrome." When management questions performances, it is because they have not identified the personal needs of the workers to provide them with a purpose or vision for doing the work. Or, the manager has not set a good example.

This also applies to good parenting skills. One of those needs is a natural drive to belong to something bigger than ourselves. Family relationships to impart needs and values plays a critical role. Single parents have a tough role being both parents while maintaining the finances of the home. This can be both spiritual and an organizational blunder for not explaining how each performer has an important team role to play in the quality of the finished product. There must be realistic conversations about the realities of living in the current environment and circumstances, so they become a shared responsibility.

The most common mistake leaders make is applying generic group needs—a mission statement, vision, values, beliefs, and then indoctrinating every member into believing these general ideals must be their personal mission, too. This is a meaningless extrinsic practice. Although common goals are essential to team development and performance, to be truly effective, leaders must be more aware of what drives human behavior and motivates every performer. Then develop a mission to help meet the personal needs and goals of the people doing the work.

The Value of The Triad's 3 Secret Skills
Awareness, Evaluation, Reward-Reinforcement

The primary Application is to the "Big Four" jobs, tasks, skills, relationships. Assumption—increasing awareness of meaningful and relevant knowledge transforms attitudes and beliefs to improve performance. The clockwise circular flow of the following figure **7 Steps to The Triad Performance Improvement System** is a visual summary to effect performance improvement for yourself and those you lead.

Strategies for Applying The Triad

1. Use the needs and abilities assessment survey in the Appendix to identify, rate, and prioritize your needs and abilities.
2. Identify and prioritize your top three tasks either on the job, at home, in a relationship, or learning to improve a physical skill.
3. In a sentence or two define your purpose for performing each skill named and include a personal need and goal to achieve.

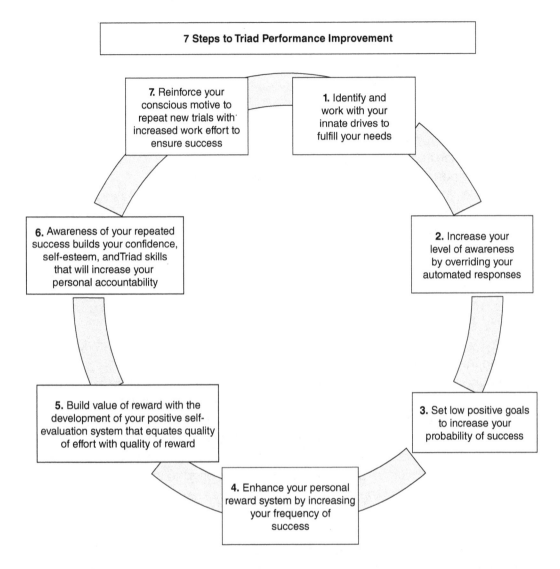

7 Steps to Triad Performance Improvement

7. Reinforce your conscious motive to repeat new trials with increased work effort to ensure success

1. Identify and work with your innate drives to fulfill your needs

6. Awareness of your repeated success builds your confidence, self-esteem, and Triad skills that will increase your personal accountability

2. Increase your level of awareness by overriding your automated responses

5. Build value of reward with the development of your positive self-evaluation system that equates quality of effort with quality of reward

3. Set low positive goals to increase your probability of success

4. Enhance your personal reward system by increasing your frequency of success

4. Identify what you value most about the activities you perform using the skills named.

5. Identify three to five strategies you will use to improve your skills performing each of the prioritized tasks named above. (Create a simple outline format.)

6. Write each strategy as an objective beginning with the words, "I will be able to (place the adverb to describe the specific strategy here)" … followed by a short description of the skilled performance. For example, I will be able to (type) 60 words per minute with no errors after two weeks of practice.

7. After you take an assessment to objectify performing each named skill to establish a baseline performance, also known as your immediate past performance, write a realistic lowest positive goal you can make for each skill.

8. List five personality characteristics used to identify several top performers in each of the tasks you have named above.

9. List five personality characteristics to describe yourself.
10. Compare and contrast your personality characteristics to the top performers in each identified task.
11. Describe how you will try to change your personality to be more like successful performers. Limit your response to two to three sentences, and record in your task performance journal.
12. Describe how you plan to create objective data to demonstrate learning and performance improvement using feedback taken from your immediate and past personal performances. (Keep a task performance journal).
13. For tasks you have previously stated, list five strategies to increase your awareness to improve your performance skills.
14. Using the tasks previously stated, list five strategies to enhance your self-evaluation for performing those skilled tasks.
15. Using the previously stated tasks, list the primary reward you will be consciously aware of to reinforce your motivation to continually improve that skill.
16. Describe the objective and goal you have met, and your conscious awareness of the steps you used to accomplish them in your performances.
17. State a new goal for each task when you accomplished your previous goal using the goal setting strategy suggested in chapter four, Goals.
18. Rate the value for achieving each goal by assigning a percentage of perceived reward divided by perceived effort to derive a positive index between 1.0–1.5. Consult the Value Activity Index in chapter 3, Values.
19. Self-evaluate the performance value index for each goal accomplished to determine its reinforcement value and suggest a need to change how you will set a new goal, stay focused, and increase your work effort to insure your success.
20. Keep a workout log to journal your daily activities and specific cues to focus on recognizing with selective attention to enhance your response.

The following **Triad Performance Improvement System Flow Chart** is a visual schematic diagram for learning intrinsic motivation as a leadership skill.

The value of RROSR—recognize, receive, organize, store, retrieve information

Use the RROSR strategy to …

- identify a specific task and list the top two or three cues you want to immediately recognize
- list two primary ways you prefer to receive performance feedback (visual, verbal, or kinesthetic)
- describe how you plan to organize the new information …
  - comparison to immediate past performance or average

The Triad Performance Improvement System Flow Chart

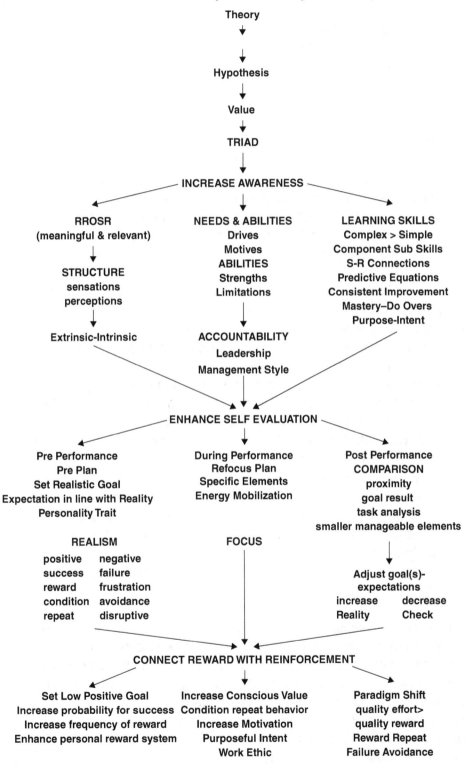

Theory

↓

Hypothesis

↓

Value

↓

TRIAD

↓

INCREASE AWARENESS

RROSR
(meaningful & relevant)

↓

STRUCTURE
sensations
perceptions

↓

Extrinsic-Intrinsic

NEEDS & ABILITIES
Drives
Motives
ABILITIES
Strengths
Limitations

↓

ACCOUNTABILITY
Leadership
Management Style

LEARNING SKILLS
Complex > Simple
Component Sub Skills
S-R Connections
Predictive Equations
Consistent Improvement
Mastery–Do Overs
Purpose-Intent

ENHANCE SELF EVALUATION

Pre Performance
Pre Plan
Set Realistic Goal
Expectation in line with Reality
Personality Trait

During Performance
Refocus Plan
Specific Elements
Energy Mobilization

Post Performance
COMPARISON
proximity
goal result
task analysis
smaller manageable elements

REALISM

positive	negative
success	failure
reward	frustration
condition	avoidance
repeat	disruptive

FOCUS

Adjust goal(s)-
expectations

increase	decrease
Reality	Check

CONNECT REWARD WITH REINFORCEMENT

Set Low Positive Goal
Increase probability for success
Increase frequency of reward
Enhance personal reward system

Increase Conscious Value
Condition repeat behavior
Increase Motivation
Purposeful Intent
Work Ethic

Paradigm Shift
quality effort>
quality reward
Reward Repeat
Failure Avoidance

- visual bit maps of the whole performance using visualization technique having observed yourself on tape or a top performer from in front or behind as having a "third eye"
- verbal breakdown of the complex skill into specific S-R sequence using perceptual cues to selectively focus on immediately prior to performing, during performance, and in a post-performance evaluation
- kinesthetically to increase awareness for fine motor skills during the warm-up activity to suggest a positive feeling anticipating success and performing with confidence
- creating a complete positive continuously improved subroutine movie to execute on autopilot during the performance after frequent mental rehearsal trials using visualization techniques prior to performing
- describe the value of each learned subroutine to select whether you want to store for immediate short-term use or archive for long-term use later by associating and scaffolding new performance knowledge to prior knowledge and understanding described in task familiarity
- use the activity value index to store information for immediate short term or long-term, and list key multi-sensory associations to readily retrieve stored information at will on demand ...
  - create new visualizations with other senses to make the experience as realistic as possible
  - recall from storing your successful performances how your warm up felt, pre-performance routine, kinesthetic feelings from your muscles, auditory sounds like crowd noise or energizing music like the theme from 'Rocky', what you tasted in pre performance meals, and pre performance visualization and mental practice routines
  - recall the primary trigger or cue to start the performance sequence
  - recall and reflect previously created and stored performance predictions and projections to determine congruence between the goal and actual performance to increase realism essential for consistent top performance and building confidence
  - realism increases positive reinforcement value and raises personal expectation for success

Top performing salespersons visualize and rehearse important sales pitch features and benefits, incentives and close prior to getting in front of the customer. They are confident with less stress by getting familiar with the process beforehand. For sports practice with a recording of the background crowd noise and imagine the game to be on the line with the clock running down.

You cannot possibly practice all kinds of actual game experiences so use visualization techniques to make the practice experience seem real. You control the emotional stress and learn cues to efficiently respond with earlier recognition awareness skills and get familiar with the task. The more familiar you are with a task, you increase your awareness of new cues, focus on positive goals, objectives, and outcomes to create MaS>MaF.

Qualities of Top Performing Leaders

Some so-called experts believe some performers are born leaders. Leadership may be observed early in few individuals. In my view, leadership takes time to develop the philosophy, personality, experience, and accountability to lead oneself or followers. They make tough and sometimes unpopular decisions to be a lonely job. Outstanding leaders are usually top performers in jobs, tasks, skills, and relationships.

What concerns me are those who judge others with little or no leadership experience to know the job, scrutiny, and stress. Their evaluations are based on emotion instead of proven results to compare to past performances of others. I may not like a leader but I respect their results.

Good leaders and top performers seldom wait for the approval of others. They are guided by a strong philosophy to serve the best interests of the people. They pay less attention to critics and form a vision to accomplish the mission of the company or organization.

Quality leaders guide large groups of performers and decision influencers. Good leaders acquire and display the same performance skills before trying to lead others. They are comfortable, natural, and confident in their abilities to communicate a clear message. They are forthright. Their experiences make them familiar with the needs and results to predict positive actions.

I moved into leadership roles as director of aquatics, head swim coach, company owner, and school superintendent. My father's advice was, "Be yourself. If you talk up or talk down to people, either way they'll know the difference." From my experience, I put everything in writing so I would not be misquoted or misunderstood. You can correct your words in print, but not if misspoken. Clear communication skills are hallmarks of strong leaders.

Leadership Philosophy

Philosophy is a study in the truth. Idealism, pragmatism, existentialism are the main areas. The idealist leader speaks in promises of their vision for future performance outcomes. The pragmatist leader offers a vision to finance proposals for change. The existentialist leader envisions the individual existence and free will to assume responsibility for performance and accountability.

My high school swim coach was an existentialist without knowing it. The day before competition he posted our line-up and would not change. He did his job all week and as individuals learned free will accountability to do ours. He sat in the stands with parents and an assistant coach took splits on the deck.

I liked the Philosophy of Education course I took in my Master of Science degree. Mid-semester the professor used the whole period for us to write our personal philosophy of education. Other education majors with BS degrees and a few years of teaching experience wrote pages. I wrote a couple paragraphs of some thoughts and condensed to one sentence that has since guided my career with an existentialist philosophy. "To teach how to learn, to think, act, and do for yourself and eventually others."

I knew true needs, values, and goals to be meaningful and relevant must come from within the performer. My extrinsic words meant little by comparison. My leadership role was to create independence and self-reliance. I never wanted my children to be dependent on me or anyone. They were expected to educate themselves and hold themselves accountable for their behaviors.

All good leaders have a foundation in philosophy. It is the inner compass to guide their words and actions. They are good listeners to gather knowledge from a variety of credible sources and then make decisions. Weak leaders prefer management by committee. They blame poor decisions on the committee and no one person is held accountable.

If you need to be a strong quality leader you must identify and refine your philosophy to live by and guide all your decisions for the benefit of all performers. This takes focused effort to increase awareness of past experiences proven to get results with all performers. Your philosophy is your guide to sound character and integrity qualities of leaders. A philosophy provides a set of intrinsic standards to excel and persevere in a passion when critics may disapprove of a single performance.

Good leaders are human to make mistakes and grow from the experience. Reflect on the body of your work. How is your philosophy guiding you to improve? You cannot be a copy of someone else.

Dr. Wayne Dyer (2004) in his book The Power of Intention suggests you only regret things you did not try to accomplish. It is not your failures, but your awareness and ability to act with a purpose will define your life's work as a leader.

Leadership Personality Traits

Would you or could you change your personality to be a more effective leader or performer? Personality is composed of traits and patterns. Your traits are mostly formed before age three. Patterns continually evolve from traits with experience. You may be trait insecure and untrusting. But as you become more familiar with a task or socialized with people who are family, friends, or co-workers you may display patterns of trust and security.

To be an effective leader is more than your brand or image. You must know your personality make up to understand the kinds of personalities you want to lead or marry. It may not be wise to marry or lead until your pre-frontal cortex is fully developed around age 23–25. Early marriages and relationships do not have a good track record.

Observe the inner workings of top performing leaders of political parties, government agencies, companies and organizations, and professional sports teams. Chemistry among the performer's personalities co-exist with the leaders including the managers.

Understand the personality requirements of the leadership positions before you hire or promote. Are the personality patterns inherent in the top performers similar for the promotion to be effective? Hiring a staid and rule bound leader may not work for a gregarious self-directed staff. Secure leaders are familiar with performing the tasks they lead others to learn and improve. They build confidence and trust in their leadership.

Top performing leaders know and accept their purpose to lead and communicate positive strategies to predict success. They accept suggestions from subordinates as positive feedback to improve their leadership skills. Insecure leaders are bosses who are not familiar with the performance tasks. They surround themselves with buffer agents who are rewarded to protect their egos from the critical scrutiny of subordinates.

Insecure leaders are intimidating and controlling personalities and create more stress and less creativity within the company or organization. These leaders or managers are less likely to alter their personality traits and may need to be removed from authority positions.

It is essential leaders in the human resource department eliminate this problem in the hiring process. Hire secure leaders who understand personality psychology to build teams of intrinsically motivated performers. My experience is HR Directors evaluate candidates based on textbook resources with little or no experience with the positions they are tasked to hire. Quality applicants are missed. Performance improves when all performers subscribe to a common company philosophy, needs, values, and mission as their own.

This saves company dollars eliminating costly middle management conflicts and salaries, decreases employee turnover, and personnel costs to advertise, interview, hire, induct, train, and mentor new people. Top performing leaders improve the company profit and personal welfare of the performers doing the work.

Top performing leaders with secure personalities empower creative performers. Intrinsically motivated performers do more to improve according to their preferred style for learning. Boss leaders who perceive defiance of their "my way or the highway" authority maintain their control. They use demotions, and poor evaluations to cover their inadequate performance from subordinate critics. This practice ruins intrinsic motivation and performance.

When used, this coercive discipline consistently holds back a company's growth potential. Leaders of successful companies hire likable leaders who permeate the entire organization with a positive vision. Companies lead by unchallenged insecure egos the growth is retarded, and morale is low. They are top heavy in "yes men" managers to protect the boss, and there is higher than average worker turnover to seriously hurt company production and profit margins.

Specific Experience

Top performing leaders delegate responsibilities, authority, and accountability especially in larger companies and organizations. To delegate they are good at identifying talent to lead and manage. This takes experience and knowledge of the specific duties and responsibilities for each hired position.

Younger performers question how to get experience when positions require experience. My answer is the same. While learning specific skills in school find internships and volunteer for organizations to put on your resume. Then be willing to start at the bottom being mentored by a top performer. There are numerous captains of industry who started in the mail room to learn the business from the ground floor up.

Identifying talent and hiring performers too often falls out of the leadership role. The directors of human resource or marketing may hire talent in a resume with results but lack the personality of the company or organization. From my business experiences outside of education I questioned the human personality and behavioral and product knowledge of these directors.

When I was in medical sales as a distributor rep and regional manager the marketing team put together new product slicks for representatives in the field to impress our customers. The slick looked great, but the content focused on the product features and not the customer benefits. It appeared they had no knowledge of sales training.

Human resource directors hire sales representatives without vetting to learn why they really left their last position. Did they have integrity being honest with customers to build relationships? Or, were they ruthless to gain the sales commission and screw the customer? What does their social media look like? How professional is their voice mail message? You can tell a lot about a person by the friends they keep.

With some experience in sport psychology I enjoy analyzing the performers and leaders of professional sports teams. Studies of college coaches and their student athletes and programs have similar personalities. Observe athletes and coaches of championship teams at the end of grueling seasons. There is a togetherness and trust between the owners, management, coaches, and athletes. They are a family willing to make personal sacrifices for the group benefit they can enjoy. The owners and management give all the credit to the coaches and players. Those personalities work together for a common mission.

Leadership needs and values analysis must come from experience on the job and not out of a textbook. Leaders who start at the bottom communicate and often socialize with a variety of performers on the job. They learn about families and the personal needs and values of those performers. Are they happy? If not, why not? What do they like? What don't they like?

Those same questions can be asked of customers marketing and selling a product. Those kinds of questions come from personalities with experience who care about helping the customer benefit from their product or service.

As the leader or manager what you think of a performer's performance matters more when your performer has learned to think, evaluate, and value their performance quality and effort to build accountability. This process varies from performer to performer based on the value system they bring to the organization or you can teach them.

To create intrinsically motivated people, periodically do the needs analysis to align the needs of your organization with the personal needs of your performers. Leaders need to value and respect the opinion of every performer to improve their accountability and intrinsic motivation. You build value with trust.

Empowering performers to write their own job description and do that job in a creative way according to their personalities will put them on the same page and produce expected outcomes. An intrinsically motivated performer with the ability creates the need to improve. The leader needs to provide performers with the training and tools to do the job. The organization creates the need in the outcome value of the quality product.

Cognitive Leadership—Understanding Needs of Customers and Employees

Good leaders are made not born. Using their cognitive thinking skills, leaders quickly learn to assign relative value to all incoming information. They use past experiences to compare with projected results to determine value. Some call this gut instinct. Cognitive implies a purposeful thought process brought to a conscious level.

Good leaders are highly observant. They continuously sample new information compared to what they know from their experience. They observe trends and project a vision to guide planned events. They evaluate competitor's products and services and customer needs.

Top performing leaders self-evaluate their performance and hold themselves accountable for their application of knowledge to succeed. A cognitive leader "sees" the big picture to have vision based on successful performance.

Skilled leaders define the mission with a purpose. They are respected by top performers in the company or organization. Careful consultations and planning go into every decision. When leaders act unconsciously without thoughtful purpose to plan, performance is impulsive and inconsistent.

What protects us human animals is cognitive thinking. There are built-in innate flight or fight survival skills leaders learn to override. The greatest of those skills is projection. Focus on success but have contingent disaster plans.

Our bodies are biological organisms designed to self-regulate processing simple or mundane tasks. This decreases the need and value for performing simple tasks and skills. Leaders must be aware how this affects their performers during production resulting in serious injury or poor performance.

Intrinsic Motivation Meta-Cognition Flow Chart

Meta-cognition is your ability to construct personal knowledge and gain experience on the job or in school. Nothing can replace first-hand experience to get familiar with new tasks. The value of coaches, mentors, and trainers is how they create the need to be lifelong learners. They provide age-appropriate meaningful and relevant methods and strategies compared to prior knowledge. They can also shorten your learning curve.

Top performing leaders demonstrate sincere caring for their performers and their personal performance improvement. The performers feel the caring and are intrinsically motivated to produce outstanding quality production or service.

The flow chart below shows how to increase cognitive awareness for learning. Body nerves transmit and store information, and the mind-body connection transforms sensations and lower levels of primate thinking into higher level perceptions and predictions for personal accountability.

Intrinsic Motivation Meta-Cognitive Flow Chart

Structure		Awareness		Learning	
Central Nervous System		**Sensations**	**Perceptions**	**Learning Models**	**Natural Drives**
Brain	Body	Unconscious	Conscious	Mastery Do Overs	Improve
Frontal Lobe	Synapse	Stimulus S	Response R	Input-Output	Meaningful, Relevant
Pre-Frontal	Association	Conditioned SCR	Response	Transfer Identical Elements	Motives Motivation
Cortex (PFC)	Neurons	Paired-Associate	Conditioning	Feedback	Long-Term Memory
Short-Term Memory	Reflexive	Information Processing	RROSR	Identify Needs	Identify Abilities
Micro-processor	Fight-Flight	Sensory Satiation	Task Familiarity	Planer Thinking	Practice Repetition
Fine Motor	Gross Motor	Selective Attention	Cue Recognition	Sequence	Pattern
Kinesthetic	Receptors	Stimulus Generalization	Response Generalization	Serial Loops	Chaining
Personality		Feeling	Reward	Open-Closed	Backward-Forward
Traits	Patterns	Intent	Purpose	Complex Tasks	Subroutines
Types	PAP	Immediate Past Performance	Past Performance Average	Visualization	Mental Rehearsal
Group	Group Performance	+/– Goal Shift	Low + Goal	Paradigm Shift	Quality Effort-Reward
Verbal	Verbal Statements	Extrinsic	Intrinsic	Leadership	Top Performance
Self	Past Performance	Effort	Reward	Desire to Repeat	Work Ethic
Realism	Top Performers	Increase Probability of Success	Increase Probability of Reward	Reward	Reinforcement

Leadership and Personal Accountability

Leaders start learning personal accountability in the home. My father was "old school." The contract was your word and a handshake. Say what you mean and mean what you say. Choose your words carefully. However, as a superintendent leading a school district, I put my vision and comments in writing to not be misunderstood or misquoted. I found putting my thoughts and words on paper for others to read saved discussion time in board meetings.

The primary job of leaders is understanding their purpose. Purpose is every performer's job and the guiding light to personal behavior and accountability. As a leader setting up job descriptions and holding performers accountable is not nearly as effective as when every performer holds themselves accountable.

Performers who blame others for poor performance is a clue. As a leader you need to clarify every performer's role in the company, organization, or team to provide a personal purpose. Describe personal performance feedback methods using immediate past performance to self-evaluate improvement.

Who Are the Leaders and What Are The Accountability Measures?

Leaders are administrators, directors, managers, supervisors, commanders, professors, teachers, coaches, captains, students, parents, civic volunteers, and organizers of all kinds. Each leader must identify common needs to create a uniform purpose in their performers. And their personal needs cannot supersede the group's or performer's needs. Performers is used interchangeably with workers.

Have you experienced a manager who pounded and berated you? Did you believe they only cared about showing improvement in their division to impress their boss? It was not about your needs and values. Unfortunately, this kind of management rules when performers are not viewed as partners.

If you want your performers to be partners and accountable for positive outcomes, help them identify their short and long-term needs. We are in an age of immediate gratification and a literal functioning society. I am hungry, feed me. I expect everything I want to be free. There is less emphasis on behavioral accountability and more emphasis on "big brother" micromanagement.

The problem this creates is young inexperienced performers do not know how to perform basic process skills to motivate performance improvement. They were not taught personal accountability and values in the home. Performers are motivated best by guiding intrinsic motives to satisfy personal needs or goals with a specific purpose. This must be more than a paycheck.

As a rule, you cannot build accountability in a micromanagement system. If your intent is to control the behaviors of your performers, you must assume they will blame you the leader and not be accountable for their poor performance behaviors. "I did what you told me to do!"

Most performers are conditioned to follow directions and take orders. Extrinsically managed performers do not take ownership for their behaviors or performance outcomes. They blame management for their poor performance. They resist being empowered and held accountable for their decisions and performances. Leaders can create all the necessary rules and consequences. Your performers will still misbehave because of your extrinsic management controls.

To build accountability your performers must perceive intrinsic value to their performance outcomes to hold themselves accountable. Management must balance the alignment of extrinsic management motives with the personal intrinsic motives of the performers. Natural human behavior is to challenge and defy the odds to achieve what others say you cannot perform. The other is to root for the underdog. Despite big challenges, it is always better to set low positive achievable goals to exceed and feel rewarded. Those performances get repeated.

Leaders who make tough decisions citing rules and regulations may seem convenient and speedy. But better to engage conversation in personal performance accountability to meet the needs of the workers.

Set low positive performance standards and let the performers comply with their personal skills. Show them how to feel rewarded from improving personal performance feedback to measure their output. If the output is not up to standard change the input cues or goals to recognize before the performance.

Weak leaders who do not know how to motivate their performers create more coercive rules to instill conformity. This may control the masses but destroys creativity in the intrinsically motivated future top performers.

Unskilled teachers teach to the lower end of the performance spectrum. And the *system* produces a wealth of underachievers. Weak governments seek to control the masses because they do not trust people to make decisions for their own welfare. It is easier to provide more dependent social programs.

A leader must balance hope with facts. Hindsight is 20/20 and easy for critics with poor knowledge of the facts and leadership experience. This creates more fear and worsens the problem to get personal accountability.

Poorly trained managers feel threatened by top performers to find more faults than positives to reward producing stagnation and malcontent. Corporations and trainers are trapped in the middle. They are top heavy in management spending billions to increase work output in unmotivated performers.

Neither rewarding irresponsible behavior or modeling responsible behavior improves personal accountability. As a rule, the more you do for people, the less they will learn to do for themselves. When organizations and systems need to use rules and conditions to coerce and qualify performance behaviors, their micromanagement costs increase. This hurts profitability and performer confidence.

A behavioral leadership rule is do not make unenforceable rules or laws to regulate extrinsic accountability. Top performers will disregard them in favor of their personal accountability rules.

More rules lower morale and change the focus as the performers feel less in control over their work environment and hold themselves less accountable. Student performers and handbooks focus more on negative what not to do instead of the positive effects of learning.

Change Your Leadership From BS to RS

You have the natural ability to sense more than you think, and so does your customer. To paraphrase Abraham Lincoln, "You can fool some of the people some of the time, but you can't fool all of the people all of the time." In business, you fake it until you make it.

BS can mean bull—, or a Bachelor of Science degree. Or, be the abbreviation for bright stuff and back stabber. Who are you kidding when you lie to a customer? You are the customer when you do not hold yourself accountable for your performance. Why are you not improving? What is your problem? What do you need to succeed?

Quit blaming others and making excuses for your inability to do more to ensure your success. Any average IQ performer can condition a sequence to improve any job, task, skill, or relationship. Simply set low positive goals only one point higher than your immediate past performance or average.

RS is the right stuff. It is what astronauts and top performers are made of in their field. As a leader, how do you find and determine top performers who demonstrate a forward vision to improve? It is no one who has all their needs provided by others. Look for performers who have a work ethic and give them the chance to keep improving.

Objectively compare past performance results and observe performance improvement. Use visual graphs or charts to plot improvement over time to predict future growth, expansion, and leadership opportunity. Subjectively observe each performer's unique behavior by what motivates them. Is it money, promotions, more responsibility, recognition from superiors or respected colleagues? Or is it job satisfaction meeting personal goals, personality patterns of stability, realism, persistence, and will power?

The answer determines whether leaders must hire more management. Better to hire right than micromanage performers to extrinsically motivate them with greater rewards.

Meaningful and Relevant Knowledge Value to Improve Leadership Training

What do you really need to learn? The answer lies in the application of knowledge to improve performance for any job, task, skill, or relationship. According to W. Edwards Deming who helped rebuild Japan after World War II, knowledge is king.

Knowledge retention improves with intrinsic motivation methods. Simply teaching a performer anything important is still regarded as extrinsic. However, a skillful teacher instructs with age appropriate applied examples to create an intrinsic meaningful and relevant relationship. Performers perceive the value and retain the new information as knowledge.

Companies and organizational systems have missions. The leader imposes an appropriate vision with challenging performance achievement goals. Managers, coaches, supervisors, mentors, parents, and teachers must instruct with methods and cues for performers and students to accommodate and assimilate to retain the new information.

Personal needs factor in. Leaders create a vision and need for performers to follow the mission. References are "buy-in" or in slang "a dog in the hunt." If you do not ask questions, you are barking up the wrong tree. The simple method is to ask questions so learners must discover the why. The answer creates the meaningful and relevant value in the mind of the learner.

RROSR Methods and Cues Basic to Integrating Education and Training Systems

For your review, RROSR is the anachronym for recognition, receive, organize, store, and retrieve essential cues for learning and performing skills. This strategy was described in chapter one.

Top performers store the most meaningful and relevant skills performance information directly on their brain's desktop. They retrieve and respond faster with only one iteration to access the stored data. This one fact is what I have observed separates top performers from average unprepared performers with little training.

This fact means training programs are only as good as the knowledge and experience of the instructors to identify the most meaningful and relevant methods and cues. Top performing company salespersons do not want to sacrifice their incomes and lifestyle to be stuck in the home office. Public-school systems have tenure rules, salary schedules, and labor-relations laws making removal of poor instructors or rewarding top performing teachers nearly impossible.

Knowledge of Physical and Mental Skills Essential for Improving Performance

W. Edwards Deming stated knowledge is king. Every performance has a beginning, middle, and end. A result is observed as a criterion. Performances are broken down into smaller parts called subroutines. Each part is learned independently and then in a proper sequence chained together to perform.

Those parts are variables. Leaders such as mentors and coaches and teachers must define what variables are most significant to spend time teaching and learning. This forms a multiple regression equation to predict favorable results.

Top performers are observed. Astute coaches pick out the mental and physical skills they perform with regularity getting good results. Education and training systems instructors can ask top performing players and teachers to learn best practices. Then brainstorm a list of maybe ten variables.

From subjective observations and questioning top performers you may learn out of those ten variables three of them account for the most predictive success or variance. You can never account for 100% of the variance because of the variable interaction effects. If three variables account for 50% and the other seven account for only another 20% where would you want to focus your time?

Bottom line. Ask your top performers what mental and physical skills they spend their time. Then tailor make your education and training systems to focus on teaching and learning those skills.

Turtle and Rabbit—a Fable to Teach Goal Setting and Persistence

School leaders challenge whether you can teach young children how to set low positive goals and The Triad leadership skills. I talked to children kindergarten through grade three as a K-12 school superintendent in a rural farm district. I would start by telling the Aesop fable of the Tortoise and the Hare.

Of course, some pupils had never heard the fable, so I referred to the characters as the turtle and rabbit guy in a challenging race. I asked, "Who won the race?" Children know turtles are slow and rabbits are fast. They provide a variety of answers, but pupils who had not heard the fable guess wrong.

Then I focus their thinking why the turtle guy won. The turtle focused on the finish line goal with each small step. The rabbit was overconfident and took a nap procrastinating he could easily finish to beat the slow turtle. Like the symbolic race, learning happens by focusing on each small step with the goal to be educated.

The goal is life-long learning to help yourself be successful. You never learn everything there is to know. Skills are produced slowly over time. You cannot perfect the three interrelated skills in The Triad, but you can apply them for the rest of your life. The Triad skills help define your purpose and are based on motivational principles in behavioral psychology.

As a skill you do not make one free throw and believe you will be the next Michael Jordan. Your Triad performance and leadership skills develop as you learn to apply the principles to improve your performance for the rest of your life. Top performers are remembered for achieving their success over time. Their frequent success conditions a will to win.

Parents as leaders can share the excitement and consistent performance of their children and not offer judgment to create a faulty extrinsic reward connection. Performers with intrinsic motives are aware of their immediate past performance to slightly improve with focused practice. They make that their personal standard to improve.

Sports Business

I have frequently used sports and athletes as examples of leadership and top performers. They provide a laboratory like setting to observe the kinds of dynamics of improved performance in less time.

As I have been editing this manuscript a sports channel began a ten-part mini-series documentary, "The Last Dance." It is about the Chicago Bulls NBA team's run of six championships and the iconic effect, Michael Jordan had on the team and other players.

Watching the mini-series reinforced my views about top performers as leaders. Several points stood out. One is top performers set their own personal standards. In groups or on teams they lead by placing emphasis on mental toughness and continuous self-improvement of every member.

Like Michael Jordan, top performers speak out when they do not see the same needs and values being demonstrated by management or teammates. They work hard to keep improving and raise the goal expectations of those who surround them.

Learning to be competitive does not come from a coddling Pollyanna like parent or siblings. You suffer defeats, get knocked down, and learn to get back up and get better to avoid the pain and enjoy the pleasure of success.

Michael set low positive goals and kept improving his skills. With this knowledge from competition, he could accurately predict competitive goals he could achieve. And then he held himself accountable for achieving them.

Labor As a Commodity in Sports Teams

Professional sports teams are unique. Unlike businesses with labor-relations protections and laws, professional athletes are traded like a commodity. As players age, owners can write off a depreciation expense. Player contracts are complicated. Top performers are motivated to improve their personal worth to gain more income as their contracts are about to end.

Observe professional championship teams and consider how management gets all the player's egos and motivation to work to achieve the common mission. For some top performers it is not about the money. They want respect and to be admired by their fans. Who are the stars, role players, and reserves? Who among them appears to be unselfish for the good of the team?

Individual and Team Cohesiveness and Chemistry

In the last dance mini-series, Dennis Rodman, a great rebounder, and defensive player, said when he joined the Chicago Bulls it would be fun. He could trust Michael and Scottie (Pippen). This implied they had the same needs and values to win the NBA Championship title. It was respect for each other's talents to play as a team. This raised the expectations of the other players.

Excellent performance improvements occur when the goals are in line with reality. This projection is based on past performance experiences, and each performer's self-evaluation to hold themselves accountable for doing the work in practice.

The last person a locker room needs is a whining complainer who blames everyone else but themselves for poor performance. Great coaches counsel their top performers. They use a long leash to give latitude to the bizarre behaviors of top performers. Most top performers thrive on stress and the challenge with a high frustration tolerance. But breakdowns do occur.

To understand how much stress goes into a championship observe the winning celebrations. Top performers cry. The pressure has been relieved. They have paid the price. Nothing else matters. Championship are won starting with the exit team meeting at the end of a painful season. The new mission is laid out, and every member commits to working harder in the off-season.

Relationships, Parenting, and Effect of Early Discipline

Improving performance in less time includes relationships and parenting skills. I began to study sport psychology taking graduate level classes. My college swim coach was educated in exercise physiology. But he was a master in the growing field of sport psychology. He along with the great diving coach blended roles of top performing World Record holders, Olympians, and All-American egos into a cohesive team to win NCAA Championships. These top performing coaches were top ranked All-American athletes with experience.

In another sport psychology graduate class, a visiting professor said the single greatest predictor of later athletic or academic success was early discipline in the home. He asked, and which parent made the greatest impact? Our class was split between the father and mother. The answer was the mother with the most contact time to spend with the child to effect discipline and reinforce positive behaviors.

Tough love means never having to say you are sorry. Observe how mothers of top performers effected early discipline in the home. When the TV pans the player's fans in the Final Four NCAA basketball playoff and championship games you mostly see the mothers. After the game interviewed players credit their mothers.

Tiger Woods was asked how it was to get his father to take him to the golf course. He consistently said dad was easy, but mom was tough making sure my homework was completed first. Michael Jordan also remarked how his mother was the disciplinarian while his father offered guidance.

I cannot imagine Michael Jordan's or Tiger Wood's mother allowing him to get away with bad behaviors in her home.

Disciplined children learn to control their personalities or face painful consequences. They are held accountable for performance improvement. Spoiled children do nothing to earn rewards from parents who build relationships with free gifts and passes on poor behaviors. They have mixed ideas what their child is experiencing in social groups like a sports team. Everyone gets a sports participation trophy. Expectations are kept low and unchallenging and lack accountability for performance improvement. The way to overcome the pain of losing or being picked last is to develop a keen work ethic to ensure learning and success. You outwork your competitors.

Your performers must choose to accept the consequences of their behaviors and hold themselves accountable for performance improvement. As a school administrator my first position was a high school dean. I observed children's school performance from permissive undisciplined homes to find poor study habits, tardiness, absentee-ism, and incomplete assignments. These students were clearly unmotivated by the models in the home. Needs and values were not taught by the parents.

Early discipline in the home is a choice. When my triplet boys were born three months into my doctoral studies, the doctor advised, "the kids come to live with you, not the other way around."

I thought about raising my children, especially the triplets, when they were little. I was a young father and busy working like most dads. I would get home only to dis-cipline my boys if they misbehaved. Why didn't my wife discipline them immediately at least with a timeout to be more effective?

Observe behavioral changes in love and punishment from older grandparent generations. Times were not so affluent. Needs and values were different. A new pair of pants or shoes were valued. Your work ethic was reinforced to provide for your extra personal needs.

Discipline was to administer pain for violating warned bad behaviors. A value system was created in the home. Before making decisions, you had to ask, "What would momma have to say?" You honored your mother and father and respected your elders for the wisdom they could provide.

Then psychologists countered historical animal and human behaviors advo-cating to "spare the rod and spoil the child." Pain as punishment would reinforce violent behaviors. Laws are enacted so you cannot spank your child. Educational systems adopted "self-esteem psychology" thinking praise would reinforce positive behaviors.

As a behaviorist the first message I told my staff as a K-12 school superin-tendent was I did not believe in self-esteem psychology. I gave my reason with an example of a second-grade student being told excellent work, and nice job by the teacher. Problem is students evaluate the effort they performed to earn such praise. Unwarranted praise is a lie. When students do not trust the teacher, they may not believe anything they are taught. Ditto untruthful parental advice.

The Lasting Effect of Early Discipline

As a parent of six children and school superintendent I have observed all ages of child behaviors. My design was to offer positive advice based on my experiences to forewarn of possible errors in behavior and the consequences. I wanted my chil-dren to be tough-minded and think of positive behavioral decisions.

There were times my children did not like me. I was not their best friend. I was the parent and hopefully the smarter one. I questioned what their friends and activ-ities were like to understand the motivations. I instilled the value of an education as their responsibility. The consequence was they could not live with us after they graduated from high school. They learned how to apply The Triad Performance Improvement System.

Now years later all have college degrees with successful careers and families. And I still question all my grandchildren the same way to hold them accountable for their learning and behaviors.

Children have a marvelous way of growing up despite what parents do right or wrong. I completed doctoral studies in behavioral, educational, and personality psychology. I thought about how we condition our children to behave or enable their misbehavior.

Children need to learn a self-evaluation performance feedback system and hold themselves accountable for performance and behavior. When provided choices and forewarned of the consequences for bad behaviors, children will make the right decision.

If not, parents need to follow through with the consequence or punishment. For home or classroom rules keep it simple and few, "If you do this, I will do this." Follow through to effect discipline and condition the rules. Then reward and reinforce correct behaviors to condition respect for the rules.

Personnel Management with Companies and Schools

Managing Performers

Management has traditionally sought to control the efforts of others for their own material gain. This is true of publicly held companies offering upper level management stock options and bonuses the rank and file performers do not get. Occasionally, this backfires on management or a sales force.

Top salespersons who build trusted customer relationships and loyalty are rewarded with higher earnings. When a publicly held company lets go several high earning performers, they show higher profitability to Wall Street investors. This improves the company stock price to reward managers with bonus stock options.

Managers who benefit are conditioned to use extrinsic means to boss through coercion and retaliation if performers do not fulfill their needs. This does not motivate performers to improve performance but does build resentment toward the company and its customers. For low level task environments, large corporations want people to be smart to follow simple directions, but not too smart to strive for more out of their work environment in a valueless job. However, The Triad performance improvement system can still be applied in every instance.

Applying Extrinsic Versus Intrinsic Motives

Observe any system, whether it is education, business, religion or politics, the object is to use external rewards to modify the mass behavior of individuals. The object is to control and not motivate individuals to think, disagree, or question the practices inherent in the system.

There is a distinct dichotomy between intrinsic and extrinsic motivation applied to company leadership. For example, in a team sport, NBA pro basketball coach

Phil Jackson applied intrinsic motivation skills to win numerous NBA Champion-ships with the Chicago Bulls and Los Angeles Lakers. Each team had its top per-formers, Michael Jordan and Scottie Pippin with the Bulls and Kobe Bryant and Shaquille O'Neal with the Lakers.

What made Phil Jackson unique and successful was he unknowingly applied The Triad leadership skills. He coached his players to hold themselves accountable for their personal performances working as a team. Coach Jackson's philosophy and coaching style are aligned with The Triad skills training.

1. He personalizes every player's role with a purpose to focus on improving their personal performance in all the fundamental skills of the game. This included practice and games and their personal lives off the court.
2. He used the player's own immediate past performance or average to be the personal standard for improvement rather than comparing their generalized skills to high performers in the game.
3. He created a personal feedback system for each player to self-evaluate the worth of their performance. This personal self-evaluation feedback converts the motivation from extrinsic to intrinsic. The player not the coach is account-able for performance improvement.
4. When errors needed to be corrected, he refocused on the motives to achieve success greater than the motives to avoid failure (MaS>MaF). He would not reinforce the error but would refocus on the positive execution of the triangle offense and defense.
5. The players are conditioned to be more aware of their personal skills and abili-ties to work together as a team to improve through self-evaluation. Coach Jack-son let Michael Jordan condition those positive work ethic behaviors for the common good.

In governments, dissidents disagree with dictators because they want the free-dom to control their personal lives within the system rather than have the system tell them what they can or cannot do. This suggests performers can be taught intrinsic motivational strategies to improve their personal performance and quality of life.

The freedom of choice creates more intrinsic motivation to achieve and help others. Dictators are like boss managers who fear they will lose their power with loss of control. There is no trust in the relationship. In every instance, free people resent application of new laws and regulations that reduce their freedom of choice because of the stupid acts of a small minority.

Extrinsic motives are only effective for the short-term Quid Pro Quo result. What is in it for me (wiifm) creates selfish behaviors. Hire the right performers who fit the personality and work ethic demands of the job description. One key question to ask is, "What will this performer do when management is not looking?" When the cat is away, how will the mice play?

Micromanagement Pitfalls and Why Success Breeds Success

As a behavioral rule you cannot build accountability in a micromanagement system.

When leaders mistrust their performers, it results in more micromanagement. This creates a dependency on an inefficient system to provide for needs they must learn to provide for themselves. This kind of decision-making leader does not have a strong educational foundation in psychology to understand need-driven behavior.

Top performers leave jobs, or become apathetic, more for lack of some control over how their work is performed than for more money. Having some control over how you use your personality to do your assigned work is one of the last freedoms in America. Job freedom is violated by leaders who do not know how to motivate their teams and resort to bossing to ensure compliance. These are the leaders to target for learning powerful lessons in transformational leadership with The Triad.

Boss-managers stifle company creativity to find new and more efficient ways to improve performance. They threaten inexperienced performers to perform tasks only their familiar way. Thinking outside the box is unfamiliar and stressful to these managers. As a result, some top performers have left unrewarding jobs to form companies to compete with the company they left.

Self-motivated performers improve their personal performance to meet their needs, benefit the team, and prefer to lead by example. High achievers are often misinterpreted and mistreated by managers who are not as personally successful and are challenged by their ideas and results.

Talented performers are aware of winning cues and strategies to fit their job descriptions and ensure success. Poor managers allow bias, egos, and jealousy to not recognize talent. They are quick to criticize quality performances to control the performer. Criticism of a personal best performance reduces the intrinsic motivation of any performer.

Organizations or companies need to remove managers who have a personality threatened by top performers who resent micromanagement. Top performers are often labeled whiners and complainers. They are frustrated with company leaders not taking positive steps to improve performance with all the performers. They simply want to win and want change in effective leadership.

They are branded as not a team player by the micromanager system when they are highly motivated to win and feel personally rewarded for doing their part. Leaders who recognize top performers with a pat on the back, a kind word, or thank you note of appreciation means far more than winning an extrinsic company contest or trip.

Top performers need management to create a positive winning atmosphere starting with every performer motivated to improve their performance. The complainer-achiever wants all the players on the team to work as hard and have the same will-power strength to win.

Vocal performers must not be misinterpreted by management as threats to their leadership and removed to avoid embarrassment. Head coach Phil Jackson allowed Michael Jordan to be critical of his Chicago Bulls teammates to value teaching them his knowledge, tough-mindedness, and will power.

Scottie Pippin became one of the top 50 NBA players of all-time. After the success, general manager, Jerry Krause, wanted to take the credit for building the team. By micromanaging the achievers who did the work and taking the credit, morale dropped, players opted to be traded or retire, and the team dismantled.

This scenario happens on professional athletic teams and business systems. Recent studies in personnel management indicate most people leave their jobs not for more money, but to get away from the boss manager. The performer in question leaves, finds the new environment meets their needs and values, and has an outstanding year.

The Chicago Cub's executive management from 1908–2006 is a notorious example. This same error occurs repeatedly in not so successful organizations and companies. The focus must be on pleasing the customers or fans by providing a quality product or service. The Cubs managed to trade good talent for monetary return cutting the payroll to earn more profit for the owner. The mission was never to win a championship. For years, the joke was to win a World Series you had to have three former Chicago Cubs players.

Whether it is sport, business, education, politics, or government, observe the top performers. Model or copy what they do, how they think, and how they act when they perform.

Then lead others in the organization to perform in the same success patterns. When performers on a team apply The Triad skills, the results become conditioned and infectious. More performers in the organization will know and understand what it takes to succeed with a purpose and develop stronger relationships to trust each other.

This translates to fewer turnovers where training dollars pay dividends. Winning breeds success and happiness creates value, and both reinforce a positive work ethic. Performers and their egos learn to get along for the common good. When professional sports team management takes away credit from the players, they are motivated to save salaries in contract negotiations. The negative effect is loss of team cohesiveness and intrinsic motivation. Similar examples occur in business, education, and political systems.

Success Breeds Success

Successful people know success breeds success. When you feel successful fulfilling a need or surpassing your goal, you naturally want to repeat those behaviors and good feelings. Success is a personal feeling. You do not have to be the best in the world. What matters is if you feel you are improving against a standard you have set for yourself.

The standard most often used by top performers and the one suggested throughout this book is your immediate past performance or average. By setting a low positive goal only slightly better you increase your probability for success and frequency of reward. This conditions a positive feeling and expectation to build confidence and increase your intrinsic or self-motivation. You feel success because you apply a positive feeling to improving your performance over your perceptual anchoring point.

Boss Versus Lead Management

Psychologist Dr. William Glasser, (1990) The Quality School, described a dichotomy between boss-managers and lead-managers. The boss-manager is controlling to achieve conformity. The lead manager offers choices to allow the personality to create value from their work.

Boss-managers believe people are motivated from the outside. They fail to understand all motivation comes from within the performer. Boss-manager types continually lament how their performers are not motivated. What they mean is they do not know how to motivate their performers.

The boss-manager type does not believe internal rewards can possibly motivate a performer because they are not internally driven. They are only driven by the external reward of a pay increase and more power to provide temporary job security from a promotion. These managers believe it is their demeanor and coercive leadership style, along with fear of reprisals that motivates people to work harder to please them before themselves. Unfortunately, those who are promoted follow in the same footsteps.

In their mind, the performers are incapable of deciding when and how much effort to put out on the job. Inexperienced boss leaders believe they can motivate performers to conform to their thinking with the promise of a good evaluation or grade.

Leaders who are not able to discriminate between extrinsic and intrinsic motives interchange motives to confuse performers and achieve inconsistent results. A purpose or connection between the quality of performance and quality of personal reward is not established. Consequently, the boss-managed performer is focused more on keeping the boss happy than to be motivated in ways to improve their performance.

The motivation to meet personal needs is reduced, and so is accountability. You can blame the boss management for your failures and mistakes. Boss management leads to unproductive status quo and avoidance behaviors. Your motive to avoid failure is greater than your motive to achieve success (MaF>MaS).

Conversely, lead-managers recognize the innate needs in others and align them with the needs of the company in fulfilling their roles and contribute to successful job performance. They align the mission and needs of the corporation with the personal needs of the workers who gain personal satisfaction beyond the paycheck for their results.

The corporation can turn a fair profit but not at the personal expense of the performers doing the work. Success comes from a positive focus on a mutual goal to align the needs of the corporation to build a familial trusting partnership with the personal needs of the performers. The motive to achieve success will be greater than the motive to avoid failure (MaS>MaF).

Highly paid performers still leave their jobs for less money to achieve personal job satisfaction and recognition. Underpaid top performers who are made to feel valued and meet their personal needs develop company loyalties and remain on the job improving their work. Scottie Pippin with the Chicago Bulls was a perfect example. He was underpaid and undervalued by management and conflicted. But his pal Michael Jordan and coach Phil Jackson convinced him of his value to the overall success of the team. Gratefully, Scottie was loyal to enjoy winning NBA Championships to gain public recognition that meant more than what management provided.

Lead-managers consistently recognize and increase their awareness skills to point out positive feedback in every performer. This communicates a feeling of value about the work quality. Performers for lead managers report their performances are enriching and fulfill their personal needs for survival, love, power, fun, and freedom.

Intrinsic motives are a matter of trust. The boss-manager does not trust the worker to be self-motivated. They are motivated to satisfy their personal needs before the needs of the performers and impress their supervisor. The lead-manager trusts the performers to fulfill their needs by accomplishing quality services in production and customer relations to improve the company or organization.

The Effect of Affluence and Work Ethic Motives

Economies in countries all over the world have become more affluent. There are more families with refrigerators, TVs, Internet, and cell phones to process communication. This increased awareness has motivated performer's needs and values and goals for themselves and their children.

The natural drive is to provide for the needs of the children and give them benefits parents did not have at their age. In that zest to provide, the children have been gifted many things without benefit of working to provide for them as was required in the previous generation. These children are labeled "millennials" as most were born at the turn of the century.

As a rule of universal human behavior in all affluent countries, people do not value things that are free. Value can only be created by personally working to earn the reward. A teenager may be gifted a used car so the parent can avoid transportation nightmares with multiple children participating in all their activities. Will the teen wash the car or ask for gas money? Forget about who pays the insurance.

America has been generous to help countries develop with foreign aid. The carrot on the stick was they would embrace democracy with free elections. Behaviorally several of those governments in desperate need gratefully accept the money but never respect the giver.

As a rule, people in need will accept the offer but not respect the giver. Parents who gift the child must realize it is an external reward. However, if given an allowance for work in the home, the child buys a baseball glove, they will value and take care of it.

Leadership Assumptions and Applications

Boss leaders falsely assume they can create stronger group motives all performers will follow. Political leaders gain favor making promises they know they cannot keep, to meet the personal needs and values of voters to get elected. They get rich when people buy in to their message and put money in their tin cup.

Educational systems do not seem to develop critical and creative thinkers or knowledgeable about how government works. The Constitution is the rule of law so government of the people, by the people, shall be for the people.

Traditional leadership models separate leaders from their performers for fear of loss of control, or to effect discipline without showing favoritism. In this kind of boss-management leadership style, performers face negative extrinsic motives like loss of their job or bonus if they do not do what the boss demands.

Today, successful companies demonstrate lead-management leadership styles using positive intrinsic motives to personally reward and reinforce good qualities. Morale and performance output are improved. The work environment is friendly and trusting. Companies care enough for their "families" to provide day care, fitness gyms, extended lunch workout breaks, and other services for their employees.

As I was editing the highly contagious Covid-19 virus became a worldwide pandemic with hundreds of thousands of lives lost. To avoid the virus "shelter in place" and "6 feet social distancing" became the rule as economies shut down. Everyone was advised to wear a mouth and nose mask covering, use disinfectants on hands and not touch the face, and frequently wash hands with disinfectant soap for twenty or more seconds.

With improved technology more office performers can work from home. This implied trust and companies are reporting performance improvement. Sadly, production of real industrial goods and services in the restaurant and hospitality industry are not so fortunate.

There are roles reversing as more men are home with the children and their wives are the principal wage earner. Needs can and do change. Corporations are becoming more worker friendly. Company owners realize they need to make a profit to stay in business. A fair profit can treat their customers and performers like family and provide a more desirable quality of life to meet their personal needs.

How they do business and treat customers relates to how they satisfy the needs of their employees who in turn care to meet the needs of the customer. This provides a win-win-win scenario for the company, performers, and customers. The hidden benefit is these companies spend the least amount of money on human resources recruiting, hiring, and training middle management to supervise and motivate their employees. This appears to be the model for privately held companies. Publicly held companies must answer to a CEO, President, Board of Directors, and shareholders who invest to make a larger profit to gain a dividend.

Performance Evaluation Systems

Individual Performer Self-evaluation Versus Group Evaluation

Evaluation systems rely on a standard instrument to uniformly assess performance improvement. The constant is a comparison of past performance to immediate performance. Specialized tasks are usually broken into categories or sub skills to objectify scoring.

The evaluator and the performer use the same instrument. Then they meet to compare self and manager ratings. If in agreement there is congruence. The object of any self-evaluation is to improve performance with intrinsic motivation. The evaluation provides positive feedback for what is going well, and areas needing improvement.

Rubrics, pre-set objective evaluation tools, and portfolios are used to compare immediate to past performance. Performers given the opportunity to evaluate their work develop intrinsic feedback skills. Top performers usually set personal standards higher than the average performers.

They prefer to set low positive goals slightly better than the immediate past performance. This increases the probability for success in small increments and the preferable reward system. The personal feeling has more value especially when there is loss of respect for the job of the supervisor.

Group evaluations differ in overall performance rating. The job of the trainer or leader is to ensure each performer is aware of their role in the group performance. Then hold the individuals accountable for their contribution.

The RROSR strategy applies to every performer in the group. Overall performance evaluation is dependent on every performer doing well. Learning to learn in a group implies trust for each performer to improve and help the team to succeed. Before leaders start educational sessions, they point out the essential cues.

Consensus by Committee

Educational and political systems use consensus by committee more often than businesses, and organizations. Leaders are not allowed to make unilateral decisions for the performers or constituents. Consequently, neither do they take the blame for poor decisions. In fact, no one committee member is ever singled out for a bad decision and be held accountable.

Good leaders do ask for input from others to make good decisions. The final decision is on them. Top performers accept decisions by quality leaders who act in their best interests. A balance occurs between satisfaction of the needs and values of the performers with those of the company or organization.

Performance Feedback Design

The key to intrinsic motivation and personal accountability is using The Triad to develop a personal feedback system. Each performer learns to tell their brain what they feel is meaningful and relevant to assign value to new information.

RROSR was introduced to show how the brain processes information. Understanding the purpose introduces value and need to satisfy a goal. To intrinsically motivate performance progress is shown in The Triad Feedback Loop. This figure provides a template to check your progress in learning and evaluating performance improvement. It serves as a blueprint for leaders to follow.

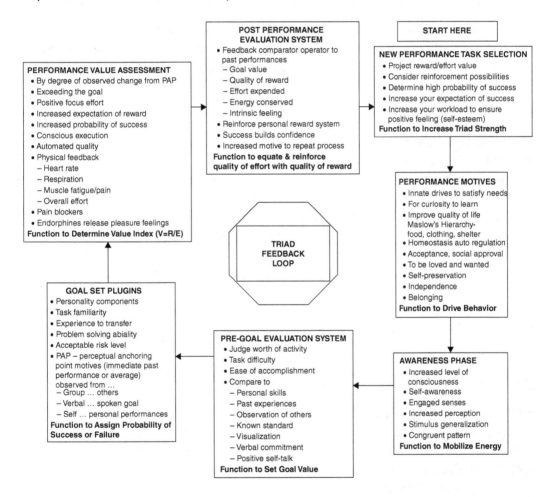

POST PERFORMANCE EVALUATION SYSTEM
- Feedback comparator operator to past performances
  - Goal value
  - Quality of reward
  - Effort expended
  - Energy conserved
  - Intrinsic feeling
- Reinforce personal reward system
- Success builds confidence
- Increased motive to repeat process

Function to equate & reinforce quality of effort with quality of reward

START HERE

NEW PERFORMANCE TASK SELECTION
- Project reward/effort value
- Consider reinforcement possibilities
- Determine high probability of success
- Increase your expectation of success
- Increase your workload to ensure positive feeling (self-esteem)

Function to Increase Triad Strength

PERFORMANCE VALUE ASSESSMENT
- By degree of observed change from PAP
- Exceeding the goal
- Positive focus effort
- Increased expectation of reward
- Increased probability of success
- Conscious execution
- Automated quality
- Physical feedback
  - Heart rate
  - Respiration
  - Muscle fatigue/pain
  - Overall effort
- Pain blockers
- Endorphines release pleasure feelings

Function to Determine Value Index (V=R/E)

TRIAD FEEDBACK LOOP

PERFORMANCE MOTIVES
- Innate drives to satisfy needs
- For curiosity to learn
- Improve quality of life Maslow's Hierarchy- food, clothing, shelter
- Homeostasis auto regulation
- Acceptance, social approval
- To be loved and wanted
- Self-preservation
- Independence
- Belonging

Function to Drive Behavior

GOAL SET PLUGINS
- Personality components
- Task familiarity
- Experience to transfer
- Problem solving abiality
- Acceptable risk level
- PAP – perceptual anchoring point motives (immediate past performance or average) observed from ...
  - Group ... others
  - Verbal ... spoken goal
  - Self ... personal performances

Function to Assign Probability of Success or Failure

PRE-GOAL EVALUATION SYSTEM
- Judge worth of activity
- Task difficulty
- Ease of accomplishment
- Compare to
  - Personal skills
  - Past experiences
  - Observation of others
  - Known standard
  - Visualization
  - Verbal commitment
  - Positive self-talk

Function to Set Goal Value

AWARENESS PHASE
- Increased level of consciousness
- Self-awareness
- Engaged senses
- Increased perception
- Stimulus generalization
- Congruent pattern

Function to Mobilize Energy

Performer Self-evaluation Versus Peer Evaluation

Peer evaluations are another means to provide performance feedback. They can never be used for hiring or dismissal purposes. In educational systems an experienced teacher observes a class taught by a new or inexperienced teacher. There is usually no formal evaluation form, and comments are shared only between the two teachers.

I am not familiar with peer evaluation frameworks for business in production management. Perhaps two performers doing the same job evaluate each other informally for an hour or some agreed time. My impression is this would build team cohesiveness and trust.

Performer self-evaluations provide a formal instrument to assess specific performance objectives. The assessments would annotate categories mutually identified by the performers and management. Records of previous evaluations would be kept in the personnel file to compare year to year or perhaps quarter to quarter.

Evaluating the Evaluator—Management Performance Evaluations

Managers and supervisors of performers can make or break performance improvement. Personality plays a role. Insecure and unrealistic managers may feel pressure to control top performers and write poor evaluations to keep the focus off their inability to motivate their performers.

Any evaluation system needs checks and balances to evaluate the managers evaluating performers. In a business there are management layers. Sales representatives are evaluated by sales managers. And sales managers are evaluated by regional or district sales managers.

The regional and district sales managers are evaluated by the Vice-President of Sales and Marketing. And the Vice-Presidents and Department Directors are evaluated by the CEO or Chief Executive Officer. There is a chain of command. In publicly held companies, a Board of Directors reviews policies set forth by the CEO and CFO or Chief Financial Officer and evaluates those executive positions.

In school systems, the Board of Education comprised of five to seven members evaluates the Superintendent. Contracts must be followed according to Labor Relations Laws. The point of evaluation is to provide feedback to improve performance. Proper self-evaluation instruments are a powerful intrinsic motivator.

Management Performance Evaluations

Evaluations of other's performances are extrinsic and less valuable. Performers may have a different opinion especially if they do not respect the manager. Self-evaluations are intrinsic for performers to value their skills and abilities and hold themselves accountable for performance improvement. There is no one to blame for poor performance.

Evaluations are awareness reminders of the correct cues and methods used to produce quality products and services. A certain safety review occurs on a frequent schedule. This is essential in routine production jobs like assembly lines when skills become automatic.

Grading systems in schools are extrinsic. Student's work is evaluated by teachers. Where a certain number of "do-overs" are permitted, students can improve the performance and final grade. This is no different than the adult world where a marketing team evaluates a mock-up of a marketing flyer several times before printing.

Rubrics are excellent to provide an evaluation matrix for students to self-evaluate a project or writing exercise prior to submission. Elementary school portfolios provide a file of a student's assignments and classroom work to compare for improvement week to week. This comparison evaluation creates the need to learn how to learn and hold oneself accountable for performance improvement.

The recurrent teacher-management theme is, "I will decide what is meaningful and relevant, and be the one to tell you if your work is good or bad." Performers know quality when they see it but cannot describe it. All performers can self-evaluate their performance by learning feedback and awareness skills to compare immediate to past performance or averages. Identifying personal needs and values from wants creates intrinsic motivation to achieve success with the self-imposed personal standard.

Board of Directors

School Boards are elected by the public. Public companies and organizations have Boards of Directors elected by proxy votes of the shareholders. These Boards have come under scrutiny for members with little or no experience to contribute or guide the company or organization. Their appointments appear political pay backs for influence in governing and policy making.

Organization and Corporate Culture

Entrepreneurial Engines Change the Task

The life blood of any economy is privately held small business. Large corporations combined may employ less than twenty percent of the workforce. Small to medium sized businesses avoid middle management. Large corporations spend billions of dollars employing middle management with the premise performers are incapable of being self-motivated.

Boss managers rely on intimidation and micromanagement to destroy more powerful intrinsic motives in their people. Performance improvement suffers along with possible ideas to enhance the product quality or service.

Transforming to The Triad Performance Improvement System of intrinsic motivation from traditional micro-management is difficult for companies. The process is related to task familiarity as a personality phenomenon. Change implies improvement but upsets and stresses out conditioned and familiar routine behaviors. Any transformation to a temporarily unfamiliar routine creates more apprehensive, insecure, and less confident personality patterns. Patience is required.

Think about an accountant routinely working with concrete financial data every day and now suddenly having to draw up abstract plans for a new office. There are performers on your team who have very rigid personalities and others who are very adaptable to change. Start the transformation with performers who are adaptable to change. Performers will self-select various jobs suited to their conditioned personality patterns to reduce inner conflicts and stress.

Leaders need to focus on quality outcomes more than the process. Then enable performer's personalities to define an efficient process to accomplish the work in realistic timetables. They are trusted to do their jobs and function as a team to reach projected goals and outcomes. Southwest Airlines appears to be a good example.

Decision Making Process—http://TheBehavioristView.com

I am a behaviorist and not a licensed clinical psychologist. The simple truth is I believe in B.F. Skinner's "Black Box" feedback design shown in an earlier chapter. Self-evaluation is a powerful intrinsic motivator. Cues go into the black box (your brain) as input to process. The response is the output and sends a feedback loop back to the input phase. If the response is incorrect or not as desirable, then modify or change the input cue until you get the expected response.

One of my concerns about self-motivation or intrinsic motivation is how to advise performers to make better short and long-term behavioral decisions. I decided to take the top two psychological principles and top two behavioral rules from my first book, Purposeful Intent. If any one or more are violated, it will not make a favorable decision.

My posts on the website use the same four points applied to news stories and reports as examples of violations that are not probable for good short or long-term decisions.

The oldest psychological principle is to go for pleasure over pain. No one gets an electrical shock, jumps up, and yells let's do it again! The other is anyone can rationalize anything to get what they want. Try telling a friend to stop smoking, doing drugs, lose weight, etc. and note how they rationalize their behavior.

The two behavioral rules are more pliable unlike principles being irrefutable. The first is the more you do for people the less they will learn to do for themselves. There is little connection between the value of effort and reward when the process is done by others for you. The second is you cannot build accountability in a micro-management system. If you demand or do the work for others, they will not take accountability for their performance and blame the leader instead.

Resistance to Empowerment

Where businesses and organizations fail to perform and improve, they lose their focus on developing The Triad skills process. They are top heavy in management with boss leaders engaged in fault finding more than on improving the quality product or service outcome.

Boss leaders are conditioned to keep their job by finding the faults in others. It is their job to correct errors in the organization to make it more efficient. The focus should be more on positive ways to improve employee and customer relations to produce the product quality or service outcome.

Needs and values of the customers and performers must be aligned with the needs and values of the business or organization. Lay boards who micromanage their professionally educated CEO's can expect personality clashes. And companies laden with boss managers do not intrinsically motivate talented and creative performers.

In my opinion, local lay boards of education have retarded the growth of American public education. Legislators, without knowledge of behavioral psychology, have enacted poor legislation rewarding performers not to work and be held accountable for meeting their own election needs. Offers of free government services have less personal value for accountability. Now millennials are demanding free college education. This will demean the value of a college education.

Resistance to empowerment always occurs when performers are never held accountable for performance. No one wants to take the blame for poor performance outcomes. Programs designed to help the needy hurt motives to help oneself. Redistribution of wealth with socialist ideals removes the incentive to improve a quality of life. Necessity is still the mother of invention.

Setting a worthy goal, doing the work to attain the goal, and taking all the credit for the achievement improves personal pride and integrity. To ease the economic pain of The Great Depression, President Franklin D. Roosevelt created The New Deal. This put people to work to value an income to provide for their needs and self-respect.

Growing Company Trends

The growing trend for successful companies and organizations is to align their company mission stated as a need and value with the personal needs and values of the people doing the work, and customers who benefit. This is not an easy task, but worth the effort.

The benefit is stronger performer loyalties, less turnover, and outstanding production. They realize, as educators must, you cannot beat performance into people with a stick. You cannot demand a customer buy your product or service. You must create needs and value, and then be able to demonstrate how to fulfill those needs with value.

In any relationship for business or family, if you care to meet the needs and values of the other party more than your own it will be sensed, and your relationship improves. This goes back to increasing awareness, the first part of The Triad.

One bit of advice I offered my children was about bias and egos. Whatever your brain is thinking you may as well be saying out loud because your body language is speaking those thoughts. My dog Greta was a golden retriever and she could sense who was friendly to let them pet her. Be like a golden retriever and practice the Golden Rule—Do unto others as you would have them do unto you.

The great advice my father gave me was never talk up or down to people. Either way people will know the difference. Just be yourself. But I must admit as an author, I use simpler words to convey the same meaning. When you care more about meeting the needs of others like customers and treating your performers as family, you share a valuable message.

Intrinsic motivation is more powerful than extrinsic motivation and all its worthless incentive plans. Nothing means more to a loyal employee than for the boss to recognize the worth of their small contribution with a handwritten note as opposed to the cold fact you were not the best to win a vacation trip.

Promoting Positive Leadership System of Need Satisfaction

Top performers consistently know how to identify and meet their own needs. They are self-reliant and not dependent on others. They seldom blame others for not meeting their needs or for poor performances. They set personal standards and are accountable to achieve them. They create personal intrinsic value for all their activities.

Organizations and companies do better to provide a positive leadership system to encourage empowerment, personal growth, and more efficient operations. These low-cost suggestions promote a positive need to improve performance in less time.

1. Move from boss management to lead management.
2. Align the mission, vision, needs and values of the organization with the personal needs and values of the performers doing the work.
3. Allow performers who do the work to have some say in how they would like to accomplish the results.
4. Call attention to smaller segments of the process to increase frequency of success with positive results.
5. Managers must remove all conscious thought for "my way or the highway" to get more "buy-in" from people doing the work.
6. Value the worth of every employee and their ideas to remove formal titles and lines of communication.
7. Everyone gives credit where credit is due. No one takes credit for another performer's ideas or job performance.
8. Treat your workers like family.
9. Set performance goals only slightly higher than the immediate past performance or average performance of each performer.
10. Develop a positive feedback system and show each performer how to use it.
11. Encourage routine self-evaluation of performance congruent with semi-annual performance evaluations from management.
12. Reward the positive by looking for the good in your performers.

13. Extinct the negative by placing emphasis on MaS>MaF.
14. Have your performers periodically assess their personal needs and the needs of the company to determine the impact of their job or role in the company growth.
15. Recognize and celebrate personal performance improvement without extrinsic rewards.

APPENDIX

Go to http://The3SecretSkillsofTopPerformers.com/Survey
to download a printable PDF on full-sized page

Name _____   **Date** _____

Personal Awareness Survey: An Enhancement Exercise

This exercise is designed to help you learn your strengths, weaknesses, preferences, and ultimately your passion to excel or exhibit quality performances. This will determine your past, current, and future needs to develop your personal Triad strength. Moderate changes may be required to your personality to increase your level of awareness over time. If you are conscious of your strengths and weaknesses, you increase your awareness to perform at a higher level. Focus more energy to improve your weaknesses and strengthen your personality.

Sections

Part I: Talents, Abilities, and Skills
Part II: Attitudes, Values, and Beliefs
Part III: Activities, Preferences, and Goals
Part IV: Performances, Achievements, and Planning
Part V: Personality
Part VI: Needs, Drives, and Motives

Measurable Objectives

- Raise your level of awareness.
- Move from unconscious to conscious awareness.
- Record general and specific responses.
- Assign a Likert Scale rating of 1 low to 5 high for your personal selections.
- Make an honest appraisal of your talents, abilities, and skills.
- Learn your awareness level is associated with your personality.

General Directions

- **Make a copy of your blank survey BEFORE you begin.**
- Go to a quiet place to eliminate distractions or possible interruptions.

- To be more accurate record your initial spontaneous responses.
- Do not spend overly think your responses to be a more realistic indicator.
- Control your sensory input to access the thought that pops up in your mind.
- Close your eyes to block visual stimulation in the room and create mental images of past performances.
- Refrain from music or watching TV or people.
- This is a worthwhile time-consuming exercise.
- Your first pass through will be incomplete. Do not stop too long to answer any question.
- The object is to obtain spontaneous answers.
- Go back to fill in your responses with additional passes.
- **After you have made it through all the questions once,** you can enlist help from significant others like parents, grandparents, siblings, aunts and uncles, cousins, or a close friend.
- You can ask people who know you like teachers, coaches, ministers, peers, neighbors, employers, bosses, or people you report to.

You may be surprised to learn how they see things in you that you may not see in yourself. This alone is worth the time of doing this personal survey.

Specific Directions

- Use your blank survey copy to give to a significant other to survey you. Then compare their responses with your copy.
- After you have filled in the blanks, you can replace suggested responses made by others to best fit your personal description. **But you must not replace any of your personal selections so you can see how others view you.**
- You can add additional selections beyond the number asked for.
- Rate, 1–5, every response you have made on your personal copy.
- Be honest with your initial first impression. There are no right-or-wrong answers.
- Do others rate you the same to provide congruence?
- Use a blank sheet of paper to draw a line down the middle to create a dichotomy.
- On the left-hand side of the paper include selections you or others rated 1 or 2.
- On the right-side place all the items rated 4 or 5 corresponding to each question and shorten into a header.

For example:
1. Academic talent

1 or 2	4 or 5

Shakespeare wrote, "To thine own self be true." This exercise is designed to provide you with a better feeling for your tendencies that when brought to a more conscious level of awareness can yield more positive performance results. If honest, this forms an accurate personal awareness to enlighten your future choices and strengthen your Triad skills. Later, in Part II, self-evaluation, and Part III, reward-reinforcement you will understand how awareness is interrelated to these areas.

Carry this survey with you. Answers will come to you at the strangest times you will want to record. Jot down on a note pad or scrap paper your thought to record later. Keep a pen and paper handy with a small flashlight next to your bed. Thoughts may come to you in the middle of the night.

Part I: Talents, Abilities, and Skills

1. Name five academic talents you have.
2. Name five athletic talents you have.
3. Name five talents that are neither academic nor physical.
4. Name five mental abilities you have.
5. Name five physical abilities you have.
6. Name five abilities you have that are neither mental nor physical.
7. Name five specialized mental skills that you have demonstrated.
8. Name five specialized physical skills that you have demonstrated.
9. Name five neither mental nor physical specialized skills you have demonstrated.

Part II: Attitudes, Values, and Beliefs

10. Name three attitudes you have had toward people, places, or things in the last five years.
11. State five values you have thought about in the last five years.
12. State five beliefs you hold without question or doubt of any kind.

Part III: Activities, Preferences, and Goals

13. Name five activities you have consistently strong preferences for performing.
14. When you make a personal goal, do you think about the performances of …
    a. groups of other people
    b. what you tell people you plan to do
    c. what you have performed in your immediate past performance
15. If you were given a crystal ball to see your future, what three things would you most like to see?
16. If given the technology, would you want to be programmed and not worry about all the work required to learn?
17. Circle activities you prefer and demonstrate some ability to perform.

Concrete	Abstract
Numbers	Concepts
Deductive	Inductive
Mathematics	Psychology
Accounting	Sociology

English grammar	Creative Writing
History	Social Studies
Reading	Speaking
Government	Political Science
Auto Shop	Art
Industrial Arts	Music

18. Name two sporting activities you consider to be the most proficient (they can be non-competitive like fishing or water skiing)?
19. When you read a book what two things interest you the most?
20. What two ways do you like to organize your daily activities?
21. When you see a movie for a second time, what three details do you notice you missed the first time?
22. When you write a paper and let it sit for a few days, what areas do you look to correct and make the paper better?
23. When speaking face to face with another person, what body language do you attend to the most?

Part IV: Performances, Achievements, and Planning

24. In the last five years, name your three most quality achievements.
25. At what age did you realize you were independent enough to argue with your parent(s)?
26. How much time do you spend planning your activities?
27. How do you prefer to prepare for a significant performance?
    a. Paper and pencil test on a core academic subject?
    b. National test like SAT, ACT or license of any kind?
    c. Athletic contest?
    d. Job interview?
    e. A first date?
    f. An extracurricular activity (name the activity _____)?
28. Rate your ability to …
    a. Communicate
    b. Understand
    c. Think
    d. Create
    e. Learn to learn
    f. Focus
    g. Use tools
    h. Make decisions
    i. Solve problems
    j. Increase awareness
29. Name three performances you demonstrated attention to details.
30. I prefer to plan my activities.

Part V: Personality

31. The following is a list of common personality traits taken from IPAT 16PF test profile (2008). Review them but wait to rate each of them until instructed to do so.

a.	Reserved	Outgoing
b.	Concrete thinking	Abstract thinking
c.	Affected by feelings	Emotionally stable
d.	Conforming	Assertive
e.	Serious	Impulsive
f.	Expedient	Persevering
g.	Shy	Bold
h.	Self-reliant	Dependent
i.	Trusting	Suspicious
j.	Practical	Imaginative
k.	Forthright	Calculating
l.	Confident	Apprehensive
m.	Traditional	Free-thinking
n.	Group-dependent	Self-sufficient
o.	Undisciplined	Controlled
p.	Relaxed	Tense

32. Name the two best performances of your life and the activity you were doing.
33. If you had the opportunity to do these performances again, what would you do differently?
34. If you had a choice, would you choose another kind of activity instead, and if yes what would that activity be now?

Part VI: Needs, Drives, and Motives

35. Think of your life on a continuum from birth to now. Project into your future and list your needs. Beside each need if not yourself indicate who has provided or will provide for each future need.

Infancy	0–1
Early childhood	1–5
Pre-school—elementary school	5–10
Junior High School	10–13
High School	13–18
Post High School	18–23
Post College/Trade School	23–30
Settling Down	30–49
Maturing	49–62
Early retirement	60–70 (if applicable)

36. Describe what typically drives your behavior every day.

37. Name two prominent drives that have motivated your behavior most all your life.
38. If you could dream the biggest dream possible to achieve in the next five years, describe what that would be and how it would affect your life.
39. How do you prefer to entertain yourself with physical or mental activities?
40. Do you like to use all your senses?
41. On average, how many minutes a day do you spend ...
    a. Listening to music with a portable player and earphones?
    b. Watching mindless non-specific learning TV programs?
    c. Reading?
    d. Eating?
    e. Sleeping?
    f. Communicating?
    g. Learning something meaningful?
42. In relation to your peers, would you rate yourself as having more-or-less experience to perform difficult thinking tasks to solve problems?
43. In terms of travel to gain world experience, you have been ...
    a. Out of the country
    b. Out of the state
    c. Visited 10 or more states
    d. Flown in an airplane
    e. Seen one of the Great Lakes
    f. Seen an ocean
    g. Been to a major city in the last two years
    h. Been on vacation with a parent regularly
    i. Taken a passenger train ride
    j. Camping
    k. Seen a sunrise and sunset in the same day
    l. Gone fishing
44. What was the last project you created by yourself?
45. What is the best quality performance you have ever seen, and why did you enjoy it?

Rate every response from 1 weakest to 5 strongest you have indicated on your paper. Be patient, this will take some time. You may add another item to your incomplete lists, but you cannot replace one of your initial responses.

ABOUT THE AUTHOR

Peter Andersen, Ph.D. is a behaviorist, author, speaker, and publisher. He has observed top performing athletes and successful educational, medical, publishing, and business systems for over fifty years. He has been a top performing athlete as a 5-time All American, setting Masters' Swimming World and National Records, and winning 25 Senior Olympic Summer Nationals Championship Gold Medals with several records.

His educational training comes with a B.S. and M.S. degrees at Indiana University and Ph.D. from The University of Toledo majoring in Perceptual-Motor Learning and Sport Psychology. Emphasis was placed on principles of learning using behavioral, educational, and personality psychology research. His dissertation subjects included the 1972 U.S. Men's Olympic Swimming Team.

After completing graduate degrees, he coached All-American collegiate women, and later high school boys' swimmers before entering business to gain experience in sales and marketing. In succeeding positions, he became a regional sales manager, and company owner in the medical systems and publishing business. During this time, he published, The Sport Psychology Advisor, a weekly newspaper column a decade before sports teams and athletes accepted this training.

After twenty years in business he returned to education as a school principal and superintendent. During this tenure he gave presentations on an intrinsic motivation model for transformational leadership at many teacher conferences.

After retiring he authored Purposeful Intent and Teach Yourself to Swim and over a dozen e-books on swimming and water safety instruction. He has associated with top performing athletes and Internet marketers to present transformational leadership strategies to improve performance in less time. Married for over thirty-five years to his wife Marcy, together they have six children and fourteen grandchildren.

Personal Notes

CPSIA information can be obtained
at www.ICGtesting.com
Printed in the USA
LVHW020044260321
682548LV00018B/501